American Nov

The Discoverers :

American Novelists In Italy

The Discoverers: Allston to James

by

Nathalia Wright

Philadelphia
University of Pennsylvania Press

7383

Printed in the United States of America

To

the Memory of my Father

"Considerate la vostra semenza :
  fatti non foste a viver come bruti,
  ma per seguir virtute e conoscenza."

Inferno, **XXVI**, 118–120.

Preface

THIS STUDY IS PRIMARILY CONCERNED WITH THE INFLUENCE OF their experiences in Italy on the fiction of the first group of American writers to be notably affected by travel in that country. It largely disregards their knowledge and conception of Italian culture acquired through books, reproductions of works of art, and other means available outside Italy. It is only incidentally concerned with other matters bearing on these writers' Italian experience : their awareness of other travellers in Italy, predecessors as well as contemporaries; their influence on each other; their travel in other foreign countries; their motive in leaving and general attitude toward America; the varying conditions in Italy during the span of their several visits. Nor does this study evaluate, except incidentally, the literary worth of the Italianate works. It aims to consider these writers above all as a group, the first of several such groups to be inspired by personal contact with the Italian scene.

The discussion of each writer begins with an outline of his Italian itinerary. Next his comments on his experiences in Italy in such factual accounts as letters, diaries, and travel books are summarized. The use of Italian material in all his published works is then briefly surveyed. Finally the treatment of Italy in his fiction is analyzed in detail.

In assembling the background material used in the introductory chapter, I was greatly aided by Guiseppe Prezzolini's

Come gli Americani Scoprirono l'Italia (Milan, 1933), the fullest account of American visitors to Italy before 1850. I also drew upon Van Wyck Brooks' *Travellers in Arcadia* (New York, 1956). In the chapter on Howells I am deeply indebted to James L. Woodress' *Howells & Italy* (Durham, N. C., 1952), the only full-length study which has been made of the Italian experience of any American writer. His purpose in writing differing from mine, Mr. Woodress did not examine Howells' Italianate fiction as particularly as I have done.

I am very grateful to the American Association of University Women for its Founders Fellowship for the academic year 1959/60, during which time most of this book was written.

I also wish to express my gratitude to Miss Eleanor Goehring and Mrs. Ella Jo Hinton of the University of Tennessee Library, to Mr. John E. Van Kohn of New York City, and to Mr. Howard Mott of Sheffield, Massachusetts, for assistance in obtaining copies of relatively rare publications; to Mrs. Lida Mayo of Washington, D. C., for information about George Alfred Townsend; to the Cincinnati Art Museum, the Frick Art Reference Library in New York, Sig. Marcello Piermattei of Rome, and Mrs. Lou Spears of Maryville, Tennessee, for assistance in securing photographs; and to Professors Richard Beale Davis of the University of Tennessee and Norman H. Pearson of Yale University for suggesting revisions in the manuscript.

I have the kind permission of the following publishers, institutions, and individuals to quote from books and manuscripts and to reproduce works of art : The Boston Athenaeum; The Boston Public Library; Mrs. William Burnham, Brookline, Mass.; Giovanni Castano, Boston; The Cincinnati Art Museum; The Concord Free Public Library, Concord, Mass.; The Detroit Institute of Arts; Prof. Leon Edel of New York

University, who has permitted me to quote from his forth-
coming edition of James' letters; Harvard University; Harvard
University Press; The Historical Society of Pennsylvania,
Philadelphia; The Library Company of Philadelphia; The
Metropolitan Museum of Art; Roger Michahelles, Florence,
Italy; The Museum of Fine Arts, Boston; The New-York
Historical Society; The New York Public Library; The
Newark Museum; Oxford University Press; Paul R. Reynold
& Son, agents for the Henry James Estate; Prof. Norman H.
Pearson, who has permitted me to quote from his forthcoming
edition of Hawthorne's letters; David Richardson, Washing-
ton, D.C.; The Royal Academy, London; The Smithsonian
Institution; The Valentine Museum, Richmond, Va.; Wads-
worth Atheneum, Hartford, Conn.

N. W.

Maryville, Tennessee

Contents

List of Illustrations

American Novelists In Italy

The Discoverers: Allston to James

BUT ITALY HAS A MAGNETIC VIRTUE QUITE PECULIAR TO HER, which compels alike steel and straw, finding something in men of the most diverse temperaments by which to draw them to herself. Like the Sirens, she sings to every voyager a different song, that lays hold on the special weakness of his nature. The German goes thither because Winckelmann and Goethe went, and because he can find there a sausage stronger than his own; the Frenchman, that he may flavor his infidelity with a bitter dash of Ultramontanism, or find fresher zest in his chattering boulevard after the sombre loneliness of Rome; the Englishman, because the same Providence that hears the young ravens when they cry is careful to furnish prey to the courier also, and because his money will make him a *Milor in partibus*. But to the American, especially if he be of imaginative temper, Italy has a deeper charm. She gives him cheaply what gold cannot buy for him at home, a Past at once legendary and authentic, and in which he has an equal claim with every other foreigner. In England he is a poor relation whose right in the entail of home traditions has been docked by revolution; of France his notions are purely English, and he can scarce help feeling something like contempt for a people who habitually conceal their meaning in French; but Rome is the mother-country of every boy who has devoured Plutarch or taken his daily doses of Florus. Italy gives us antiquity with good roads, cheap living, and, above all, a sense of freedom from responsibility. For him who has escaped thither there is no longer any tyranny of public opinion; its fetters drop from his limbs when he touches that consecrated shore, and he rejoices in the recovery of his own individuality. He is no longer met at every turn with "Under which king, bezonian? Speak, or die !" He is not forced to take one side or the other about table-tipping, or the merits of General Blank, or the constitutionality of anarchy. He has found an Eden where he need not hide his natural self in the livery of any opinion, and may be as happy as Adam, if he be wise enough to keep clear of the apple of High Art.

—JAMES RUSSELL LOWELL, "Leaves from my Journal in Italy and Elsewhere" [1851–52]

I

The American Literary Discoverers of Italy

THE FIRST AMERICANS TO GO TO ITALY AND TO PRODUCE significant records of their Italian experience were artists. Benjamin West, the first American of all known to have visited that country, went as a youth in 1760 to see its celebrated works of art. As a result of his four years there he became the founder of a new school of painting—the neo-classic. At least three of his contemporaries followed him. The most illustrious was John Singleton Copley, whose work became significantly broader in scope, if somewhat less original, after his study in Italy of the work of other artists. By the end of the colonial period, indeed, a tradition of an Italian sojourn, for the twin purposes of study and stimulation, had been established among American artists.

This tradition was revived after the Revolution by Washington Allston, who went to Italy in 1804. Profoundly influenced by his experience there, Allston more than any other American may be said to have introduced that country to his countrymen. He was the first American artist to depict to any extent the Italian landscape. He was, moreover, the first major American artist to return home after visiting Italy—West and Copley having settled in London. Through Allston a recognizable body of American intellectuals for the first time became conscious of Italy and of the stimulus to the mind and the imagination which it could be.

American sculptors in this period found in Italy also the best marble and the best stone cutters in the world, and on that account many established residence there. The first was Horatio Greenough, a disciple of Allston, who went to Rome as a student in 1826 and lived in Florence almost continuously from 1828 until 1851.

Partly because of the precedent set by American artists, a tradition of travelling to Italy emerged among American writers early in the nineteenth century. Some of the earliest and much of the later American writing about that country was done by the artists. Several of the writers were relatives of the artists, and a few of the writers—for example, F. Marion Crawford and Francesca Alexander, whose fathers were artists residing in Italy—grew up there. For nearly a century a close association existed between American artists and writers in Italy. The tradition of Italian travel among the writers grew chiefly, however, out of the general movement of Americans as tourists to Europe, and with this movement American writing about Italy has retained vital connections ever since.

The first book produced by an American drawing on experiences of his own in Italy was the first of a long series of American accounts of travel in that country : *Letters from Europe, during a Tour through Switzerland and Italy, in the Years* 1801 *and* 1802, published in 1805 in Philadelphia by Joseph Sansom, who spent a winter in Italy with his wife for the sake of her health. The second such book was *Grecian Remains in Italy* (1812), by the South Carolina archeologist and painter John Izard Middleton; it was illustrated by engravings from drawings he had made in the vicinity of Rome. The next year the first Italy-inspired American belles lettres appeared : three sonnets about Italian paintings in

Washington Allston's *Sylphs of the Seasons*. The first fiction laid in Italy by an American who had been there was also by Allston : his novel *Monaldi*, which was finished by 1822 though not published until 1841.

The first professional American writer to visit Italy was Washington Irving, in 1804. Not yet decided about a profession, he was travelling primarily for his health. The ten tales with Italian settings in his *Tales of a Traveller* (1824) were the first such fiction to be published by an American with first-hand knowledge of Italy. Nowhere else (except in his journal), did Irving make substantial use of Italian material. (Irving's brother Peter visited Italy in 1807, but the historical novel laid in Venice which he published in 1820, *Giovanni Sbogarro*, was only a translation of the French work *Jean Sbogar*.)

The next professional American writers who travelled to Italy were historians and journalists : Theodore Lyman, William Hickling Prescott, George Ticknor, Edward Everett, George Bancroft, and Theodore Dwight the younger, all between 1817 and 1821, and George Washington Greene in 1827. Ticknor, Everett, and Bancroft had gone abroad primarily to study at Göttingen, and all were just beginning their careers. All wrote of Italy to some extent—notably Lyman and Dwight in books on its politics and Prescott and Greene in essays on its literature—but none did so in a major work.

Not until 1827 did a second belletristic American writer reach Italy. This was Henry Wadsworth Longfellow, who had recently graduated from college and was preparing himself in Europe for the teaching of foreign languages. He stayed in Italy a year. Of all European countries Spain delighted him most, but he made the greatest literary use of his knowledge of Italy and of Italian—in travel sketches and other prose (including the semi-autobiographical *Hyperion*, whose Mary Ashburton has been to Italy) in translations, and in some two dozen poems. Dante, whose *Divina Commedia* he translated, was a major influence on him. He was less interested in the country itself, however, even after revisiting it in 1858–69, than in its literature and legends, with which he became acquainted for the most part in America.

In 1828 James Fenimore Cooper, on a tour of Europe with his family, became the third professional American writer of belles lettres to visit Italy. With him Americans began at last to reckon in literature with that country. He was the first of them to write of it extensively and enthusiastically. As a novelist, moreover, he was the first of the particular group of American writers who were most affected by personal contact with the Italian scene.

In the early 1830's the number of American writers in Italy rose sharply, and from then to the present it has grown steadily. Ever since the cessation of the Napoleonic wars, indeed, travel in Europe among all nationalities has been increasing. As Italy has always had a peculiar appeal for the inhabitants of more northerly European countries, it has proved to have such appeal for Americans also. In the nineteenth century at least a hundred professional American writers travelled to that country and subsequently published works concerning it, and at least as many other Americans published records of their visits there. In the twentieth century, the number has been still greater.

The greatest number of literary works produced by Americans in consequence of going to Italy have been, of course, in the category of description and travel. Among the authors of these works have been artists, scholars, novelists, poets, journalists, navy men, clergymen, diplomats, and merchants.

In the nineteenth century notable studies of Italian literature, art, folklore, and politics were made in connection with Italian residence by Richard Henry Wilde, Charles Eliot

Norton, James Jackson Jarves, Charles C. Perkins, Francesca Alexander, Charles Godfrey Leland, and F. Marion Crawford. Most of the major American historians of that century— Prescott, Bancroft, John Lothrop Motley, Francis Parkman, and Henry Adams—travelled as young men in Italy, where their sense of history must have been heightened. None of them, however, devoted himself to the study of Italian history.

Many American poets have been inspired by sojourns in Italy, and several—including Longfellow, the sculptor William Wetmore Story, Elizabeth Stedman Kinney, Joaquin Miller, T. B. Aldrich, Clinton Scollard, G. H. Boker, and Josephine Preston Peabody—have published one or more volumes of poetry or poetic drama on Italian subjects. Most of these poets have been minor ones, however. On only one of importance— Ezra Pound—has residence in Italy exerted a major influence. The major American poets have tended, indeed, not to go abroad at all. In this respect those in the nineteenth century were in striking contrast to contemporary English poets, many of whom spent long periods fruitfully in Italy.

A few notable nineteenth-century American men of letters who visited Italy gave no sign of having been deeply influenced by their experience there. Chief among them were Ralph Waldo Emerson, William Cullen Bryant, Oliver Wendell Holmes, and James Russell Lowell.

The most imposing body of literature produced by Americans as a result of going to Italy has been fiction. At least twenty-five Americans in the nineteenth century and over twice that many in the first half of the twentieth have written novels—and, in addition, a few others have written short stories—with Italian settings. Among these writers are many of the major American novelists, and some of these novels are among their most distinguished achievements. Nearly all the nineteenth-century American novelists of importance went to

Italy, and on nearly all of them this country exerted a major influence. Melville and Clemens were the only exceptions. Melville, most of whose prose was written before he went, drew on his Italian experiences in poems, however, and Clemens incorporated some of his in travel books. Other nineteenth-century American fictionists who visited but took little or no fictional account of Italy include Catherine Sedgwick, J. W. De Forest, Caroline Kirkland, Helen Hunt Jackson, and Sarah Orne Jewett, all of whom except Miss Jewett published accounts of their foreign travels. The chief novelists thus far in the twentieth century who have visited but been little if at all inspired by Italy are Hamlin Garland, Ellen Glasgow, Theodore Dreiser, F. Scott Fitzgerald, Willa Cather, John Dos Passos, and William Faulkner. Compared with Americans, few Europeans in either century have produced notable fiction in consequence of exposure to the Italian scene.

The Americans who have written novels or stories dealing with Italy after visiting that country comprise three large groups. The first consists of those whose writing was done before or begun by 1870, chief among them Cooper, Nathaniel Hawthorne, William Dean Howells, and Henry James. The last Italianate work by a member of this group, James' *Golden Bowl*, appeared in 1904, one hundred years after Allston first set foot on Italian soil. A sense of discovery, both geographical and experiential, pervades the Italianate works of most of these writers. Nearly half of them wrote books about travel in Italy, and much of their fiction laid there has the basic pattern of such books. The characters in this fiction are primarily concerned, however, with moral problems. Though nearly all these writers depicted the Italian scene realistically, they tended to endow it with symbolic values.

About 1870 the fiction produced by Americans under the influence of Italy—with the conspicuous exception of that by

Howells and James—began to exhibit other patterns, which continued to distinguish it until about 1940. Among these writers in this period were Mary Agnes Tincker, Virginia Wales Johnson, William Wetmore Story, F. Marion Crawford, Constance Fenimore Woolson, F. Hopkinson Smith (who was also a painter), W. W. Astor, Henry Blake Fuller, Henry Harland, Clinton Scollard, Edith Wharton, W. D. Orcutt, Norval Richardson, Thornton Wilder, Louis Bromfield, Ernest Hemingway, and Sinclair Lewis. Most of these writers represented Italy explicitly or by implication as a place of refuge from materialism and treated their material romantically. They tended to be particularly interested in the Italian past. Crawford, Astor, Scollard, Mrs. Wharton, Orcutt, Wilder, and many others wrote historical novels laid in Italy. Several made it the scene of fantasies: Crawford in *With the Immortals*, Fuller in *The Last Refuge* and other works, Wilder in *The Cabala*, Bromfield in *The Strange Case of Miss Annie Spragg*.

A third group of American writers of fiction inspired by sojourns in Italy has emerged since World War II. Among the most noteworthy are John Hersey, Alfred Hayes, John Horne Burns, Tennessee Williams, Irwin Shaw, William Styron, and Elizabeth Spencer. Whereas most of the earlier writers dealt repeatedly with Italian material, nearly all these have done so only once or twice. Like those of the first group, however, these writers have taken an essentially realistic view of the Italian scene. The characters which they portray often seem to be in search of something and often acquire in Italy a sense of direction or a feeling of human brotherhood. Many of these characters, moreover, are in effect returning to that country, as Italian-Americans, as veterans of war, or as descendants of Americans who had previously travelled there.

Throughout the Italianate fiction of all three of these groups certain broad patterns persist. Most of it concerns American

Washington Allston, SELF PORTRAIT. Rome, 1805.
(Courtesy of the Museum of Fine Arts, Boston)

Frederick Church, Jervis McEntee, George Peter Alexander Healy, THE ARCH OF TITUS. Rome, 1871. (H. W. Longfellow and his daughter Edith in the center; Church, McEntee, and Healy on the right.)

(Courtesy of The Newark Museum)

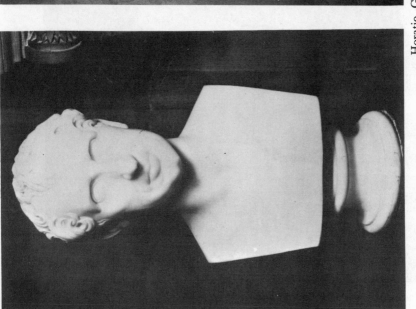

Horatio Greenough

JAMES FENIMORE COOPER.
Paris and Florence, 1831–ca. 1833
(Courtesy of the Boston Public Library)

NATHANIEL PARKER WILLIS.
Florence, 1832–ca. 1834.
(Courtesy of Mrs. William Burnham, Brookline, Mass.)

Thomas Hicks, SARAH MARGARET FULLER, MARCHIONESS
OSSOLI. Rome, 1848. Engraved by M. Haider.
(From the Century Magazine, *April, 1893)*

Maria Louisa Lander, NATHANIEL HAWTHORNE. Rome, 1858.
(Courtesy of the Concord Free Public Library)

characters in an Italian setting rather than exclusively Italian material. The setting, moreover, for all its realistic details, is commonly more symbolic than literal. Historically or politically it is the epitome of Europe; intellectually and morally it represents experience not available in America. In any event it is a scene larger than the American scene, one where Americans may have intercourse with the world and the past, form fruitful attachments, or escape frustration. No other foreign country has figured so provocatively in American fiction. Indeed, under the influence of Italy American novelists may be said to have opened intercourse with the world. Beginning with Cooper these novelists, for all their tendency toward introspection, have been to a great extent concerned with the relation of America to other societies, and for many of them this concern originated in their visitation of Italy.

The first group of these writers thus doubly merits attention. Not only were they the American literary discoverers of Italy. In their Italy-inspired fiction they originated motifs which became perennial in such fiction by Americans and which have affected the main course taken by the American novel.

At least thirteen American novelists, and one short-story writer, had gone to Italy and subsequently written fiction about it before the end of 1870. Cooper, Howells, and James wrote more than one novel laid there; Allston, Theodore S. Fay, Henry T. Tuckerman, Nathaniel Parker Willis, Henry Greenough, Hawthorne, Harriet Beecher Stowe, Sarah Loring Greenough, Henry P. Leland, and Anne Hampton Brewster wrote one novel each; Irving wrote a series of tales. Of the few Americans who made only incidental use in fiction of their Italian experiences during this period—in portions of books or in single stories—the most prominent were Francis Parkman,

Donald Grant Mitchell, George William Curtis, and George Alfred Townsend.

Discoverers though they were, these writers were not without preconceptions of Italy or precedents for writing about it. Their chief precedents—and the chief source of their preconceptions—were Elizabethan tragedies and Gothic romances having Italian settings and characters. In most of these works an atmosphere of terror and mystery prevails; intrigue and crime constitute the action; and the central character is a villain-hero, sometimes a priest, derived from the character of Machiavelli's Prince. The Italy thus represented is, however, almost totally a product of the imagination. Few of the authors of these works had visited the country. Their descriptions of the scene, for which they were often indebted to travel books and histories, were sketchy.

Throughout most of the nineteenth century the influence of the Gothic romance on American fiction was pronounced. In consequence such fiction of this period as is concerned with Italy largely reflects the Elizabethan-Gothic tradition about the country and its inhabitants. Nearly all the Italian-laid fiction produced by nineteenth-century Americans who did not visit Italy—a large body in itself—is stock romance of the Gothic and tale-of-terror variety. So is most of the considerable amount of nineteenth-century American drama laid in Italy, written as it largely was by playwrights who had never been there. Commonly in the Italianate works of the first group of American fictionists inspired by that country, Italian villain-heroes appear, crimes and sins are committed, and Italian scenic details are frequently Gothic in nature. The most striking fact about this fiction, however, is its deviation from the Elizabethan-Gothic tradition about Italy.

This deviation is three-fold. Unlike the creators of the tradition, the authors of this fiction treated the Italian scene realistically or objectively. With their native esteem for observed phenomena, they almost invariably described the scene as eye-witnesses, commonly adopted the pattern of the travel book in constructing sequences of events, and often incorporated in their narratives some of their own experiences in Italy. Many of the typically Gothic details in these narratives, indeed, are taken directly from Italian life. In this fiction, moreover, (as in other productions) these writers took a dominantly American point of view. Much of their picture of Italian life is colored by American political, social, and religious convictions, and they often dealt with specifically American issues. At the same time, they tended to idealize their material, projecting essentially moral themes, and employing to a great extent the technique of symbolism.

The early nineteenth-century Europeans who wrote fiction laid in Italy after visiting there also broke with the Elizabethan-Gothic tradition. Chief among their works were Mme de Staël's influential *Corinne* (1807), a virtual guide book to Rome; the historical novels of Bulwer-Lytton, *The Last Days of Pompeii* (1834) and *Rienzi* (1835); Hans Christian Andersen's *Improvisatoren* (1835), distinguished for its local color; Henri Beyle's *Chartreuse de Parme* (1839), a study of character in the modern world in which the scene is of incidental importance; and George Eliot's historical novel *Romola* (1863). The Americans followed Mme de Staël's method of projecting the Italian scene, and like Beyle they were primarily interested in the development of character. They tended, however, to exhibit a stronger nationalistic bias and a greater tendency to idealize than the Europeans. In the latter respect these American writers were most comparable to the English romantic poets, in whose connection with Italy several of the later Americans were much interested.

It was, indeed, essentially as Americans that these writers

made their discovery of Italy. There they found areas of experience and patterns of life virtually unknown in the New World, and in their writing about that country they addressed themselves primarily to marking out these areas and tracing these patterns.

Above all, these American writers acquired in Italy the conception of a way of life more purely delightful than any they had previously known. To this conception the moderation of the climate and the cultivation of the landscape in Italy— in marked contrast to these phenomena in America—together with the simple and natural aspects of the life of the Italian lower orders contributed. The keenest pleasure, however, which most of these writers had in Italy came from viewing scenes and objects associated with historical or legendary events familiar to them, and the chief aspects of the ideal life which they projected in Italian terms were intellectual stimulation and freedom from commercial pressures. For nearly all these writers, the life led by an American artist in Italy best served to represent this ideal.

As a group these writers also acquired in Italy a deeper sense of the past than they previously had. Unlike typical historical novelists, they were most interested in that phase of time as it impinged on the present. Though most of them recognized certain evil influences emanating from the Italian past, nearly all felt that experience was enriched when it overlay layers of previous experience, as it did to an unusual degree in Italian history. Most of them, moreover, regarding the Italian past as the fountainhead of classical-Christian culture, took much of it as part of their own heritage. The particular period of Italian history commonly appearing in the background of their narratives is consequently not the Renaissance, which had dominated the imaginations of most belletristic writers about Italy before them, but the time of the Roman state, which they evoked chiefly through references to Roman ruins.

In the third place, these American writers found in Italy a world where—strikingly unlike the situation in America—art objects abounded, artistic sensibility was widely diffused, and artists enjoyed enormous prestige. For American painters and sculptors these aspects of the Italian environment were of more immediate practical value than they were for American writers. For the writers, the implications of these facts were what mattered. They bore out the hypothesis, nowhere else so convincing, that the creative imagination was the source of a life independent of society and even of time—an inner life, entailing danger as well as delight. These writers commonly projected such a life, and in so doing in their Italian-laid fiction they relied heavily on artist characters and Italian objects of art. In this connection they particularly tended to employ symbolism.

In Italy, finally, this group of American writers apprehended moral issues more pressing and more complex than those familiar to them in the New World. They often depicted Italian civilization as corrupt, particularly as it was manifested in the Roman Catholic Church and in a conventionalized society. Yet they also saw in these institutions, as in the Italian past, influences for good. In dealing with moral issues in their Italianate fiction these writers commonly employed two imagistic configurations: the innocent American girl exposed to pernicious influences on foreign soil and the Garden of Eden. The character type of the American girl abroad developed in American fiction, indeed, almost exclusively in an Italian setting. The myth of the Garden of Eden was freely employed by American writers of all kinds throughout the nineteenth century, it is true. Yet many of the first group of fiction writers who visited Italy found that country peculiarly comparable to Eden, and several produced among their Italianate works some of the most brilliant and provocative variations on that myth in American literature.

Figuratively speaking, nearly all these authors discovered in Italy another native land—a home of the spirit or intellect. Several of them were also deeply drawn to England and in their writing, both fiction and non-fiction, juxtaposed the two countries as though to combine the values of each. They were, like other Americans in this youthful period of their nation's history, in quest of a cultural heritage. Chiefly for political reasons, they were generally not quite comfortable in England. Italy represented to many of them, moreover, (as it did to many of the English) an area of experience wanting in the Anglo-Saxon world, which was to that extent incomplete. Most of them felt for that country a unique attachment, quite unlike what they felt for their own. Relatively few spent a long period of time in Italy, in contrast to a good many American artists and English writers of the day. This fact, however, but points up both the intense national consciousness of these American writers and the essential inwardness of their ties with Italy.

II

The Untrammelled Life

ALLSTON, IRVING, TUCKERMAN, FAY, WILLIS, THE
GREENOUGHS, STOWE, LELAND, BREWSTER

IN NEARLY ALL THE NOVELS ABOUT ITALY WRITTEN BY
Americans who produced only one such work under Italian
influence, and in the Italianate tales of Irving, the country
appears as a scene of delightful experience and artists are
prominent characters. Hawthorne's *Marble Faun* projects a
more complicated scene. For this reason, and for the reason
that this is the only major one of these works, Hawthorne calls
for separate consideration.

The authors of the rest of these works, however, may be
considered as a group, so far as their Italianate writing is concerned. Though they range through the whole period of the
American literary discovery of Italy—from Allston at its
beginning to Miss Brewster, who lived well beyond it—they
may, moreover, conveniently be considered first. In their
limited and relatively simple treatment of their material, they
are in effect forerunners of the major fictionists of the period.

Washington Allston

Washington Allston arrived in Italy as a twenty-five-year-old art student in the fall of 1804. He had gone abroad shortly after graduating from Harvard, spent three years in London —the center of the most celebrated school of painting of the day—and stopped briefly to see the collections of art in Paris on his way south. He stayed three and a half years in Italy, most of the time in Rome. From there he returned directly to America. Though he later lived longer in England and re-visited Paris, he never went to Italy again. His Italian experience, nevertheless, constituted one of the most profound and pervasive influences on his art and thought.

The high points of that experience were Allston's study of works of art in Italian collections, his observation of the Italian landscape, and the beginning in Rome of his friendship with Coleridge, to whom he said he owed more intellectually than to any other person. Remembering years later his walks and talks with Coleridge in the grounds of the Villa Borghese, he said it almost seemed that he had listened to Plato in Academe.

Technically Allston benefitted most as an art student in Europe from studying the use of color by the contemporary English and the Renaissance Venetian painters. He was most drawn to Italian painters of the Renaissance—especially Michelangelo and Raphael, whom he praised for their imaginative and intellectual power. The most obvious foreign influence on his painting, however, was the Italian scene, as some fifteen Italian landscapes and figures by him reveal. These works are distinguished by a mood of meditation or reverie; most of them, in fact, were painted after his return to America. Their character is especially notable in view of his early enthusiasm for the Salvator Rosa tradition, with its

Washington Allston, ITALIAN LANDSCAPE. Boston or Cambridgeport, *ca.* 1830.
(Courtesy of The Detroit Institute of Arts)

emphasis on wild Italian scenery and banditti. Such subjects were Allston's favorites in his youth; not until he had been in England more than a year did he recover from what he called his "banditti mania." The pensive landscape and the dreaming figure became, indeed, virtual hallmarks of his painting. Both may be traced to his contact with the Italian scene.

The greatest influence under which Allston came in Italy was, in fact, neither strictly artistic nor scenic but intellectual. All works of art were to him communications of one mind to another, expressions of the life of the mind or spirit or imagination, which alone had the power of generating such life and inspiring such works. He found the very color in Venetian painting, as he put it later, to be "procreative in its nature, giving birth to a thousand things which the eye cannot see, and distinct from their cause." Because of the abundance of art objects in Italy and his preference for Italian artists, he was more conscious of this vital force there than in any other country. He was surely drawing on his own experience when he urged the sculptor John Cogdell in 1836 to go to Italy because of

the renovation which that delightful country, with its thousand monuments of human genius, would produce in your spirit. . . . You will find yourself growing younger in body and more elastic in mind, and I should not be surprised if the consequence prove a development of powers of which you are now unconscious.

He was sure, he wrote Cogdell a few years later, that

the glowing works of art by which you will be surrounded in Rome . . . will breathe new life into you. Even at this distance of time I live upon them in memory.

He must have recalled his own experience, too, when in his essays on art, written about 1830, he described the results of Claude Lorrain's seeing works of art for the first time in Rome.

There, in the "great University of Art," Allston wrote, the simple pastry-cook experienced a birth of intellect, found "new forms of language" ready for his use, and finally had a rush of thoughts of his own.

Allston's three books were *Sylphs of the Seasons* (1813), a collection of poems; a novel, *Monaldi* (1841); and the posthumous *Lectures on Art, and Poems* (1850), consisting of four essays, all his poems, a story, and some aphorisms. The artistic theories set forth in the essays were fostered by Allston's study of European art, and both the essays and the aphorisms contain references to Italian art and artists. It is chiefly in the poems and the novel, however, that Allston's Italian experiences are reflected. These works generally project, moreover, like his paintings of Italian subjects, the image of a delightful interior life.

Some dozen of Allston's poems have Italian subjects or contain Italian references. In three—dealing with paintings by Michelangelo, Raphael, and Pellegrino Tibaldi—the author marvels at the embodiment in these works of art of abstract conceptions and the creation of forms unlike any in nature. In "Michelangelo" the artist is represented as a planetary source of light and life, and in an untitled sonnet on art he is cited as the type of true artist, who "brought to view / The invisible Idea." "The Tuscan Girl," a literary companion piece to Allston's painting by the same title, describes the girl's maturing consciousness. One of the two poems entitled "A Fragment" is about a Florentine, who, like the title character in Allston's novel, is named Monaldi. The subject of the poem "Rosalie" is a counterpart of the girl, apparently an Italian, in his painting by the same title, and both are possibly related to Rosalia, the heroine of *Monaldi*. In "To the Author of 'The Diary of an Ennuyée'," which Allston called "one of the truest and most beautiful books ever written on Italy," this country is described as it is brought to his recollection by this book of Mrs. Anna Jameson's. The Italian landscape appears to the poet

> As 't were by passing Angels sportive dropped
> From flowers of Paradise, but newly cropped,
> Still bathed and glittering with celestial dews!

He sees the "Tuscan Zephyrs" laugh and run, "As if their touch another sense had given," and calls them "pure play-mates of the soul." Though "the long-sealed fountains" of his youth cannot be released, his "breathing, bounding, *present* youth" is awakened. Indeed, Italy is, he declares,

> that vision clime,
> Which, having seen, no eye the second time
> May ever see in its own glorious truth;—   ·
> As if it *were not,* in this world of strife,
> Save to the first deep consciousness of life.

Incidental Italian references occur in the poems "The Young Troubadour," "The Two Painters," and "Myrtilla."

Monaldi was ready to appear in 1822 in *The Idle Man,* edited by Richard Henry Dana, but, that periodical being suspended, its publication was delayed nearly two decades. Generically it is a Gothic romance. Allston was sympathetic to this literary tradition, as he was to romantic melodrama in general and to Gothic architecture. (He painted during his college years scenes from Schiller's *Räuber* and from Mrs. Radcliffe's *Mysteries of Udolpho* and later the vision of Spalatro from Mrs. Radcliffe's *Italian.*) In several signifi-cant particulars, however, *Monaldi* is not typical of Gothic fiction. The story purports to be the work of an American traveller to Italy in the eighteenth century. The first sentence sounds a passing but definitely realistic note in the reference to the "striking . . . resemblance between the autumnal sky of Italy and that of New England at the same season." The title character is a painter, and the plot conveys a moral theme.

Monaldi is a passive, introspective type, who is contrasted with both his ambitious, intelligent but unimaginative friend the poet Maldura and the crafty, licentious Count Fialtro. When Maldura, jealous of Monaldi's professional success and rejected as a suitor by Rosalia Landi, learns of the marriage of Monaldi and Rosalia, he employs Fialtro to trick Monaldi into suspecting Rosalia of infidelity. The deception of Monaldi follows the pattern of that practiced on Othello by Iago. Eventually Monaldi stabs Rosalia and, supposing he has killed her, flees. In the denouement, a repentent Maldura finds Monaldi deranged, helps him back to sanity, and then plunges him into madness again by confessing the plot against him. In the end Monaldi dies, but in his right mind and reconciled with Rosalia.

Beneath the revenge-tragedy pattern in *Monaldi* lies a moral conflict : that of a pure interior life with a world of crass and base men. The former is chiefly represented by the artistic consciousness of Monaldi. Apparently sluggish and even vacant, he shuts out the external world in order "to combine and give another life to the images it had left in his memory." To him every object had a charm, and its harmony and beauty, its expression and character, all passed into his soul in all their varieties, while his quickening spirit brooded over them as over the elementary forms of a creation of his own.

His painting of Noah's sacrifice, "unnatural" to one "who *sees only with his eyes*," is pronounced great for the reason that in it nature is bent to his will. It is to his "thoughts and feelings" that nature speaks. Looking from Maldura's apartment upon the Campo Vaccino in Rome, he declares :

. . . there *is* a chain that runs through all things. How else should the mind hear the echo of its workings from voiceless rocks? Mysterious union! that our very lives should seem but so many reflections from the face of nature; and all about us but visible types of the invisible man! Even the works of man, the passive combinations of his hand—they too have found a tongue in the elements, and become oracular to his heart—even as that proud pile of Titus, so dark and desolate within, now speaks from without, in the gorgeous language of the sun, to mine.

In contrast to Monaldi, Maldura lives "only in externals," can not see "beyond the regions of discovered knowledge," and lacks the *"realizing* quality" or the individualistic, subjective touch that "gives the living principle to thought." It is presumably for this reason that he has only temporary success as a poet.

The interior life is also represented in *Monaldi* by the works of Raphael and Michelangelo. Monaldi carries on the tradition of Raphael, is commissioned by the Pope to paint a companion piece to one of Raphael's *Madonnas,* and first sees Rosalia in the gallery where this work is exhibited. The lovers become acquainted with each other in their discussion of that artist and of Michelangelo. Monaldi and the Landis agree that, for all Michelangelo's technical faults, "there is a *something* in his works that . . . lifts one above our present world," that his forms are those "of a race which minds of a high order might call up when they think of the inhabitants of the planet Saturn," and that the current fashion to talk of his "extravagance, of his want of truth, and *what not*—as if truth were only in what we have *seen!"*—is a "matter-of-fact philosophy" which "has infected the age."

In *Monaldi* the life of the imagination is, indeed, seen as closely related to the religious life. Monaldi is overcome partly because he is not fortified by religious convictions, and just before his death—which occurs in a convent—he is converted. His acquisition of knowledge about evil has drastic effects on his artistic consciousness. During the time in which he believes Rosalia unfaithful he loses his appreciation of the natural scene and in a fit of rage accidentally destroys a bust in his house. The only painting he produces after hearing Maldura's confession depicts Satan enthroned in hell with the figure of a man kneeling to him. It is perhaps significant that Monaldi's early life with Rosalia is said to be "like one of fresher ages; like the first stream that wandered through Eden."

WASHINGTON IRVING

A few months after Allston settled in Rome, Washington Irving arrived. A twenty-one-year-old, reluctant law student, he had been sent to Europe by his older brothers in the hope of improving his spirits and his health. During his sojourn of a year and a half, he spent some eight months in France, six in Italy, and three in England, and passed through Switzerland, Belgium, and Holland. During his two subsequent European residences—lasting altogether twenty-one years—he lived for the most part in England and Spain. Of all European countries Spain most delighted and stimulated him. He never returned to Italy and, except for scattered references, treated it in his writings only in *Tales of a Traveller*.

Irving was in Italy from October 1804 to May 1805, stopping chiefly in Genoa for two months, in Sicily for one month, in Naples for two weeks, and in Rome for one month. He saw most of the tourist attractions along the way, but his chief pleasure was in the society of certain English and Americans. He prolonged his time in Genoa in order to enjoy the circle around Mrs. Bird, wife of the British consul there, and her daughters; consorted with American naval officers in

John Izard Middleton, VIEW FROM THE GROTTO OF THE CONVENT OF THE
CAPUCHINS AT ALBANO. Rome? *ca.* 1809. Engraved by M. Dubourg.

(From Middleton's Grecian Remains in Italy)

Sicily; and cut short his tour of the country (to his brothers' disgust) in order to travel with the young Virginian J. C. Cabell, who was going from Rome directly to France.

Irving's most memorable association at this time was with Allston, whom he met in Rome. Fifty years later he recalled how one of their rambles had almost changed the course of his life. They had been returning to the city from a villa on the outskirts, he wrote Evert Duyckinck in 1854 :

The blandness of the air, the serenity of the sky, the transparent purity of the atmosphere, and that nameless charm which hangs about an Italian landscape, had derived additional effect from being enjoyed in company with Allston, and pointed out by him with the enthusiasm of an artist. As I listened to him, and gazed upon the landscape, I drew in my mind a contrast between our different pursuits and prospects. He was to reside among these delightful scenes, surrounded by masterpieces of art, by classic and historic monuments, by men of congenial minds and tastes, engaged like him in the constant study of the sublime and beautiful. I was to return home to the dry study of the law, for which I had no relish, and, as I feared, but little talent.

An amateur artist himself, Irving suddenly had the idea of remaining in Rome with Allston and becoming a painter. For several days he considered embarking on such a career, connecting it always with "beautiful Italian scenery, palaces, and statues, and fountains, and terraced gardens" and with the society of Allston and other artists, and picturing "forth a scheme of life all tinted with the rainbow hues of youthful promise."

In fact Irving felt the charm of the Italian landscape before reaching Rome. On the Mediterranean between Genoa and Sicily he did not wonder that the climate of that region "should have been particularly productive of poetry & romance." "There is a poetic charm," he wrote in his journal,

. . . that diffuses itself over our ideas in considering this part of the globe. We regard every thing with an enthusiastic eye — thru a romantic medium that gives an illusive tinge to every object. 'Tis like beholding a delightful landscape from an eminence, in a beautiful sunset. A delicious mistiness is spread over the scene that softens the harshness of particular objects — prevents our examining their forms too distinctly — a glow is thrown over the whole that by blending & softening and enriching — gives the landscape a mellowness — a sweetness — a loveliness of coloring — not absolutely its own, but derived in a great measure from the illusive veil with which it is oerspread.

On the road from Naples to Rome he decided that

There is no country where the prospects so much interest my mind and awaken such a variety of ideas as in Italy. Every mountain — every valley every plain tells some striking history. On casting my eyes around some majestic ruin carries my fancy back to the ages of Roman splendor. I am lost in astonishment at the magnificence of their works, at their sublime ideas of architecture and their enormous public undertakings.

On the other hand, Irving found "present circumstances & objects" in Italy deplorable. Everywhere he saw "misery indigence & ignorance," "beggary," "the Arts languishing— neglected, the progress of knowledge impeded and man gradually returning to a state of brutality," "the land scarcely cultivated." All these phenomena he attributed to "the baneful effects of despotic governments—of priest craft & superstition, of personal oppression and slavery of thought."

Yet Irving was favorably impressed by certain aspects of Roman Catholicism in Italy. He admired the "long & dimly lighted aisles & vaulted chapels" of churches, the "pomp and sublimity" of religious services, and above all the liturgical music. This music had, he felt, "a simplicity and Grandeur best calculated to produce the sublime." A vesper hymn which he heard chanted by the crew of a vessel in the harbor of Messina seemed to him to come from "a choir of Æreal spirits that were traversing the air," and, "being in the country of romance," he was almost tempted to "indulge the fancy that they were so."

Irving did not make use of his Italian experiences in fiction until two decades later, in *Tales of a Traveller*. Ten of these tales have Italian settings and characters : the eight of Part III, which is entitled "The Italian Banditti," and two others— "The Adventure of the Mysterious Stranger" and "The Story of the Young Italian." All are typical of the Gothic, more specifically of the *Räuber* tradition established by Schiller and other German romanticists. (Among the books Irving took abroad with him in 1804 was Mrs. Radcliffe's *Italian.*) At least six of these tales are based on stories he heard in Paris in 1823 and 1824, and for background material in several he drew on such books as Alberti's *Descrittione di tutta Italia*. Nearly all of them, nevertheless, reflect his experiences in Italy.

Eight tales are laid in places Irving had visited : the town or neighborhood of Terracina, where he and Cabell spent a night en route from Naples to Rome; the mountains above Frascati, which he visited while staying in Rome; Genoa; and Naples. In describing the Roman Campagna in "The Painter's Adventure" and Genoa in "The Story of the Young Italian" he drew on his decriptions of these scenes in his journal.

During his sojourn in Italy Irving acquired first-hand knowledge of professional robbers like those featured in most of his Italian tales. In Genoa he saw the celebrated young bandit Joseph Musso, whom he described at length in his journal; and between Genoa and Sicily the vessel on which he was travelling was attacked by the crew of a privateer— *"Banditti of the Ocean,"* as he called them. At Terracina, in a region of Italy most infested with bandits, he saw the skull of a murderer exhibited in an iron cage over the town gate. This scenic detail presumably prompted that in the tale "The Inn at Terracina," where banditti are said to be hunted and shot by gendarmes and "their heads put in iron cages, and stuck upon posts by the roadside."

"The Story of the Young Italian" incorporates a greater number of Irving's particular experiences in Italy than any other of his tales. The fact is notable in view of its being one of the most derivative, having parallels with Schiller's *Räuber* and C. R. Maturin's *Fatal Revenge* as well as allegedly having been told Irving by Coleridge. In this tale the productions of the monk in the convent near Vesuvius who paints and makes wax models of human bodies in the process of decay evidently memorialize the similar wax figures, made by a monk, which Irving saw in the Capuchin convent near Syracuse. The association of Ottavio, the young Italian, with the celebrated painter in Genoa reflects Irving's association with Allston in Rome. The location of the villa belonging to the guardian of Bianca, Ottavio's beloved, corresponds roughly to that occupied by the Bird family at Sestri Ponente near Genoa, and Ottavio's glowing recollections of his time spent there with Bianca match Irving's delight in the company of Mrs. Bird and her circle.

More broadly speaking, *Tales of a Traveller* projects the image of an artist's life in Italy, which had loomed so alluringly before Irving in Rome. Two groups of these tales—seven of the ten laid in Italy and one other—deal with painters who have lived there. "The Adventure of the Mysterious Picture" (laid in England), "The Adventure of the Mysterious Stranger," and "The Story of the Young Italian" are concerned with Ottavio, a Neapolitan painter, or with his work. After an unhappy childhood, spent partly in a gloomy convent, Ottavio finds himself as an art student in Genoa. "Another being seemed created within me," he declares; "or rather, all that was amiable and excellent was drawn out." His life at that time was "a blissful period," passed

in storing my mind with lofty and poetical ideas; in meditating on all that was striking and noble in history and fiction; in studying and tracing all that was sublime and beautiful in nature.

His master, a painter of note, seemed " a benevolent genius that had opened to me a region of enchantment." Given the task of painting one of the portraits in a large work undertaken by the master, he falls in love with its subject, Bianca. She, however, is tricked into marrying another man. Ottavio kills him and is thereafter haunted by his phantom. In an attempt to banish the phantom, Ottavio paints a portrait of it—the "mysterious picture" which he gives the English baronet prominent in Part I of *Tales of a Traveller*. (Toward the end of the narratives especially there are parallels between Ottavio's story and Allston's *Monaldi*.)

A French historical painter in Italy appears in four of Irving's tales: "Adventures of the Popkins Family," "The Painter's Adventure," "The Story of the Bandit Chieftain," and "The Story of the Young Robber." For several years this artist lives with the family of a prince in his villa near Frascati, assisting him in making archeological researches nearby. The artist's "mode of life" during this time is "delightfully serene, diversified by interesting occupations and elegant lesiure." When he is captured by bandits in the neighboring mountains, he forgets his plight in admiring and sketching the scenery, ingratiates himself by his art with the bandit chieftain, and eventually paints the chieftain's portrait—recalling as he does so Salvator Rosa's sojourn among bandits.

References to Italy are scattered through several of Irving's other works, but most of them have little or no significance.

Those in "The Author's Account of Himself" in *The Sketch-Book* (1819–20), his first avowedly professional work, are, however, noteworthy. The title and the general point of view of this work were largely influenced by Irving's association with artists, including Allston, in England from 1817 to 1819. Yet his memory carried him back to his Italian experiences when he wrote that in his "sketch-book," which was "crowded with cottages, and landscapes, and obscure ruins," he had "neglected to paint St. Peter's, or the Coliseum; the Cascade of Terni, or the Bay of Naples; and had not a single glacier or volcano in his whole collection."

    *   *   *   *   *   *

In the 1830's four Americans besides James Fenimore Cooper who subsequently wrote fiction about Italy visited the country: Henry Greenough from 1830 to 1833; Nathaniel Parker Willis between 1832 and 1834; Henry T. Tuckerman in 1833/34 and from 1836 to 1838; and Theodore S. Fay, in 1833/34. Greenough and Willis, who knew each other before going to Italy, met there and both they and Fay knew Cooper abroad. Willis and Fay were associated as editors on the *New-York Mirror,* and Fay was partly following Willis's example in visiting Italy. Willis was the first of the four to write about that country—in travel letters, but Tuckerman was first—a few months earlier than Fay—to produce fiction laid there. Greenough was last to do so. Sarah Loring Greenough, his sister-in-law, who went to Italy for the first time in 1850, was the next American to make substantial use in fiction of personal experience in Italy.

Three other Americans travelled in Italy in the 1840's—Francis Parkman in 1844, Donald Grant Mitchell in 1846, and George William Curtis in 1846–47—and later referred incidentally to the country in fiction. In Parkman's novel *Vassall Morton* (1856), the hero briefly touches Italian soil.

Mitchell's *Reveries of a Bachelor* (1852), in which the bachelor recalls his love for a Roman woman, Enrica, reflects some of the author's experiences in and around Rome. (Mitchell, who was the American consul in Venice from 1853 to 1855, also wrote several magazine articles describing Italian life.) Curtis' "A Story of Venice" (1859), a melodramatic tale, was allegedly told him in that city. These works, however, hardly merit further attention for their treatment of Italian material.

HENRY T. TUCKERMAN

In the fall of 1833 Henry Theodore Tuckerman, who had prepared himself to enter Harvard but was too frail to do so, went to Italy in the hope of improving his health. He was twenty at the time. Landing at Le Havre, he passed quickly through France and reached Italy late in October. He stayed a little over six months : about three in Florence, two in Rome, and the rest of the time travelling, seeing notably Naples, Venice, and Milan. His return to America was by way of Switzerland and France. Two years later he went directly to Sicily, where he spent most of the time from the end of 1836 to the summer of 1837, when an epidemic of cholera drove him away. From then until the following spring, when he left the country, he travelled chiefly in northern Italy, visiting Florence at length and Lucca, Pisa, Carrara, Genoa, Turin, Bologna, Modena, Ravenna, San Marino, and other points briefly. Again he passed through France on his way home. During both Italian sojourns he saw a good deal of the American artists in Florence, particularly Horatio Greenough. His third and last trip abroad, which consumed about a month in the winter of 1852–53, took him to England and France only.

Thomas Hiram Hotchkiss, TAORMINA, THE ISLAND OF SICILY. Taormina, *ca.* 1869.

(Courtesy of The New-York Historical Society)

Italy and its inhabitants appealed to Tuckerman far more than any other foreign country or people. He called France prosaic by comparison and the French character "delusive." Though he admired the English, he missed in them the Italian esthetic sense and "devotion to the ideal."

In Italy he found the mild climate and the slow tempo of life especially agreeable. Above all, he found intellectual and social influences there which were in striking contrast to the commercialism and competition in America, and which seemed to him more conducive to the development of human capabilities and values. His Sonnet XXV most succinctly describes this contrast and most explicitly states what he felt the influence of Italy to have been on himself:

> In my first youth, the feverish thirst for gain
>   That in this noble land makes life so chill,
> Was tempered to a wiser trust by pain,
>   Hope's early blight — a chastening sense of ill;
> And I was exiled to a sunny clime,
>   Where cloud and flower a softer meaning caught
> From graceful forms and holy wrecks of time,
>   Appealing all to fond and pensive thought;
> Enamored of the Beautiful I grew,
>   And at her altar pledged my virgin soul. . . .

The great effect of works of art in Italy was, he wrote after his first Italian visit, to produce the character of "the amateur": one who had a genuine and disinterested "appreciation of the results of mind, whatever their character or origin," and who exerted a beneficent influence, especially in contrast to those devoting themselves "with fatal exclusiveness, to the purposes of ambition." The "imaginative, the purely intellectual character of the enjoyments" offered in Italy were, he conceded, "at war with the ultra-utilitarian spirit of the age." Yet for this very reason he felt that the country had valuable lessons to teach. "There are few countries," he declared, "better calculated to nourish and bring out the latent *ideal* of existence than this."

The more he saw of artists in Italy the more attractive Tuckerman found their life and the more assured he became that they were valuable members of society. "Often subsisting upon the merest pittance, indulging in every vagary of costume," he wrote of them after his second Italian visit,

they wander over the land, and yield themselves freely to the spirit of adventure, and the luxury of art. . . . They seem a privileged class . . . these gay wanderers.

The office of all artists, he thought, was to keep alive the truth that "man does not live by bread alone." American artists (as examples he named sculptors Horatio Greenough, Hiram Powers, and Shobal Vail Clevenger, all living in Florence) further served to keep the "national heart" from being "wholly corroded by gain."

The Italian people were to a great extent responsible for Tuckerman's pleasure in Italy. Their sympathetic nature and deep capacity for feeling—especially manifest, he thought, in Italian women—endeared them to him. He apparently fell in love with a Sicilian girl, to judge from his poem "To a Brunette," and he was charmed by the Italian countess and her daughter with whom he lodged during his first visit to Florence. Italians were, he declared, "a kind of primitive humanity," supreme users of "natural language," "the poets of the nations." In consequence he felt that "life in Italy—in the deepest sense of the term, is to a great extent *latent.*" "Italy is, indeed," he wrote in his review of J. T. Headley's *Letters from Italy* in 1845,

every where written over with the hieroglyphics of antiquity, yet nowhere have we so realized youth—the youth of humanity, of the individual, the real youth of warm feeling and quick sensibility and credulous imagination—the youth that speaks in the kindling eye, in the ready tone of sympathy, in childlike abandonment to the fresh and honest impulses of the heart.

In contrast, America exhibited the "uniform aspect of precocious age," uniting the youthful characteristics of "activity, excitement, and self-confidence" with

an incessant care and ambition which transforms the boy almost in a day, to an anxious, plodding man, and transforms the pretty child, as it were at a bound, from the nursery to womanhood—not reposing, sunny and joy-dispensing, but careful, worn and "troubled about many things."

In his essay "New England Philosophy" he called the "pervading theory of life" in Italy an artistic one. More significantly, in analyzing this philosophy, which he equated in general with the national philosophy in America, he contrasted what he regarded as its first and most deplorable principle—deference to public opinion—with the determined and fruitful individualism which he thought typical of Italians.

A lifelong sympathizer with the movement for Italian independence, Tuckerman visited Silvio Pellico in Turin in 1838 and befriended many Italian exiles in America after the Revolution of 1848. In recognition of his literary services to the government of Victor Emmanuel II, an Italian order of nobility was conferred upon him.

Italy exerted an extensive influence on Tuckerman's writing. Indeed, his first visit there indirectly led him into the profession of letters. On his return home in 1834, he spent a short time at the Harvard Divinity School and then began to contribute to the *Boston Pearl and Literary Gazette* a series of descriptive sketches, tales, and poems inspired mainly by his recent Italian experiences. In the following year he collected some of these and other prose pieces in his first volume, *The Italian Sketch Book* (1835), obviously modelled after Irving's

Sketch-Book; it was slightly enlarged in 1837 and almost doubled in length as well as much revised in 1848. His second and third books capitalized on his second visit to Italy : *Isabel, or Sicily* (1839) and *Rambles and Reveries* (1841).

Approximately half of Tuckerman's two dozen volumes, and twenty-two of his hundred-odd uncollected pieces, deal wholly or in part with Italian subjects, and most of his works on other subjects contain Italian references. His distinctly Italianate writings consist of some two dozen descriptive sketches; sixteen biographical and critical essays or reviews, chiefly on leading figures of the Risorgimento; about twenty poems; two book-length and thirteen shorter pieces of fiction; and a few translations of Italian poems and prose narratives. Of the works indirectly reflecting his Italian experiences, the most notable are *Artist-Life* (1847; revised as *The Book of the Artists,* 1867), *A Memorial of Horatio Greenough* (1853), and *America and her Commentators* (1864).

Of Tuckerman's poems dealing with Italy, five touch on the Italian revolution ("Italy," "The Siege of Rome," and three sonnets to Pius IX); five are descriptive ("Il Ponte Santa Trinita—Florence," "The Contadina," "Rome," "Lord Byron at Venice," "Syracuse"); three are narrative ("The Fate of Pia," "Giulia," "The Apollo Belvedere"); three are autobiographical (the lines to R. C. Waterston from Rome in "Excerpts from the Diary of Thoughtville," "To a Brunette," and Sonnet XXV); and three describe works of art ("The Apollo Belvedere," "Washington's Statue," "The Unknown Portrait"). In six (including the autobiographical ones) foreigners appear on the Italian scene and some fall in love with Italians.

All Tuckerman's fiction except one story and one sketch is laid in Italy. Of the shorter pieces one appeared in the first edition of *The Italian Sketch Book,* four in the second edition of that work, three in *Rambles and Reveries,* and all in the last edition of *The Italian Sketch Book.* Several have Gothic details. (Mrs. Radcliffe and C. R. Maturin were, Tuckerman recalled, "clandestine intimates" of his childhood.) Most of these pieces, however, are related in the first person and purport to be tales heard by the narrator while travelling in Italy. All Tuckerman's fiction laid in Italy reflects in a general way his Italian experiences, and some incorporates specific details of those experiences. The journal he kept in Italy, on which he drew at least in the first edition of *The Italian Sketch Book* and which might have revealed other details in his fiction to have been derived from fact, has apparently not been preserved.

All these fictional works of Tuckerman's except two stories are laid in specified Italian places, all of which he had visited : three in Rome, two in the city or on the bay of Naples, and one each in Florence, Venice, Genoa, Pisa, Milan, Leghorn, Massa, and Sicily. All these places are described, in more or less detail, with the eye of an observer. In the first of these works, "The Florentine," the characters Anina and her mother are drawn from Tuckerman's landlady in Florence in 1834 and her daughter. The central character in this story is an Italian painter, and in three other stories or sketches—"The Disclaimer," "Harry Clinton," and "A Reminiscence of Shelley"—there are non-Italian painters, such as Tuckerman had known in Italy. Four of his later pieces contain American characters travelling or living in Italy : "Love in a Lazzaret," describing the courtship of an American, Delano, and an Italian girl, Angelica de Falco, on a vessel quarantined in the Bay of Naples; "Speculation; or Dyspepsia Cured," which concerns a former Maine schoolmaster, now a New Orleans speculator, who has come to Italy to invest in marble; "Harry Clinton," in which the central character is an American travelling abroad for his health and an American painter in Rome, Charles Arlington, briefly appears; and "Kitty Mayo," concerning an eccentric Quaker heiress from Philadelphia, who has wandered about the Mediterranean for twenty years and now presumably lives in Naples. In two other stories—"The Rose-Colored Packet" and "The Thespian Syren"—Britishers travelling in Italy fall in love with Italian women.

Tuckerman's novel, *Isabel,* written partly during his second Italian visit, concerns the journey through Sicily of an American girl, Isabel Otley, who has come from America to meet her father. With her uncle, who has accompanied her across the Atlantic, and a young Italian count, whom she has met on shipboard, she spends several months travelling on the island, following a route which was probably Tuckerman's own. From Messina the party goes to Catania and Syracuse; thence across to Palermo, from where they make an expedition to see the antiquities of Segesta, Selinunte, Sciacca, and Agrigento; back to Catania; and from there by way of Etna back to Messina. The novel thus has the basic structure of a guide book. Besides detailed descriptions of all these places and of the routes between them, it contains a sketch of a novitiate, accounts of several famous Sicilians, and a brief discussion of Sicilian literature.

More significantly, Tuckerman's novel has an international theme. Isabel's father, Frederic Otley, had been forced early in life into commerce, had found it uncongenial, and had been confirmed in his attitude during a year spent in southern Europe. After the death of his wife, he had gone abroad again. "It is on revisiting southern Europe, especially," Tuckerman wrote apropos of this trip of Otley's, "that an American is best prepared, justly to estimate, and duly to feel, all that is peculiar in the two hemispheres." The "legitimate gratifications of southern Europe are eminently meditative," he explained, "incompatible with a spirit of restless ambition, or gainful passion"; they are addressed to

the imaginative and enthusiastic, to the contemplative and intellectual; to those who believe there is a greater good than worldly success, a richer boon than the distinctions of office; to those who believe that the process of improvement does not consist wholly in action . . . to those who have faith in the refining influences of art and nature, and a life of "meek self content," passed in the free and independent exercise of thought, imagination, and love; and who . . . recognise the truth, that the mind, like the earth, is enriched by lying fallow, and that a tranquil life, if permitted by an individual's destiny, may be rendered more truly profitable than one passed in the most successful and renowned course of active usefulness.

Isabel, "an ardent and gifted idealist," like her father appreciates Italy. In sharp contrast to them is her utilitarian uncle, Clifford Frazier, who frequently asserts the superiority of American to Italian institutions.

As Isabel discovers, however, a deplorable disparity exists between the attractive natural scene and the great achievements of Italy in the past on the one hand and the tyranny, immorality, and poverty of contemporary Italian civilization on the other. The young count, Vittorio, acknowledges as much. A supporter of the Risorgimento like his father, who has died in exile in England, Vittorio is instinctively drawn to American political and social philosophies. Early in their acquaintance he commends Isabel not only to her patron saint but to

that self-dependence, that trust in individual mind and energy, that confidence in the native and personal power of the soul, characteristic of northern nations, and than which there is no greater mystery of character to a southern European.

Repelled by the spectacle at the Royal Theatre in Palermo on the last day of the carnival, he urges Isabel's uncle to

"pierce the artificial gloss; read the evidences of exhausted resources, unprincipled lives, and frivolous pursuits which make up the true history of society here, and thank heaven your lot was cast in a young republic."

Vittorio and Isabel are eventually married, on an American frigate in the harbor of Messina, shortly after the arrival there of Isabel's father. Thus the best elements of the civilizations of Italy and America are in effect united.

Tuckerman's last piece of fiction, *Leaves from the Diary of a Dreamer* (1853), is also based on his second trip to Italy. Ostensibly the diary of a young writer travelling for his health who has died at the town of Massa, it follows this character through several places in Italy visited by Tuckerman, presumably describes some of his acquaintances there, and expresses many of his own sentiments about the country. In a mountainous neighborhood the Dreamer puts up at a dwelling where "the whole scene was precisely such as Mrs. Radcliffe is fond of describing." His view of Italy, however, is a highly personal one. Though he recognizes the prosaic aspects of this country—its "garlic and mendicity, filthy staircases and cold ungarnished apartments . . . narrowness of mind and petty species of action"—he has there "a delicious sense of independence, an exhilarating consciousness of individuality." There he is convinced that a "sequestered but intense experience, a private but satisfying activity is the need of many a spirit"; that dreamers or imaginative natures as well as practical ones "were created for specific ends"; that "what is termed 'idleness,' is properly their element." He finds individuals more interesting in Italy than in northern latitudes, partly because of the "keener sympathies of the people," especially of the women.

Theodore S. Fay

In the late summer of 1833, the New York author and
editor Theodore Sedgwick Fay, then twenty-six years old and
recently married, set out for Italy, intending to spend a year
there to benefit his health. He travelled by way of Gibraltar
and Marseilles, spent a few days in Genoa, and reached
Florence about November. He visited Rome during the carnival season early the next year but was back in Florence by
Easter. During most of his stay in that city he lived in an
apartment in the Palazzo Ferroni. In addition to visiting the
chief places of interest and attending a good many social
events, he studied Italian with a priest and wrote a series of
descriptive sketches and a portion, at least, of a novel laid
partly in Italy. About June he left Florence, proceeded to
Venice and Milan, and thence to Paris and London. A few
years later he was given a minor diplomatic post in London.
In 1837 he became secretary of the American legation in
Berlin and in 1853 resident minister to Switzerland. On his
retirement in 1861 he returned to Germany, where he spent
the remaining thirty-seven years of his life. He never went back
to America.

During his first nine months abroad, Fay recorded his
experiences in a column, "The Minute-Book," for the *New-
York Mirror*. Subsequently, he wrote for the same magazine
a few sketches of Italy and England and, when he journeyed
to Germany in 1837, a series called "Original Letters from
Abroad." He was favorably impressed by London and
delighted by Germany, but of Italy (and the French Riviera)
sweepingly denunciatory. The scenery, he conceded, surpassed
his expectations (he repeatedly referred to it as "Eden"), but
he was shockingly disillusioned about "everything relating to
man in cities." The Arno at Florence was a "muddy brook"

Asher B. Durand, ROMAN HEAD. Rome, 1841.
(Courtesy of The New-York Historical Society)

and the Lungarno a "narrow filthy promenade." "What! that narrow creek the Tiber?" he exclaimed in Rome, where "the dream of a life-time" was "gone in a moment." "I do not like to live," he wrote from Florence,

in the midst of moral abasement, of despotism, a domineering aristocracy of birth rather than of talent; and I prefer a place where the men and women are better, though the statues and paintings may be worse.

Repeatedly he complained of beggary, dishonesty, indecency, and superstition among Italians and blamed the priesthood and the military for the depth of the depravity he saw. Only Venice truly pleased him; "never before," he declared, "did I anywhere so enjoy the sensation of beholding a brilliant dream of wild romance perfectly realized." He thought Milan probably the "cleanest and most beautiful town in Italy" and praised the cathedral there in particular. Yet his final judgment, like his first, was that America was incomparably superior in every way to both Italy and France. "New York," he wrote after travelling from Nice to Genoa,

is built of burnished silver, and strewn with roses washed in dew, contrasted with the receptacles of Europe; and through all Americans there is a moral feeling which will prevent them, for centuries to come, from dwelling in such revolting dungeons as are some of the most renowned European cities.

In Europe, especially in Italy, he added, "The pilgrim from the west feels that till now he was never actually in the world." But it was a world of the dead past, whereas America belonged to the future.

Fay's writings consist of a book of sketches and essays (his first volume, *Dreams and Reveries of a Quiet Man*, 1832), four novels (two of them written as protests against duelling), a long narrative poem, a few geographies for school use, two books in German on American history and politics, a history of Germany, many uncollected sketches and essays, and a few uncollected short pieces of fiction appearing in magazines. In only one long work did he make substantial use of his Italian experience: *Norman Leslie* (1835), his second book and first novel, which he worked on in Italy.

This work is in two volumes, the first laid in New York City, the second for the most part in Italy. Melodramatic throughout, it is typically Gothic in volume two, which abounds in mystery, intrigue, and crime. The title character is forced to flee America when he is suspected of murdering young Rosalie Romain, who mysteriously disappears. After six years of unprofitable wandering he comes to Italy, where he finds Rosalie; Count Clairmont (his mortal enemy, who proves responsible for Rosalie's fate), and his American sweetheart, Flora Temple, who, having declined after his departure, has been sent there for her health. The allegedly French Clairmont (modelled, Fay said, on a historical person), who is the chief villain, turns out to be a Neapolitan, Rinaldo; his brother, equally villainous, is Father Ambrose (whose name suggests a kinship with M. G. Lewis's monk, Ambrosio). Italy, moreover, is depicted as a land of moral turpitude, nowhere more apparent than in the operations of the Roman Catholic Church. It appears also as a land of social injustice, inhabited by both beggars and owners of magnificent palaces.

Unlike the typical Gothic romancer, however, Fay repeatedly interjects personal testimony to all this effect, thus giving his work an air of authenticity. He often contrasts Italy and America. "Oh, Italy!" he exclaims as he transfers the scene of the novel there :

who treads thy stricken and terrible domains, from the fresh and virgin dells of the new world, feels then, perchance, for the first time, appalled that he is *man*.

Toward the end, noting that the most interesting objects to a traveller are not landscapes or ruins but "the moods and standards of the moral world, as they vary according to clime and country," he opined that Italy's

systems of government and society are as uncouthly shattered into wild and accidental fragments as her immense and mouldering amphitheatres and her ruined towers; with this exception, that her dilapidated edifices and walls are the sublime wrecks of once perfect things, while her monstrous shapes of politics and morals appear but the phases of a mighty chaos, which has never had bright order and perfection. Her morals, her customs, her laws, her governments, have no general connection with truth, wisdom, and virtue. Every object, every principle is bent, warped, and distorted from the beauty and glory of happier countries. Hence, opinion is a crime — the press is a danger — religion, a cheat — and female dishonour, a fashion.

As for the Risorgimento, Leslie thinks it doomed to failure. "Italy will only be regenerated," he tells the liberal young Italian sculptor Angelo,

if she is *ever* regenerated, by the slow influence of opinion; and her first aid will come from abroad. She might be freed by her own revolutions a thousand times, and she would only fall back again into slavery and degradation. Austria, Russia, France, must be first changed : in her struggle she copes with the colossal energies of all these.

Americans, he reminds Angelo, "are separated from Europe. They breathe an atmosphere all their own; and were morally prepared to govern themselves long before they became their own masters."

The picture of America which he goes on to draw for Angelo is of a land, even more beautiful than Italy, of economic plenty and political and religious enlightment. In the end, the author takes his leading characters back to America with the words, "Back from the scathed Europe, with its footmarks of gaunt and bloody ages, we are once again in the fresh and happy scenes of a new world."

The descriptions of the Italian landscape and climate in *Norman Leslie* also are essentially personal observations. In contrast to the moral scene, this physical one is delightful. The climate is "unspeakably sweet and alluring," and "the pilgrim from a northern clime fancies" that the lower classes whom he sees living most of the time out of doors are "happy as the children of Eden." In November, as Leslie enters Florence (at about the same time that Fay did),

while London was merged in mud, fog, and smoke, and New-York lay dark and cold amid her naked trees and wintry winds, this ancient and celebrated town, sheltered from the north by stupendous mountains, and basking under a heaven all warm with hues of pearl and emerald, lay steeped in this ocean of glowing light, with the exquisite splendour of a *Claude*.

All autumns in Italy are said to be "golden" and the Val d'Arno is "an expressibly beautiful scene," "the most extraordinary scene for beauty which the globe can furnish." Yet the Italian climate, too, is compared unfavorably with the American. "But I doubt whether," wrote Fay,

the vigorous and enlivening joys of winter are not more conducive to health and happiness. An Italian vale, breathing its sweetest odours, is but a dull picture compared with Broadway on the bright morning after a heavy fall of snow. No scene can be more full of life and action.

The valleys and plains of Italy and of Asia at best seemed to him "beneficently designed for man in his more uncivilized state, or for the poor."

Norman Leslie is also given a realistic tone by the descriptions of particular places, edifices, and occasions, both in New York and in Italy. The Campanile and the Duomo in Florence and St. Peter's in Rome are admiringly pictured. "If you have never seen St. Peter's, reader," observed the author,

you are to be envied. In your prospective lies the possibility of a *new* impression. Its immensity and magnificence almost cease to be physical objects. They strike, they amaze, they exalt the mind. They awaken, impress, and overwhelm the imagination. They roll over you with the mastery and solemn thrill of something intellectual and ideal.

The details about the palace of the Marquis Torrini in Florence seem to be drawn from that of the Prince Borghese, which Fay described in "The Minute-Book," and the account of the Marquis's soirée seems to be based on the weekly balls at the villa of the Florentine banker Emanuele Fenzi, to which Fay was regularly invited.

Dissolute and dangerous as Italy thus appears in *Norman Leslie,* the novel affords two glimpses of idyllic life there. The first is that of the life of an artist, represented by the young sculptor Angelo and the old painter Ducci. Angelo (who seems to be drawn in part from the American sculptor Horatio Greenough, to whom Fay carried a letter of introduction) has handsome features, a noble though somewhat stern bearing, and the "character of melancholy and intellectuality peculiar to his profession—peculiar, indeed, to all whose studies lead them from the outer world into the higher realms of thought and imagination." His "labors were not of the body, but of the mind." Altogether "he was a *beau ideal* for genius." Ducci, though less talented than Angelo, has been committed to the same lofty endeavors. Apropos of him Fay wrote :

About even an inferior painter there rests a halo, however feeble, of genius and ambition. His mind, even if it have not reached them, has nevertheless grasped at the more radiant shapes of nature; his life has been one of floating dreams and brilliant shadows, a continual pursuit after the striking and the beautiful;

he inhabits a region half ideal, teeming with lovely groups, and steeped in gay and tender colouring. When he withdraws his eyes from his own imaginations—imaginations not only more gorgeous than reality, but even beyond his power to pour upon the visible canvass—how much he must behold to blot out from the picture of common life! how much he must feel to palsy his arm, and chill his hope, and teach him to fear that he struggles in vain!

As for the work of art itself, its peculiar charm is represented as being its immortal quality. Viewing the statue of Psyche which he has ordered from Angelo, Leslie exclaims, "When I look on a statue, it is ever with a thrill. Immortality is written on it, as well as genius." Angelo agrees.

Angelo is, moreover, a leader in the Risorgimento movement, who deplores the condition of his country and admires America extravagantly. "Oh!" he exclaims to Leslie,

. . . how I have hung over the romantic story of your country! —over its sublime moral fabric—over its godlike statesmen and soldiers, higher, because more enlightened, than those of either Rome or Greece. Your government and your heroes have been *disinterested*. The happiness of their race is their sole object. Your nation steps along the career of *moral right;* never reels with the drunkenness of glory—with the thirst after empire. . . . You possess the principle of growth hidden in an acorn, which, in its humble origin, affords you at once a hope and a lesson. . . . Oh that *I* had been born in such a land! where I could tread amid the still woods and mountains, and *feel* myself not a *slave*.

And when Leslie comments that Angelo speaks differently from many Europeans, Angelo says there are thousands like him.

The other image of idyllic life in Italy in *Norman Leslie* is projected in the scenes between Leslie and Antonia Torrini, daughter of the Marquis (whom the humbly-born Angelo loves hopelessly). Antonia is a stock romantic heroine in her innocent purity. Her garden, however, is contrasted with the world outside in a notable way :

It seemed a new world of foliage and light, the music of birds, and the liquid murmurs of bright waters as they leaped into the air, and fell back into their marble fountains. . . . high, huge, smooth walls bounded the luxuriant and summer Eden,

shutting out most notably beggars and friars. (Father Ambrose in company with Antonia, for whom he lusts, "looked like the tempter watching by Eve and studying her ruin.") Her room contains many paintings by old masters. In her company Leslie finds the sort of happiness he had enjoyed with Flora Temple, but he does not transfer his affections.

For all his antipathy to it, it is in Italy that Leslie recovers the thread of his life, clears his name, sees Rosalie rescued and justice done to Clairmont, and is reunited with Flora, with whom he returns to America. He had given up all such hopes, but in Italy he is promptly caught up in a series of coincidences peculiarly related to his history :

He seemed passed into a magic circle, where, under the wand of some enchanter, viewless phantoms of his own fate attended on his steps, whispering ever in his ear words connected with the mightiest secret of his soul. . . .

Only when he is passive do these influences operate. As it turns out, Clairmont had kidnapped Rosalie to obtain her jewels and, when Leslie became implicated in her disappearance, confined her to insure his apparent guilt. As a result she had gone mad. Clairmont is killed by a friend of Leslie's. Rosalie, somewhat recovered, returns to America but soon dies there.

In working out the final stages of his plot, moreover, Fay made particular use of certain aspects of the Italian scene. To some extent he cited works of art. Antonia's face is "like one of Raphael's madonnas." In describing the death of the Marquis Torrini to his nephew Alezzi (who eventually goes to America and settles in the South), Ambrose says, "The death-scene was a *Caravaggio. My pencil,* you know, leans toward the warmth and loveliness of Titian." It is the fictitious Ducci's portrait of the Countess D——'s son which enables Leslie to identify both mother and son as those he rescued from a run-away horse in New York.

More effective is Fay's use in the last scenes of his novel of the carnival and the Colosseum in Rome. Leslie, in disguise, first meets Flora in Italy during a carnival ball. The whole atmosphere of the carnival, moreover, with its disguises and abrupt, interrupted encounters, enforces the theme of mistaken or lost identity particularly noticeable in this part of the novel. In the Colosseum, with its history of violence and injustice, virtually the entire cast of characters is gathered at night in the climactic scene, when Rosalie, in the clutches of Clair-mont, is recognized; Clairmont, in the act of firing on Leslie, is killed; and the Countess D—— reveals that she released Rosalie in order to revenge herself on Clairmont. Subsequently her letter to Leslie identifies her as Clairmont's (Rinaldo's) Neapolitan wife, whom he had early deserted.

Fay's few short pieces dealing with Italy (appearing in the *New-York Mirror* in 1835–6–7) consist chiefly of the essays "San Zenobio, or, A Summer in Florence" and "The Present State of Italy"; and the historical tales "The Head of Clean-der," "A True Tale of the Coliseum" (both laid in Rome at the time of the Empire), "The Antique," and "Without a Rival" (both about Italian artists—Michelangelo and Andrea del Castagno, respectively). The only noteworthy one is "The Antique," a garbled version of the anecdote about Michel-angelo's having given his statue of a sleeping cupid an an-tique appearance and so captured the attention of Cardinal di San Giorgio in Rome. In Fay's story the young sculptor is said to have imbibed his love of art from the constant sight of the great works of art in Florence, which are described as possessing a noble and enduring life of their own. He

had caught the unseen fire, and it had long burned silently amid the immortal marbles of that old Italian city. . . . his eyes were ever familiar with these endless and beautiful beings. They became his companions. His imagination was imbued with them. He had felt the grandeur of a sublime character throned on a marble forehead, or breathing in an eternal attitude. He had become spellbound by the forms of this silent and ideal nation. Their nobleness and refinement—their revealings of poetry, history and romance—their haughty and unbending heroism, amid the homelier and more commonplace influences of life—the dark tales of wonder and death linked with them—their exquisite physical beauty—their moral sublimity, had touched him as if with enchantment.

The narrator, moreover, identifies himself with the young sculptor. "I share his startling reveries before the form of some stately warriour upon his steed," he wrote. Continuing, he emphasized the immortal quality of such works:

Our transitory nature crouches beside its majestic immorality. . . . We are hurried, blindly on, through chance and wo—through decrepitude and death. But this is beyond the malice of fate.

Nathaniel Parker Willis

Nathaniel Parker Willis was already a poet and journalist of note when in 1831, at the age of twenty-six, he went abroad as a correspondent for the *New-York Mirror,* of which he was an editor. He spent about six months in France, over a year in Italy, six months on a Mediterranean cruise, and two years in England. He described his travels in all these places in letters to the *Mirror,* most of which were collected in the volume *Pencillings by the Way.* First published in 1835, it appeared in a final, enlarged edition in 1844.

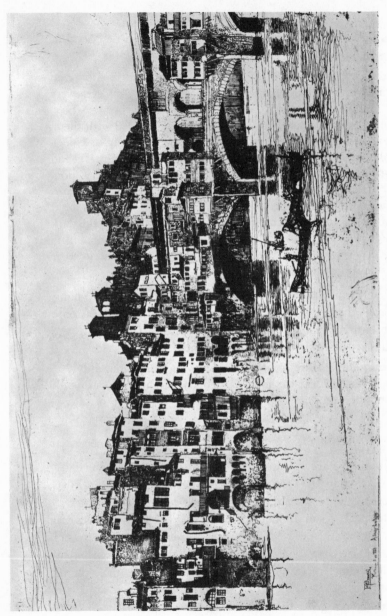

Joseph Pennell, ON THE ARNO. Florence, 1883.
(Courtesy of Prints Division, The New York Public Library)

As a traveller abroad, Willis was ever freshly delighted by new scenes yet given to few and for the most part conventional critical judgments. With his flair for society, he most enjoyed meeting celebrities and attending public gatherings. To all other foreign countries he apparently preferred England, where he associated with many literati, was to a considerable extent lionized, and married an English woman. His second trip abroad was to England, and on his next, final trip he visited only that country and Germany. He was more critical of Italians than of other Europeans, calling them "lazy, unprincipled" in contrast to the French, with their "politeness." Yet he declared that he "loved" Italy, expressing more emotion than he did about any other country. "In sober sadness," he wrote of his feelings on leaving it,

one may well regret any country where his life has been filled fuller than elsewhere of sunshine and gladness; and such, by a thousand enchantments, has Italy been to me. Its climate is life in my nostrils, its hills and valleys are the poetry of such things, and its marbles, pictures, and palaces, beset the soul like the very necessities of existence. You can exist elsewhere, but oh! you *live* in Italy!

Willis was in Italy continuously from the summer of 1832 to that of 1833, spending most of his time in Florence, and making short visits chiefly in Venice and Rome. In the course of his Mediterranean cruise and his journey north to England —in the summer of 1833 and early in 1834—he stopped briefly in Naples, Sicily, Venice, and Milan. He was apparently most diverted in Florence, partly because of the society afforded there by the Tuscan court and by several noble Tuscan families and titled political exiles from other European countries. He also enjoyed his association with several American artists in Florence—among them Horatio and Henry Greenough, Francis Alexander, John Cranch, and Thomas

Cole. He sat to Horatio Greenough for a portrait bust, briefly took up modelling under the instruction of Greenough and the English sculptor John Gibson in Rome, and even considered becoming an artist himself. Indeed, Willis seemed to think of Italy as being most distinctively a scenic embodiment of certain figments of the imagination, such as those embodied in works of art. He admired the Italian landscapes of Claude in Rome because of the meeting in them of the imaginary and the real. "I can conceive no higher pleasure for the imagination," he wrote,

than to see a Claude in travelling through Italy. It is finding a home for one's more visionary fancies—those children of moonshine that one begets in a colder clime, but scarce dares acknowledge till he has seen them under a more congenial sky. More plainly, one does not know whether his abstract imaginations of pastoral life and scenery are not ridiculous and unreal, till he has seen one of these landscapes, and felt *steeped* . . . in the very loveliness which inspired the pencil of the painter. There he finds . . . the whole delicious scenery, as bright as in his dreams, and he feels as if he should bless the artist for the liberty to acknowledge freely to himself the possibility of so beautiful a world.

Italy exerted more influence on Willis' imaginative writing than did any other foreign country. Four of his poems— "Melanie," "Florence Gray" (the name of a girl whom the poet met in Rome), "'Chamber Scene'" (the name of a painting in an artist's studio in Rome), and "To Julia Grisi"— have to do with persons in Italy, and half a dozen others contain Italian references or mottoes. The most noteworthy of these poems appeared in *Melanie and Other Poems* (1835), whose title piece is the most ambitious of them all. The English narrator of this poem, during a walk around the Cascatelles of Tivoli, tells the story of his sister, Melanie de Brevern, who in that town, on "such a day / As might have dawn'd on Eden first," met and fell in love with the Italian painter Angelo, learned at their marriage that he was her half-brother, and thereupon died. Two of Willis' three plays—the historical *Bianca Visconti* (1839) and *Tortesa the Usurer* (1839)—have Italian characters and scenes. (In the latter, Isabella, daughter of the Florentine Count Falcone, is married to the painter Angelo instead of to the wealthy Tortesa.) Eleven of Willis' twenty-five stories—two in *Inklings of Adventure* (1836), three in *Loiterings of Travel* (1840), and six others in the final, omnibus collection of his stories, *Dashes at Life with a Free Pencil* (1845)—and his only novel, *Paul Fane* (1857), are laid in Italy.

All this fiction reflects Willis' Italian experiences. Four stories—"Paletto's Bride," "Violanta Cesarini," "The Countess Nyschriem and the Handsome Artist," and "The Madhouse of Palermo"—are versions of stories or actual happenings about which he had heard either in Italy or in connection with his Italian visit. Part of the action of "Pasquali, the Tailor of Venice" occurs during the Feast of St. Anthony, on or about which day in 1832 Willis was in that city. In "Leaves from the Heart-Book of Ernest Clay" and "Those Ungrateful Blidgimses" he caricatured Miss Anna Bridgen and her spinster sister of Albany, whom he had known in Florence and at Bagni di Lucca. "My One Adventure as a Brigand" is based on his encounter with an English bridal couple on the way from Bologna to Florence, as described in one of his travel letters. Six of his stories and his novel (as well as *Tortesa the Usurer* and "Melanie") are concerned with artists in Italy, for the most part such as those he had known. The American painters F——, in "Those Ungrateful Blidgimses" and "Light Vervain," and Paul Fane are to some extent self-portraits.

The pervasive theme in Willis' fiction is the attempt of a

free-acting nobleman of nature to win a place in a society
dominated by a convention-motivated, artificial aristocracy.
In four of his Italian narratives—"Violanta Cesarini," "The
Countess Nyschriem and the Handsome Artist," "The Revenge
of the Signor Basil," and *Paul Fane* (as in *Tortesa the Usurer*)
—the humble hero is, temporarily at least, a painter. As Willis
saw them, portraitists, which most of his artists are, were particularly well suited for this role. "I have always been very
fond of the society of portrait-painters," declares the narrator
of " 'Beauty and the Beast,' " thinking of the portraitist
S——, whom he had met in Italy :

Whether it is, that the pursuit of a beautiful and liberal art
softens their natural qualities, or that, from the habit of con-
versing while engrossed with the pencil, they like best that touch-
and-go talk which takes care of itself; or, more probably still,
whether the freedom with which they are admitted behind the
curtains of vanity and affection gives a certain freshness and
truth to their views of things around them—certain it is, that,
in all countries, their rooms are the most agreeable of haunts,
and they themselves most enjoyable of cronies.

The most fully drawn of Willis' artists are the Russian Basil
Spirifort, in "The Revenge of the Signor Basil," and the
American Paul Fane. Basil, a serf by birth but a count and
diplomat by reason of his superior endowments, masquerades
as an artist for two years in Venice, while waiting for a transfer from the Russian embassy in Paris to that in Florence. In
this guise he makes advances to the Italian Marchesa del
Marmore and is repulsed. Subsequently, having become a
social lion as well as a public official in Florence, he has her
lured during his absence to his apartment, where her portrait
is painted by an artist friend of his as "The Lady Expecting
her Inconstant," and thus manages to ruin her reputation.

In Florence Basil falls in love with the English Lady Geraldine, whom he had met in Paris. "Long as he had known her," Willis wrote, "it was a passion born in Italy." In that country, indeed, Basil experiences a deepening of both feeling and thought, as a direct result of his association with artists and works of art. Coming from the "vitreous and mercurial clime of France, with its volatile and superficial occupations," to "the voluptuous and indolent air of Italy, and the study of its impassioned deifications of beauty," he finds that his "instinct of gay pleasure" has become "a thirst both of the senses and the imagination." In Italy the "idolatry of beauty," which had formerly seemed to him "sensual or unreal, kindled its first fires in his mind." "There is a kind of compromise," Willis wrote,

in the effects of the atmosphere and arts of Italy. If the intellect takes a warmer hue in its study of the fair models of antiquity, the senses in turn become more refined and intellectual. In other latitudes and lands woman is loved more coldly. . . . That divine form, meant to assimilate her to the angels, has never been recognised by the dull eye that should have seen in it a type of her soul. To the love of the painter or the statuary, or to his who has made himself conversant with their models, is added the imperishable enthusiasm of a captivating and exalted study. The mistress of his heart is the mistress of his mind. She is the breathing realization of that secret ideal which exists in every mind, but which, in men ignorant of the fine arts, takes another form, and becomes a woman's rival and usurper.

Lady Geraldine also matures in Italy, but her development, in contrast to Basil's, is essentially moral. She is a married woman, whose husband is still living. Whereas in Paris she had been free and frank with Basil, by the time they meet in Italy "the 'knowledge of good and evil' " has driven her "from her Eden of unconsciousness" and she is entirely circumspect with him. In the end she takes the Marchesa del Marmore into her household, and Basil becomes a lonely wanderer who is said to possess an evil eye.

Paul Fane, the hero of Willis' novel by that name, goes abroad primarily to study art, but his immediate motivation, occasioned by the snub which he receives from the English aristocrat Mildred Ashly, is "to know his relative rank of nature"—to discover, as he says, "what is the natural texture, coarser or finer, of my stuff and quality as a gentleman." In Florence he finds himself the equal of such genuine aristocrats as the Princess C—— (who is secretly a sculptor), demonstrates his superiority to such spurious ones as the Ashlys, and even introduces some of the latter family to larger and happier experiences than they have previously known—all in his capacity as an artist. His skill as a portrait-painter lies in his ability to reveal essential traits of character which society in general is unable to perceive. His portrait of the spinster Mildred Ashly indirectly brings about her happy marriage, and his portrait of the beautiful but shy Sybil Paleford furthers the successful courtship of her by Arthur Ashly. After visiting England, Paul returns to America. Though the Princess C—— warns him that his artistic career may suffer if he does so, he prefers the free society of his own country to the aristocracy-dominated one of Europe. Eventually he marries his youthful sweetheart, Mary Eveden, who comes to maturity during two years as a student of sculpture in Florence. Before that time she had been able to appreciate his work intellectually, but there she experiences a "gradual deepening of her character with her sense of beauty" that enables her to love him as well.

HENRY GREENOUGH

Henry Greenough was just beginning his career as an architect in Boston when, at twenty-one, he was advised to go abroad for his health. He joined his older brother Horatio in Florence early in 1830, and there he remained until the summer of 1833. Apparently he took the Mediterranean route both to and from Italy. In Florence he studied painting and architecture and revelled in all aspects of the life he led with other artists. Among these for a while was a third Greenough brother, John, who was a painter. A letter which Henry wrote Willis soon after arriving, describing typical scenes in the city on Corpus Christi Day, was printed in the *American Monthly Magazine*.

In 1845 Greenough again went abroad for his health, accompanied by his wife and children. They lived in Florence, partly to be near the Horatio Greenoughs, from the fall of that year until the spring of 1846, and from the fall of 1847 to the spring of 1850. During the intervening period they were at a water-cure establishment at Grafenberg in Austrian Silesia. On their way there they passed through Venice, and toward the end of their Italian stay they visited Rome. En route back to America, in 1850, they spent about a month in England. (Mrs. Greenough later wrote a fictional account of their European tour at this time : *Annals of Brookdale*, published in 1881.) In the winter of 1869–70 Greenough was once more in Italy with his wife, chiefly in Florence and Rome, on what was apparently his third and last European trip.

In his later years Greenough published two novels and, in Boston newspapers, a few essays (mostly those on Allston's painting *Belshazzar's Feast)* and poems. One of the poems was entitled "To Italy." Both novels concern artists : *Ernest Carroll, or Artist-Life in Italy* (1858) which has a contemporary setting, and *Apelles and his Contemporaries* (1860), laid in Greece in the fourth century B.C.

Ernest Carroll, issued anonymously, purports to be the work of an Englishman, who explains in his preface that he has

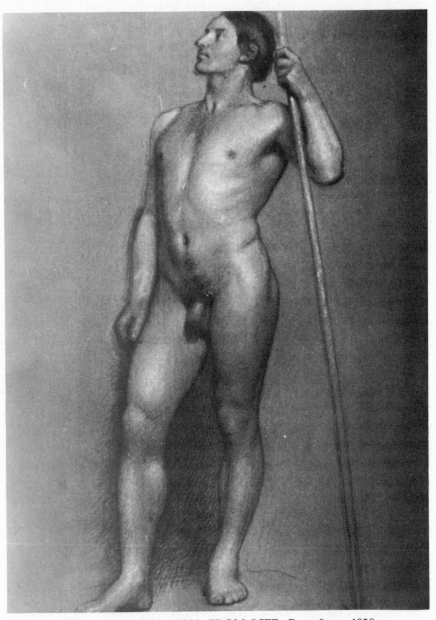

William Page, DRAWING FROM LIFE. Rome? *ca.* 1850
(Private Collection, photograph courtesy of Professor Joshua C. Taylor,
Chicago)

taken an American artist for his hero as a compliment to the Americans, many of them artists, whom he enjoyed knowing during a residence on the continent and also as a means of correcting the tendency of English writers to belittle foreigners, especially Americans. He promises also to show his fellow countrymen how severely they are criticized by other nationals. Throughout the novel the English are taken to task, particularly for their arrogance, by both Americans and Italians; and Americans are pronounced by Italians to be superior to the English in intellect and cultivation.

The explicit judgments on Italian culture in *Ernest Carroll* are also derogatory. It is depicted as morally corrupt, particularly as represented by such literature as the *Decamerone,* by the institution of cicisbeism, and by the Roman Catholic Church—"the cause of all the misery and degradation of this fair land," in the opinion of Carroll. Though awed by the wealth of art there, he likens contemporary Italy to

the skeleton of some mighty mastodon, among whose bones jackals, mice, and other vermin were prowling about. The great frame was there, but the life and strength which animated it was departed.

The Venetian Princess Zerlinski, whom he loves, proves to be innocent of her supposed vices and is at last ready to become a Protestant, but he is prevented by her death from marrying her.

The image of life in Italy projected in *Ernest Carroll* is, nevertheless, an attractive one, largely because of the descriptions of artist-life there. Part I, devoted to Carroll's involvement with Princess Zerlinski in Venice, is stock melodrama. On the other hand, Part II, which takes him to Florence, is a lively account of the activities in the art colony in that city : the gatherings in the famous Caffè Doney, a typical private class in the nude, the interminable gossip about artists of the present and the past—all drawn from Greenough's experiences in Florence in the 1830's and the 1840's. Most of the artists as well as some other persons whom he knew there are introduced by name or appear with other identifying characteristics. A chapter is devoted to reminiscences about Allston by the elderly English painter Bruce, a fictional name for the English painter and art dealer in Florence John W. Wallis, who knew Allston in Rome.

Part III of *Ernest Carroll* is based on other European experiences of Greenough during the 1840's. Here Carroll, too, travels to Grafenberg; witnesses in Florence, as Greenough did, the disturbances connected with the Revolution of 1848; and, like him and his brother Horatio, is arrested as an Austrian spy at Monselice near Venice. Numerous minor episodes and anecdotes throughout the novel are also factual in origin.

SARAH LORING GREENOUGH

In 1846, at the age of nineteen, Sarah Dana Loring of Boston became the wife of the sculptor Richard S. Greenough, the youngest brother of Henry and Horatio. Four years later she and her husband went to Italy, where he had spent several months a decade earlier. They stayed about five years, most of the time in Rome. In the late 1870's, having lived meanwhile in America and in Paris, they were again in Italy, apparently in Rome. Their son Gordon was a painter. Mrs. Greenough died in 1885 in Austria and was buried there; in her memory her husband executed a statue, *Psyche Divesting herself of Mortality*, which was placed in the Protestant Cemetery in Rome.

Mrs. Greenough was the author of two volumes of poems, a collection of short stories (which was illustrated by her son),

Richard Saltonstall Greenough,
PSYCHE DIVESTING HERSELF OF MORTALITY. Rome?
ca. 1885?
Protestant Cemetery, Rome; erected in memory of Sarah L. D.
Greenough.

and four novels. One story and the greater part of one novel are laid in Italy, and the other novels and one or two poems contain incidental allusions to that country. The story, "Domitia" (in the collection *Arabesques,* published in 1872), is an account of the transformation of a Christian woman in medieval Rome into a worshipper of Mercury.

The novel laid chiefly in Italy was Mrs. Greenough's second, *Lilian* (1863). Though typically melodramatic (like most of her work), it does not depend upon tradition in dealing with that country. Drawing upon her own and her husband's personal history, she has Lilian and Clinton, the heroine and hero, go to Rome soon after their marriage in America. Although Clinton has been in Italy before, both now experience a deeper emotion, albeit one tinged with sadness, than they have previously. They learn "the world's great lesson of the unreality of material things,—the shortness of life, the nothingness of time." They know "the sad luxury of sentiment and sensation,—which is the breath of Italian existence." Above all, the antique statues give them the sense of an inner, ideal life : "Stately they stand, and still," Mrs. Greenough wrote,

those ancient, godlike forms. A deathless life is in their nostrils, a changeless contemplation in their unswerving eyes. Empires have risen and fallen around their pedestals . . . yet still they stand serene, unmoved. . . . Their life is not as ours,—they, the immortals of the earth.

Another work of art functions symbolically in the novel : a sarcophagus in the palace which Lilian and Clinton occupy, on which two lovers are shown separated by the Genius of Death. In the face of this figure Lilian sees the likeness of Clinton's first wife, Mira.

As it develops, Mira is still alive, an inmate of an insane asylum at Naples since being injured in a shipwreck on the

Bay of Naples. In her distress at discovering this fact, Lilian runs away from Clinton and lives for a while in a Roman convent. There she reminds an Italian girl of the painting of Beatrice Cenci by Guido Reni. In the description of Lilian sitting in the Colosseum on one occasion during this period a correspondence between her unhappy state and the ruined condition and tragic associations of that structure is implied. (At this point in her narrative Mrs. Greenough was evidently influenced by several details in Hawthorne's *Marble Faun,* published three years before her novel.) Eventually Mira dies and Lilian and Clinton are remarried.

In *Lilian* Italy thus appears as the scene of the most poignant human experiences. In two curious but noteworthy instances, however, a contrast between Italy and America is suggested in which America, represented by its aborigines, seems preferable. In the opening scene, in America, Lilian comes upon an Italian boy organ-grinder swinging her kitten by the tail and shoots him with a bow and arrow. And before leaving for Italy, she and Clinton take a trip, at her desire, to the prairies, where they see Indians.

*   *   *   *   *   *

In the years from 1857 to 1860, at about the time Hawthorne was in Italy, three other Americans who subsequently wrote novels laid there visited that country : Harriet Beecher Stowe, Henry P. Leland, and Anne Hampton Brewster. Miss Brewster later returned to spend the rest of her life in Italy. Mrs. Stowe and Hawthorne met on their return voyage to America in 1860, but otherwise these writers seem not to have been personally known to each other.

A few years later—in 1863 and in 1866—the young journalist George Alfred Townsend made two visits to Italy, on which he drew in part of a story and a novel. In the story, "Married Abroad" (1865), the American art student Ralph

Flare goes to Italy after abandoning his Parisian grisette—as Townsend did in 1863. The novel was Townsend's first: *Lost Abroad* (1870), based on his European travels in 1863–64, 1866, and 1867. The hero, Applegate Shrink, as the author had done, stops in Milan and Lugano, spends a month in Florence (living in Via Parione), visits Vallombrosa, dislikes Rome but is delighted by the rest of Italy—more, apparently, than by any other country. Townsend also wrote a factual account of his first Italian visit (the chapter "Spurs in the Picture Galleries" in *Campaigns of a Non-Combatant and his Romaunt Abroad During the War,* published in 1866), several letters from Italy to American newspapers on his second visit, and a few poems on Italian subjects. The European experience which most deeply affected him and apparently most urged him to creative writing, however, was his association with a group of bohemians (including several Americans) in Paris in 1863. He drew on that experience in only two stories and a few poems partly because he feared it would shock his readers. His most notable fiction, in any case, did not begin to appear until a decade after his first, Europe-inspired pieces, and it dealt with the Delaware-Maryland area where he had grown up.

HARRIET BEECHER STOWE

On her first trip to Europe, taken in the summer of 1853 at the invitation of anti-slavery groups in Glasgow, Harriet Beecher Stowe visited England, Scotland, France, Switzerland, Germany, and Belgium. On her next, taken partly to secure an English copyright for her novel *Dred,* she stayed about three months each in England, in Paris, and—from February to April 1857—in Italy. In company with her sister Mrs. Thomas C. Perkins, she took the sea route from France to Rome,

Samuel Finley Breese Morse, THE SHRINE. Italy, 1830–1832.
(Private Collection, photograph courtesy of The Detroit Institute of Arts)

stayed there over a month, visited Naples, travelled north
again by sea, spent two weeks in Florence and about a week
in Venice, stopped briefly in Bologna, Milan, and Como, and
went back to Rome for Holy Week. She returned to America
from England late in the summer of 1857.

Mrs. Stowe's third and final European trip, made in part to
arrange for an English printing of her *Minister's Wooing*,
lasted from the summer of 1859 to that of 1860. Most of that
time she was in Italy with her two older daughters. They
spent a month visiting Como, Milan, Verona, Venice, and
other northern Italian cities; four months in Florence (where
her son Fred joined them and where she saw a good deal of
the Brownings and the publisher James T. Fields and his wife);
about six weeks in Rome; and about a week in and around
Naples. She returned to America from England in June 1860,
on the same vessel with the Hawthorne party.

Of all the European countries she visited, Mrs. Stowe
seemed to enjoy Italy most. "Rome is a world!" she wrote her
husband a few days after first reaching that city.

Rome is an astonishment! Papal Rome is an enchantment! Old
as she is, she is like Niñon d'Enclos,—the young fall in love
with her.

Venice was "all romance from beginning to end, and never
ceases to be strange and picturesque," she reported to one of
her daughters on her first visit there. Her second visit to the
southern part of the country was "a glory; it was a rose—a
nightingale—all, in short, that one ever dreams," she raptur-
ously wrote Mrs. James T. Fields.

On both visits she was keenly conscious of political issues.
Her first sight of the ruins of ancient Rome made her exult
"that the reign of disgusting, inconceivable brutality and
cruelty is over." On her second visit especially she expressed
sympathy with the Italian nationalists. In Florence she

attended the meeting of the Tuscan National Assembly at which the independence of Tuscany was formally announced, and in Rome she was much concerned over a clash between papal and national forces. With an acute American consciousness, she compared the statues on top of the cathedral in Milan to the trees in an American forest, and Neapolitans to American Negroes. (William Wetmore Story was so impressed by her impersonation of the American Negro abolitionist speaker Sojourner Truth, known as the Libyan Sibyl, that he executed a statue to which he gave that name.) The Milan cathedral and the flowers around Rome and Naples elicited her most enthusiastic comments. (In her volume of Florida sketches, *Palmetto Leaves* (1873), she declared she was more impressed by the flowers than by anthing else in Italy.) Preferring the Gothic to other architectural styles, she had reservations about most Italian buildings. She was ahead of her time, however, in her appreciation of the pre-Raphaelite painters.

Above all, Mrs. Stowe was profoundly affected in Italy by what she saw of the Roman Catholic Church. Though she found it generally devitalized and recognized its hostility to the Risorgimento, she regarded it as a virtually ideal religious tradition. Unsatisfied by the bareness and severity of Puritanism, she was strongly attracted by the elaborate and colorful ceremonies, the liturgical music, and the hagiolatry of Roman Catholicism. (Because of the recent death of her son Henry, who had not declared himself a Christian, she found special comfort in the Roman Catholic attitude to the dead.) Her shift from the Congregational to the Episcopal church a few years later was perhaps influenced in part by her contact in Italy with the Roman Catholic Church.

At the time of her first visit to Italy Mrs. Stowe was forty-six years old, the author of nine books, of which the most celebrated was *Uncle Tom's Cabin*. During both visits she wrote

travel letters for the *Independent*. In the intervening period
she published a volume of children's stories and her first non-
polemical novel, *The Minister's Wooing*. During the second
visit, when the Stowes and their American friends the John
Tasker Howards were kept indoors a day and a night by bad
weather at Salerno, Mrs. Stowe began to construct the plot of
a historical novel laid in Italy. She proposed to the party that
they pass the time collaborating on a story, wrote the beginning
of one about two women whom they had seen at Sorrento—a
young girl selling oranges at the city gate and an older woman
in the Gorge—and continued it on their way back to Rome.

On her return to America Mrs. Stowe occupied herself
simultaneously with this story, which became *Agnes of Sorrento*, and with *The Pearl of Orr's Island*. Both were serialized
during 1861 and published as books in June 1862. During the
remaining twenty-odd years of her literary life she produced
six novels, one book of poems, a dozen volumes of sketches and
children's stories, and half a dozen volumes of miscellaneous
prose. Of her imaginative work written after she went abroad,
Agnes of Sorrento alone makes intensive use of her experience
there. In the rest of that work she refers more often to the
French than to any other European culture. Italian references
occur, however, in all but two of the novels, in the children's
story "Our Dogs" (which has an account of the Demidoff
spaniel she acquired on her second visit there), in several
sketches, and in four poems. The poems, bearing the group
title "Pressed Flowers from Italy," express her feeling for the
Roman Catholic Church.

Agnes of Sorrento is unique among Mrs. Stowe's works in
being the only historical novel and the only one not laid in
America. It is also far more varied in scene, wide-ranging in
theme, and symbolic in technique than any other. Perhaps for
this reason it is one of the least sentimental of her works. It is

infused, moreover, with a warmth and a feeling for the setting which even her New England idylls lack. It was "conceived on the spot," she wrote James T. Fields,

—a spontaneous tribute to the exceeding loveliness and beauty of all things there. . . . To me, therefore, it is fragrant with love of Italy, and memory of some of the brightest hours of life.

She was working at *The Pearl of Orr's Island* "with a shiver," she wrote in the winter of 1860, and coming back to *Agnes of Sorrento* "as to a flowery home where I love to rest."

The action of *Agnes of Sorrento* takes place in 1498, against a background of the scandalous reign of Pope Alexander VI and the religious reformation led by Savonarola, who was then prior of the Convent of San Marco in Florence. The title character is the young daughter of a Roman nobleman and a commoner, who has been brought up at Sorrento, in ignorance of her paternity, by her maternal grandmother, and who aspires to be a nun. She is loved by Agostino Sarelli, a young Roman cavalier whom the Pope has dispossessed of his property and excommunicated and who is temporarily living as the head of a company of bandits. Because of the corrupt state of the church Sarelli has virtually lost his faith, but at last he recovers it and becomes a supporter of Savonarola. The novel closes with Savonarola's death and the marriage of Sarelli and Agnes.

Though it is a historical novel incorporating many motifs typical of Gothic romances, *Agnes of Sorrento* is in several respects significantly different from both these genres. Its realism, its nationalistic overtones, and its symbolism chiefly distinguish it. In these respects it may be called a typically American treatment of its subject. George Eliot's *Romola,* published a year later, which also has the Savonarola movement as a background, is more representative of historical fiction.

A generally realistic tone is created in *Agnes of Sorrento* by Mrs. Stowe's use of her Italian experiences. It is laid for the most part in places she had visited—Sorrento, Vesuvius, Florence, Milan, and Rome—and her descriptions of these places are based on her own observations. Often these descriptions are extended for their own sake and couched in the present tense. (In several passages—notably those on the Milan cathedral and on republican Florence—she drew on her travel letters to the *Independent*.) She not only described in Agnes and Elise, the girl's grandmother, particular Italians (the young orange-seller and the older women whom she and her friends had seen at Sorrento), but analyzed Italian character to a considerable extent. She also introduced many details of local color, chiefly concerning the daily life of ordinary Italians and the activities in Rome during Holy Week.

At the same time Mrs. Stowe deliberately created an ideal setting in her novel. In a letter to her publishers at the time it appeared she disclaimed "responsibility for historical accuracy" and declared it her intention to present "a mere dream-land," a "visionary region," a "fairyland." This very approach to her material, however, was inspired by her experience at Sorrento in 1860 when, as she remembered it, after she and her companions had seen the two Italian women,

The whole golden scene receded centuries back, and they saw them in a vision as they might and must have been in other days. In the novel the landscape around Sorrento is compared to Arcadia, the Garden of the Hesperides, the Isles of the Blest, Elysium, and Paradise; and the Italian atmosphere is repeatedly called "enchanting," "dreamy," "magical," and "golden." Yet these terms, for all their visionary connotations, represent precisely Mrs. Stowe's personal impressions of the Italian scene.

Agnes of Sorrento is also distinguished from both the

historical novel and the Gothic romance by its nationalistic overtones. During the period of the Risorgimento many Italian nationalists regarded Savonarola as having been the champion of a cause comparable to theirs. Perhaps partly influenced by their view, Mrs. Stowe found in him and his followers certain New England qualities. In her novel the Florentines of the republican period are called the "early Puritans of Italy" and compared to the Puritans of New England. What the latter "wrought out with severest earnestness in their reasonings and their lives," the former "embodied in poetry, sculpture, and painting"; the work of the painters is likened to the sermons of Jonathan Edwards. There seems, moreover, to be an echo of the nineteenth-century American sectional conflict over slavery in the contrast established between the voluptuous south of Italy and the north, with its reforming impulse. Other incidental comparisons of American and Italian types and scenes are scattered through the novel.

It is most of all in its symbolism that *Agnes of Sorrento* differs from the two genres to which it is related. In employing this technique, Mrs. Stowe drew mainly upon the Italian landscape, the Roman Catholic Church, and works of art in Italy. Her references in all these areas, moreover, tend to project the same general image : that of a passageway from earth to heaven. It is an image which recurs in her fiction in connection, as here, with the theme of man's moral growth. Though her favorite symbol for the passageway—a ladder—occurs only once in this novel, in no other is the image so pervasive.

To some extent scenes in *Agnes of Sorrento* are counterparts of characters : the beautiful Sorrento of Agnes, the volcanic Vesuvius of the extremist Father Francesco, who secretly loves her. Figurative references to Italian vegetation and the Mediterranean occur in several characterizations.

More significantly, theological, moral, and historical values

are attached to different sections of Italy. The section around
Sorrento is not only described in idyllic terms more often than
any other; its "glorious skies and gorgeous shores which witnessed how magnificent a Being had given existence to man"
are said to suggest that the state of man after death will be a
happy one. Mrs. Stowe thought they must have inspired "the
gentlest of old Italian souls"—as she called Seneca, whom she
did not quote quite accurately—to conclude of man's future
life, "*Aut beatus, aut nihil.*" The contrary doctrine, predicting
man's punishment after death, is vividly figured in nearby
Vesuvius, where, appropriately, Father Francesco performs his
penance. Accounting for this doctrine in terms of Italian
history, Mrs. Stowe suggests that it was crystallized by the
first Christians in Italy as an expression of revenge for the
persecutions they had suffered at the hands of Roman
emperors.

At the same time, however, the scenery and climate of
southern Italy are said to be conducive both to indolence and
to orgies, as indicated by the myths of Circe and of the
Sirens. It is significant that Father Francesco selects a mountain as the scene of his penance, turning his back on the en-
ticing plain below. The mountains of Umbria and Tuscany—
the "severe, clear heights of Florence, Perugia, and Assisi,
where the intellectual and the moral both had somewhat of the
old Etruscan earnestness and gloom"—are emblematic of the
Italian religious reform movements originating in that area.
Still farther north, the Alps and the Apennines around Milan
are described as forming the walls of a temple in which saints
and angels might worship. The Alps are "like a solemn senate
of archangels."

This geographical sequence is thus suggestive both of the
historical sequence from pre-Christian times to the Reformation and of a moral passage, from lower to higher levels on

earth and finally to an ethereal realm. As the scene of the novel's action moves from Sorrento to Florence, to Milan, to Rome, and finally back to Florence—in general, from south to north—this movement itself is therefore symbolic.

The chief aspects of Roman Catholicism dealt with in *Agnes of Sorrento* are its conventual life, its hagiolatry, and its art. Toward them all Mrs. Stowe's general attitude is that of the historical apologist, emphasizing in particular the influence of pagan practices on the development of Christian ritual and symbolism. Ultimately, however, her treatment of all these matters serves symbolic ends.

Several different convents and orders as well as types of conventuals are described in *Agnes of Sorrento* for the express purpose of presenting a picture faithful to fact: the sheltered sisterhood of St. Agnes; the Capuchins under the lax Brother Girolamo and, later, the austere Father Francesco; the Dominican San Marco, presided over by Savonarola. To Mrs. Stowe the Dominican was "one of the most enlightened and cultivated religious orders" and Savonarola "perfectly represented the attitude of the highest Christian" of the times. Her picture of life in San Marco's is, nevertheless, largely an idealized one, representing her conception of the proper relation of the spiritual to the earthly. "In its best days," she wrote of that establishment,

it was as near an approach to an ideal community, associated to unite religion, beauty, and utility, as ever has existed on earth. It was a retreat from the commonplace prose of life into an atmosphere at once devotional and poetic; and prayers and sacred hymns consecrated the elegant labors of the chisel and the pencil, no less than the more homely ones of the still and the crucible. San Marco, far from being that kind of sluggish lagoon often imagined in conventual life, was rather a sheltered hotbed of ideas, fervid with intellectual and moral energy, and before the age in every radical movement.

The references in *Agnes of Sorrento* to the Christian spiritual hierarchy, particularly to the saints, also contribute to the novel's historical realism. They are far more numerous than necessary in this connection, however, and chiefly perform two other functions: they are largely responsible for the legendary atmosphere of the early chapters, and they represent heaven and earth as closely linked.

The atmosphere of the first part of the novel is established in part by descriptions of the Sorrento Gorge, where fauns, dryads, and evil spirits are said to live and where Agnes has her shrine to the Virgin. The prevailing delightfulness of this atmosphere is created chiefly by references to Christian saints and celestial beings. Having heard about them repeatedly from the nuns in the convent of St. Agnes, the unworldly Agnes has grown up with "a poetic mist" enveloping "all her outward perceptions similar to that palpitating veil of blue and lilac vapor that enshrouds the Italian landscape." She lives in an inner world . . . peopled with martyrs, saints, and angels, whose deeds were possible or probable only in the most exalted regions of devout poetry.

Her first meetings with Sarelli, who appears and disappears with supernatural suddenness, belong in effect to such regions. At the second of these meetings he presents her with a lily like that given Mary by Gabriel; Agnes' uncle, Father Antonio (a painter-monk at San Marco's), is reminded by the episode of barbaric princes brought to holy virgins of whom he has read in "The Lives of the Saints." Subsequently Agnes dreams of Sarelli in the guise of an angel saying, "The Lord hath sealed thee for his own!" This dream comes true in a double sense when Sarelli finds his faith again partly under her influence and marries her.

Saints in *Agnes of Sorrento* are also represented as links between heaven and earth. Explaining Roman Catholic hagiolatry, Mrs. Stowe asserted that to the "really spiritual Christian" of the pre-Reformation era,

the air of this lower world was not as it is to us . . . a blank, empty space from which all spiritual sympathy and life have fled, but, like the atmosphere with which Raphael has surrounded the Sistine Madonna, it was full of sympathizing faces, a great "cloud of witnesses." The holy dead were not gone from earth; the Church visible and invisible were in close, loving, and constant sympathy. . . .

The chief character in the novel expressing this point of view is Father Antonio, who attempts to confirm Sarelli in his faith by describing to him as they stand in the Milan cathedral the company of the Christian dead.

At the same time, however, Mrs. Stowe felt that preoccupation with the other world was fatally isolating. Sister Theresa, who knows only saints' legends, is an ineffectual spiritual adviser, and Father Francesco, as long as he is bent on self-immolation, is an untrustworthy one. At the other extreme are the practical Elise and the portress at the convent of St. Agnes, Jocunda, whose allusions to religious matters are casual and even irreverent. Between the two extremes are Agnes, who corrects her false, exalted conception of the papal regime; Father Antonio, who though tending to withdraw from life into religious visions and art, is active in Savonarola's cause; and Sarelli, an artist, poet, and venerator of saints by nature, who allies himself with the reform elements in the Church. Both Agnes and Sarelli, moreover, pass from lower to higher moral levels, in accordance with Mrs. Stowe's conception of man's proper development.

The aspect of Roman Catholicism which receives most attention in *Agnes of Sorrento* is its art. Characterization is frequently accomplished by references to religious paintings. (Agnes is repeatedly compared to pictures of the Virgin.) Two larger ends, however, are served by the references to all such works of art. They themselves are represented as the chief means by which religious truth and religious devotion are expressed—in effect, as a passage between earth and heaven—and the life of the religious artist is represented as a blissfully happy one.

The religious works of art which figure most prominently are the paintings of Fra Angelico (particularly those in the convent of San Marco) and of other, unnamed pre-Raphaelites and the cathedral in Milan. The primitiveness of some of the paintings is excused on the ground that they represent the struggle of the soul toward some loftier existence. Fra Angelico painted "to show forth what he saw in heavenly visions," says Father Antonio, on whom a portion of Fra Angelico's spirit is thought to have descended.

The description of the cathedral in Milan emphasizes its loftiness. It is a

strange, pure, immaculate mountain of airy, unearthly loveliness, — the most striking emblem of God's mingled vastness and sweetness that ever it was given to human heart to devise or hands to execute.

Mounting to the roof, one seems to ascend

far beyond the tumult and dust of earthly things, to the silence, the clearness, the tranquility of ethereal regions.

The statues of saints and the Virgin on the roof seem

the fit inhabitants of the pure blue sky. One feels that they have done with earth; one can fancy them a band of white-robed kings and priests forever ministering in that great temple of which the Alps and the Apennines are the walls and the Cathedral the heart and centre.

The novel does not end, however, on any such height, figuratively speaking. Sarelli fails to secure aid for Savonarola in Milan, where he has gone for that purpose. He nevertheless returns to Florence to stand by Savonarola's cause, doomed though it is temporally, as one sure to have an eternal victory. The particular function served by the cathedral in this episode is stated by Father Antonio when he says that "it takes such monuments as these of the Church's former days to strengthen one's hopes," and calls Sarelli's attention to the statues on the roof.

The references in *Agnes of Sorrento* to religious works of art also depict the life of a creator of such works as being a supremely happy one. Naturally buoyant, Father Antonio says that as a religious artist he walks "the earth in a dream of bliss." He enjoys every aspect of nature, not only for its own sake but as a divine creation. "What higher honor or grace can befall a creature," he exclaims,

than to be called upon to make visible to men that beauty of invisible things which is divine and eternal?

"If perfect, unalloyed happiness has ever existed in this weary, work-day world of ours," Mrs. Stowe declared, "it has been in the bosoms of some of those old religious artists of the Middle Ages."

To Mrs. Stowe, indeed, the peculiar genius of the Italians, which largely accounted for their buoyant spirit, was their ability to pass between the realms of the seen and the unseen. The "Northern mind of Europe," she wrote,

is entirely unfitted to read and appreciate the psychological religious phenomena of Southern races. The temperament which in our modern days has been called the mediïstic, and which with us is only exceptional, is more or less a race-peculiarity of Southern climates, and gives that objectiveness to the conception of spiritual things from which grew up a whole ritual and a whole world of religious Art. The Southern saints and religious artists were seers,—men and women of that peculiar fineness and delicacy of temperament which made them especially apt to receive and project outward the truths of the spiritual life. . . .

The "peculiar and characteristic flowering of the Italian mind" came about, she thought, through the treatment of Christian subjects by the early Umbrian and Florentine artists. The more Italian artists came under Greek influence, the more "did the peculiar vividness and intense flavor of Italian nationality pass away from them."

Not all the works of art referred to in *Agnes of Sorrento* are Christian. Characters are often compared to paintings and statues of unspecified nature, even to likenesses on coins. Particularly telling are the references to remains of antique sculpture and architecture near Christian monuments in the region around Sorrento. The convent of St. Agnes is said to have been built out of fragments of a temple to Venus, and the statue which the sisters call "St. Agnes" at the fountain in the convent garden is actually one of a nymph. The difference drawn between this statue and the thirteenth-century frescoes in the convent depicting St. Agnes' life is significant :

their juxtaposition in the same enclosure seemed a presentation of the spirit of a past and present era : the past so graceful in line, so perfect and airy in conception, so utterly without spiritual aspiration or life; the present limited in artistic power, but so earnest, so intense, seeming to struggle and burn, amid its stiff and restricted boundaries, for the expression of some diviner phase of humanity.

The mood evoked by Mrs. Stowe's references to antique sculpture is, moreover, a melancholy one, in contrast to the happiness she associated with Christian art. In the statue of the nymph "all the silent, patient woe and discouragement of a dumb antiquity" had been "congealed." Typical of such antique works as exhibited any feeling at all, she wrote, was the statue of Psyche in the Naples Museum, with its "mournful pathos." Most of the fragments of sculpture around the dwelling of Agnes and Elise are those of sarcophagi and tombs. In the beginning Agnes is compared to the nymph, to the *Psyche,* and to other antique sculptures, as well as to Christian saints. Her moral immaturity is thus suggested and her subsequent moral growth anticipated.

Numerous parallels exist between *Agnes of Sorrento* and *The Marble Faun* (which appeared a year earlier): the characters of Agnes and Hilda, the two disturbed Capuchin monks, the depiction of a decadent Rome, the symbolic use of works of art, the background of pagan times. Probably Hawthorne's novel influenced Mrs. Stowe's.

The peculiar impression made by Italy on Mrs. Stowe's imagination is apparent, however, in the novel she wrote after her first Italian visit, before *The Marble Faun* was written. That novel, *The Minister's Wooing* (1859), is in many ways an early version of *Agnes of Sorrento.* The devout Mary Scudder, the Edwardsian clergyman Samuel Hopkins, who comes to love her, and the young sailor James Marvyn, a skeptic who becomes converted and marries her, are comparable to Agnes, Father Francesco, and Sarelli. Mary is likened to the Virgin, to St. Dorothea, to St. Catherine, and simply to a nun. If she had been a Roman Catholic, declares her friend Mme De Frontignac, "she would certainly have been made a saint." She is also characterized by means of references to the climate and the art of Italy. "Had she been born in Italy," Mrs. Stowe wrote,

under the dissolving influences of that sunny, dreamy clime, beneath the shadow of cathedrals, and where pictured saints and angels smiled in clouds of painting from every arch and altar, she might, like fair St. Catherine of Siena, have seen beatific visions in the sunset skies, and a silver dove descending upon her as she prayed. . . .

Hopkins is characterized in a similar way. He has in him, "crude and unworked, a whole mine of . . . artistic feelings and perceptions," Mrs. Stowe put it.

Had he been born beneath the shadow of the great Duomo of Florence, where Giotto's Campanile rises like the slender stalk of a celestial lily, where varied marbles and rainbow-glass and gorgeous paintings and lofty statuary call forth, even from childhood, the soul's reminiscences of the bygone glories of its pristine state, his would have been a soul as rounded and full in its sphere of faculties as that of Da Vinci or Michelangelo.

James Marvyn's mother, too, would presumably have been more fully developed in Italy. She reads in encyclopedias about Italian artists and works of art and by this means identifies as Leonardo da Vinci the painter of the head of the Madonna in the engraving in the Scudder attic. Marvyn, incidentally, gives Mary a necklace of Venetian shells after his first voyage to the Mediterranean.

In two other novels by Mrs. Stowe Italy is associated with romances of the leading characters. In *Oldtown Folks* (1869) Ellery Davenport pictures to Tina Percival the Bay of Naples and the rocks of Sorrento, "where they should have a villa some day, and live in a dream of beauty." In *My Wife and I* (1871), Harry Henderson and Eva Van Arsdel are drawn together by their common experience of having visited Italy. In her room, which is adorned with Italian pictures and which is called "Italy," they look over her portfolio of Italian views, going "back together over the brightest and sunniest passages of their experiences." After their marriage she decorates their dining room with prints of Pompeiian figures.

The only noteworthy Italian references in the rest of Mrs. Stowe's writing are those in the chapter "The Cathedral" in *The Chimney-Corner* (1868). There, the cathedral at Milan is again described, as in the chapter with the same title in *Agnes of Sorrento*, as the most celestial creation on earth.

HENRY P. LELAND

In 1857, at the age of twenty-nine, having failed to establish himself as a businessman and as an author and being in frail health, Henry Perry Leland of Philadelphia went to Italy. Evidently he hoped not only to gain physical strength but to become an artist. Possibly he was also following the example of his older brother Charles Godfrey Leland, poet and student of the occult, who had travelled in Europe a decade earlier.

Landing at Le Havre in May, Leland proceeded to Paris, visited Belgium, Holland, Austria, and Germany, and reached Italy in October. By the end of that month he was in Rome, where he lived until the following June and again for several weeks beginning late in October 1858. In the interim he was in the nearby town of Segni, in the Volscian Mountains. After a trip to Egypt he spent most of February and March 1859 in Naples. He left Italy at the end of March, travelled for about two months in Spain, evidently revisited Paris, and sailed from Le Havre for America in July.

In Rome Leland studied art at the British Academy. In that city and during part of his time in Segni he had two artists as companions: Julius O. Montalant, a landscapist and animal painter, who had lived in Philadelphia for several years before 1857; and the Englishman Charles H. Poingdestré, a landscapist and figure painter, who for many years was president of the British Academy in Rome. At Segni, Leland perhaps fell in love with an Italian girl, as the poem "Giulia di Segni" in his novel based on his Italian experiences suggests.

Leland's Italian studies did not, however, make him a professional artist. Only two of his sketchbooks—one kept during

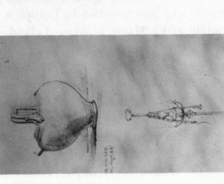

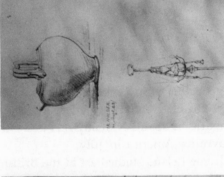

Henry Perry Leland, SKETCHES OF THE SARACEN'S GATE IN THE CYCLOPEAN WALLS, SEGNIANS IN THEIR NATIVE DRESS, C. H. POINGDESTRÉ, WATER HOLDER AND LAMP, J. O. MONTALANT. Segni, 1858.

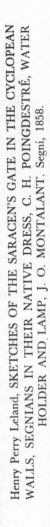

his European trip—and a few miscellaneous drawings seem to have been preserved. On his return to America he took up writing once more. Before going to Europe he had published *The Grey-Bay Mare, and Other Humorous Sketches* (1856). Afterward he produced a play, *Americans in Paris* (c. 1858); a novel, *Americans in Rome* (1863); and a few poems and short prose pieces, which appeared in the *Continental Monthly*. He and his brother collaborated on the illustrated *Ye Book of Copperheads* (1863). He was severely wounded in the Civil War in 1863 and died as a result five years later.

Leland's most ambitious work—and the only one in which he dealt substantially with Italy—was his novel, first printed in the *Continental Monthly* in 1862–63 under the title of "Maccaroni and Canvas." He supplied ten drawings by two artist friends of his (probably Montalant and Poingdestré) to illustrate the book, but the publisher who finally brought it out did not use them. In the preface Leland claimed that it was a work

almost to the minutest details true in spirit, there being scarcely an incident, even, or jest in it for which I am not endebted to my own observation or that of friends. . . .

Yet it was, he declared, "of higher aim than of mere entertainment, or even of simply faithful detail." In it he intended primarily to depict Rome as representative of "a past, by which we may still profit much," "the most living specimen of a rapidly vanishing, yet cultivated age, in existence," whose popular life was still largely unrecorded.

The opening lines of *Americans in Rome* establish both its theme and its tone:

Rome is the cradle of art—which accounts for its sleeping there.

Nature, however, is nowhere more wide awake than it is around this city. . . .

The three chief characters—James Caper, Rocjean (born in France but having lived in America for several years), and Dexter—correspond to Leland, Montalant, and Poingdestré. All are genre painters, and Caper and Dexter specialize in animal subjects. All virtually ignore the collections of art in Rome and are chiefly interested in the life of the ordinary Romans, the contadini on the Campagna, and the rustic inhabitants of Segni and other nearby villages. All these patterns of life are depicted directly—there is a great deal of dialogue —and with gusto. Leland had a particularly keen ear for the nuances of dialect and of English as spoken by foreigners. Insofar as he treated the life of artists as a group, it was in such gathering places as the Caffè Greco and the life schools in Rome, where the human interest was at least as strong as the artistic. As seen in both the city and its environs, an artist's life is above all, as Rocjean declares, "about as independent a one as society will tolerate."

Chiefly through artists of various nationalities—Italian, English, French, German, and Russian, as well as American— a good deal of international contrast is introduced in *Americans in Rome*. There is also a variety of American types, chief among them Caper's unsophisticated but intelligent uncle, William Browne, of St. Louis; the refined Mrs. Buren and her beautiful, sensitive daughter, Ida, of Boston; and the brash sculptor Chapin, with his ignorance of history and his passion for inventing labor-saving devices. (By this time there were several American sculptors of this sort in Italy, among whom Hiram Powers, in Florence, was most conspicuous.)

Intermittently throughout his novel Leland asserted the superiority of America to Italy. "The advantages of foreign travel to an intelligent American," he declared,

are to teach him . . [*sic*] the disadvantages of living anywhere save in America. And though the artistic eye dwells with such loving repose on the soothing colors of Italy, and particularly on the subdued white and gray tones of Roman ruins and palaces, walls and houses, yet the owner of that artistic eye should restrain his wrath at the fiery-red bricks of our own cities; for let him reflect, that this color goads him on, as it doth a bull to make valorous efforts—to do something!

More than once he looked forward to the improvements that he thought would accompany Italian independence.

Yet even in its decadence Rome is said to slumber "artistically, and not manufacturingly." The view from the Pincian hill is such that

Once thoughtfully noted, you will remember this glowing scene years after sublimer and wilder views are lost to memory, or grown so faint that they are to you but as dull colors seen in dreams of old age compared to the flashing brightness of those presented to the closed eyes of youth.

Caper's time spent in Segni is the high point of his Italian sojourn. Spectacularly situated on a mountain top, the town is, in the words of an army chaplain whom he knows, "air and Cyclopean walls." On one occasion it is called "Arcadia." "Superficial let our examinations be," Leland exclaimed in the concluding paragraph of his book, after citing instances of clerical tyranny and chicanery among the citizens there, unsanitary conditions and even murder in neighboring villages;

we must not dig too deep; we would disclose dirt and superstition, ignorance and prejudice enough to make angels weep; and yet, there is a contentment apparent among the Segnians, that we do not find anywhere else, save among savages and the uneducated peasants of the rest of Europe, who, like these their brothers, have never yet had intelligibly explained to them that they had souls, and were immortal; and that they were made in the image of God, and that the keys of heaven were in every man's hands—not hung up in the Vatican.

ANNE HAMPTON BREWSTER

In the spring of 1857, distraught by a long series of dis-
agreements with one of her brothers, chiefly over their mother's
estate, the thirty-eight-year-old Philadelphia spinster Anne
Hampton Brewster went abroad in hopes of restoring her
spirits. After spending several months in Switzerland, she went
early in 1858 to Naples, at the invitation of Robert Dale
Owen, then American minister in that city, and his wife.
There Miss Brewster stayed from February until July, when
her financial and legal affairs made a return to Philadelphia
seem advisable. With her went Mrs. Owen and the Owen
children.

Miss Brewster's stay in Naples was a happy interlude in her
life at this period. She admired the natural scene, made trips
to nearby points of interest, repeatedly visited galleries and
churches (she was a Roman Catholic convert), and attended
many social gatherings and theatrical and musical programs.
A musician herself, she often played the piano and sang for
friends. Among those whom she met in the city were Mrs.
Anna Jameson, the English spiritualist David Hume, and the
William Cullen Bryants. She became especially well acquainted
with two Italians: the sculptor Angiolini and a thirty-five-
year-old married man named Circolesi, who paid court to her.
Much impressed by him, she wrote in her diary that he was
the first man she had ever met

who united the fresh spring, the poetical enthusiasm of a cul-
tured youth with the experience and calm thought of mid age.

He seemed to her more like an Anglo-Saxon than a southern
European. By April she had no doubt that he

would be head over ears in love with me (his sort of love) notwithstanding the wife and all that, and be proposing a variety of

George Loring Brown, VIEW OF VESUVIUS AND THE BAY OF NAPLES. Rome, 1853–1854.

(Courtesy of Giovanni Castano, Boston)

sinful little private amusements but for my saucy piquant *froideur*.

Yet he was one of the few men, she felt, with whom she could have "no nonsense, no flirtation, no love making but honest downright friendship." By June she had given up seeing him on account of the gossip about their relationship.

Miss Brewster also occupied herself at this time in writing. She worked on a novel she had begun in Switzerland and evidently made notes at least ("journal leaves," she called them) for another. She felt a strong creative impulse in Naples. The memory of its "sun, soft air, fragrant vegetation and gentle minor music" would be, she thought, a source of later inspiration. "Ah this is the good of this coming to this 'old Europe of the Southe,' " she wrote in her diary;

the very atmosphere and sounds quicken the artist germ, life commences and then the poor soul who pined so long fearing to be barren glows and throbs with the delicious hope of at last bringing forth a mind child.

Soon after returning to America Miss Brewster moved to New Jersey, where she lived for nearly ten years, teaching music and French, and continuing to write. During this period she published her two novels and contributed several articles, mostly on musical subjects, to periodicals. Still at odds with her brother, she longed to return to Italy, but was unable to do so until after the Civil War.

In 1868 she went to Rome, where she lived until 1889. In that year she moved to Siena, where, in 1892, she died. She made several trips to Germany, France, and England, but she never went back to America. In Rome she was prominent in the expatriate group, which often gathered in her quarters in the Palazzo Maldura on Via Quattro Fontane. Her closest friends in the city were the Thomas Buchanan Reads, the

William Wetmore Storys, and the sculptor Albert E. Harnish, twenty-two years younger than she, with whom she shared a residence for fourteen years.

During most of her years in Rome Miss Brewster wrote news letters for American newspapers, among them the Philadephia *Bulletin* and the Boston *Advertiser*. She also published a few articles—chiefly descriptive, historical, and reminiscent—in periodicals, among them *Lippincott's*, the *Parisian*, the *Continental Monthly*, the *Century*, and *Blackwood's*. Though she projected other novels, she apparently wrote no more fiction.

Miss Brewster's first novel, *Compensation or Always a Future* (1860), which is laid in Switzerland, is largely based on her stay in that country. It contains a few incidental references to Italy. Her second, *St. Martin's Summer* (1866), is a thinly veiled account of her visit in Naples in 1858. The central characters are three American women who travel from Switzerland to Naples and spend six months in that city: Ottilie, the narrator, who writes in the form of a journal; and Janet and Venitia Howard, daughters of a one-time consul in southern Europe. Venitia is named for Venice, where she was born. Ottilie and Venitia both represent the author. Several other characters are drawn from persons she had known in Naples. The Rochesters—the American minister there and his wife—represent the Owens. The early life of Paul Dale, Janet's husband, also parallels that of Owen in certain particulars. The American poet B—— is Bryant, the spiritualist H—— is Hume, the sculptor Angelini is Angiolini, and Luigi Luini is modelled after Circolesi. (Ottilie's friend Philip, who arrives from America, apparently represents Miss Brewster's cousin Harry Welsh, who, however, was not in Italy at this time.) Ottilie and Luigi (who, she suggests, may be descended from the Renaissance painter Bernardo Luini) are like a sister and a brother together, but Venitia and Luigi fall in love. When Luigi finally parts from Venitia he kisses her on the forehead, as Circolesi had kissed Miss Brewster when she broke with him.

St. Martin's Summer consists largely of descriptions and historical accounts of the Italian places and objects seen by the chief characters, interspersed with conversations among them about music, art, and literature. Loose and often incoherent though it is, it has an underlying theme, which is set forth most explicitly in references to certain Italians and Italian works of art and to the way of life in Italy.

The theme is a dual one : the birth of the soul through the experience of love and the superiority of spiritual to physical love. Most of the physical love experienced by the characters in *St. Martin's Summer* is involved with pain, whereas the spiritual love which Ottilie shares with Luigi and Philip and which Luigi and Venitia come to have for each other is serene. Most of the other examples of spiritual love come from the lives of Italians of the past : St. Benedict and his sister St. Scholastica, Dante and Beatrice, Petrarch and Laura, Michelangelo and Vittoria Colonna, and Raphael and his "Beatrice" (as one legend identifies the Fornarina). According to Ottilie, moreover, this sort of love produces the greatest art.

The soul's experience with love is most clearly defined in *St. Martin's Summer* in terms of the myth of Psyche and Eros as represented by the torso of Psyche in the Naples Museum. It is Ottilie's favorite piece of statuary there. "That strange myth of Psyche!" she exclaims.

The ancients were forever representing it tenderly, as if throwing "the shadow before" of what the moderns are living so fiercely. The human soul, aspiring after the divine, loses the sweet, child-like confidence in the first mysterious presence of happiness, and seeks to make this happiness tangible and positive. This was the antique thought; but it exists actively in the spirit of the present age. Everything must be tasted, held, and possessed. Nature is forever punishing this bold, rash curiosity; for penances and expiations must continue, until the human soul perfected will enter into full possession of the divine, and all the lovely fore-shadowings of ancient myths and modern faiths and hopes, Eden and Psyche, Prometheus, and that Holy Sorrow, which, like the Jews' Jehovah, must be nameless, shall be made manifest.

Ottilie's second and third preferences among the works of sculpture in the Naples Museum also have a bearing on this myth : the *Eros and Dolphin* group and the statue of Agrippina, which represents to her courage in the face of loss and grief.

The process of the soul's coming to birth is seen in *St. Martin's Summer* chiefly in the experience of Venitia when she falls in love with Luigi. It is noteworthy that this experience comes to her in Italy. In this connection, the fact that she has an Italian birthplace and an Italianate name takes on significance. Before meeting Luigi, she is said to resemble the "imperious" Ludovisi statue of Juno in Rome. At Mrs. Rochester's ball she wears some onyxes in mountings made by a Neapolitan, among which are a diadem like that of the *Ludovisi Juno* and two figures of Psyche.

In conspicuous contrast to the undercurrent of pain and sorrow in *St. Martin's Summer* is the image of unalloyed happiness evoked by descriptions of the Italian scene and way of life. The title suggests such happiness (though it is inappropriate to the time of the action, the months from January to August). She chose it, Miss Brewster explained in her preface, because the novel was composed during a period of pleasant calm in her life—presumably in part, at least, in Naples. Ottilie's visit to Italy is a delightful interlude in her troubled existence also. In Genoa she feels that she is "living awake a beautiful dream." During most of her time in Italy the series of disturbing letters written to her from America while she is abroad is intermitted. In Naples she is able to write, "Every cause of annoyance . . . appears to be withdrawn from me; it is as if I stood on charmed ground."

The chief source of happiness in Italy as depicted in *St. Martin's Summer* is the life of *dolce far niente*. "In our frigid climates," declares Rochester, "we can form no conception of the delight of simple living and breathing in this part of Europe." Ottilie agrees, exclaiming of the inhabitants,

"Happy souls! they leave that illusion, that Sisyphus labor of life, eternal progress, to nations whose rugged, inhospitable soils force them to advance."

"The simple act of living, the breath Nature gives us here, is a priceless luxury in itself," Angelini tells Ottilie in farewell, in virtually the same words that Angiolini had spoken to Miss Brewster on her departure from Naples. That city, Ottilie decides, is the best place in which to experience Machiavelli's *nobile ozio*—"a noble idleness of delightful society, with classical associations, under a heaven of beauty." She quotes similar comments on Italy by Heine and Goethe.

At the same time, however, Italy is depicted in *St. Martin's Summer* as supremely a scene of intellectual activity. The conversations of the chief characters about art and history are largely stimulated by what they have seen there. Italy, Rochester reminds the others, has "produced more eminent men than any other country on the face of the globe." It is not only "the intellectual home of all artists, where they can best commence true study, and develop themselves most satisfactorily." "Its history is the base, and gives the key-note to all aesthetical and philosophical study." Italy, it would seem, is in relation to the myth of Psyche the closest the soul can come in this existence to pure happiness.

III

The Fruits of Civilization:

COOPER

WHEN JAMES FENIMORE COOPER TOOK HIS FAMILY TO EUROPE in 1826, his avowed purposes were to improve his health and to have his children learn French and Italian, but he was also realizing a long-cherished desire to travel for pleasure. Except for his touching at a few European ports as a young sailor, this was his only time abroad. He stayed seven years, nearly five of them in Paris, the rest of the time in other parts of France and in England, Holland, Belgium, Germany, Switzerland, and Italy. Of all these countries, Italy most delighted him and most affected his writing.

The Cooper party—which included Cooper's wife, five children, and a nephew—were in Italy from October 1828 to May 1830, during Cooper's thirty-ninth and fortieth years. They spent about nine months in Florence, five in Naples and Sorrento, five in Rome, and ten days in Venice. With great expectations, Cooper doffed his hat "in reverence" when they first sighted the country, approaching from Switzerland. At the same time he was prepared to encounter bandits; he decided Italy's reputation for them was exaggerated. He also had a romantic preconception of Italian buildings, engendered by the novels of Mrs. Radcliffe, but nowhere did he see any such as she described. Throughout his travels in Italy, indeed, he took a characteristically independent and a notably realistic view. Yet he was inclined here as nowhere else to surrender himself to the environment, taking even local legends at their face value.

In Florence, Cooper finished *The Wept of Wish-ton-Wish;* sat for a portrait bust by Horatio Greenough and ordered from Greenough a small marble group—a copy of two cherubs in a painting by Raphael; enjoyed the galleries, churches, and theatre; and became acquainted in the chief social and intellectual circles of the city. In the summer he and his family occupied the Villa Sant'Illario on the hill of Bellosguardo just outside Florence. On a trip to Marseilles by way of Genoa he delighted in the water. Italian ports, with their greater variety of vessels, he thought more picturesque than American ones, and floating again in the Mediterranean after twenty-one years gave him the feeling of "a schoolboy, broke out of his bounds." En route south he and his family sailed from Leghorn to Naples in a chartered felucca. In Sorrento, where he was happiest, they lived in the birthplace of Tasso—a "castle," he called it, spectacularly built on the cliffs overlooking the Bay of Naples. While there he wrote most of *The Water-Witch,* made numerous sea and land excursions, and revelled in the luxurious aspect and the classical associations of the area. It was, he thought, a "splendid country." "Oh! Napoli!" he exclaimed in retrospect a few years later; "glorious, sunny, balmy Napoli!" Rome most impressed him by its "recollections." It gave him a unique sensation, which was "masked in the melancholy void of the past." Here too he circulated in Italian and foreign society and commissioned a work from an American artist—a copy of a Guido Reni painting to be made by John G. Chapman. Venice, where he knew no one, he soon found monotonous. Yet "no other place," he declared, "ever struck my imagination so forcibly." It "seized" his "fancy" with such a "deep hold" that he had to "disburthen" it in a novel. He did so in his next, *The Bravo*. When at last he left Italy for Germany it was with more regret, he declared, than he had had upon leaving any other country. He felt "that reluctance to separate, that one is apt to experience on quitting his own house." Italy was the only country, his wife said, that he ever "quit looking over a shoulder."

Italy and Switzerland, Cooper decided in Germany, were "the only two countries, simply as countries . . . worth crossing the ocean to see." He found Switzerland's attractions, however, limited for the most part to the natural scene. "Italy . . . haunts my dreams and clings to my ribs like another wife," he wrote Greenough from Paris. France was, in contrast, a "cursed country," which put him "in mind of a country inn, lighted with tallow candles for a ball." During his brief visits to England, made chiefly to see publishers, he was unusually self-conscious, because of his determination to maintain his national character. As he prepared to return to America it was Italy—"dear Italy," to which "my heart yearns," he declared—that he hated to leave. "That glorious play of light and shade, as seen from Belloguardo," he wrote Greenough apropos of revisiting Florence, "comes across my imagination at times, with the force of reality." He hoped to return to Italy in a few years, perhaps with his son Paul.

Throughout the remaining two decades of his life Cooper continued to express such feeling for this country. "Italy !" he exclaimed in 1836. "The very name excites me, for it is the only region of the earth that I truly love." "There is no place," he wrote George Washington Greene, "where mere living is such a luxury." "Your grandfather," his daughter Susan recorded for her nieces and nephews, "fell in love with

Italy at first sight. And it was a love which lasted through his life-time."

Cooper published four books about his European travels—one each about those he made in Switzerland, France, England, and Italy. In these works he was hypercritical of England, though conceding to it fundamental respect; tolerant of France, even relishing certain aspects of its society; duly admiring of Switzerland; about Italy overwhelmingly nostalgic.

Cooper's Italian travel book, *Gleanings from Europe: Italy* (1838), leaves no doubt about what charmed him most in this country. It was the landscape, with its numerous associations and its mild atmosphere. A "soft," "bewitching," "refined" landscape it seemed to him; a distinctively feminine one, which he likened to "an extremely fine woman," "a beloved and lovely countenance," and which aroused in him a feeling of affection and love. It put him in a mood of reverie, partly by its "physical representation of things past" but chiefly by a certain "ideal" quality of its own. The view from Sorrento across the bay—which Chapman painted from a spot near the Tasso house—was unique, Cooper thought, not only for its combination of natural and historical elements but for the way in which a

bewitching and almost indescribable softness . . . a blending of all the parts in one harmonious whole, a mellowing of every tint and trait . . . threw around the picture a seductive ideal, that, blended with the known reality in a way, I have never before witnessed, nor ever expect to witness again.

The landscape in America was nothing like it, he repeatedly observed. "What dunce," he inquired, writing of the Bay of Naples, "first thought of instituting a comparison between the bay of New York and this?"

Cooper was also especially attracted, as his account of his Italian travels indicates, by two aspects of Italian culture : its art and its Church. His first pleasure in works of art he saw in Italy, he candidly reported, was in recognizing the originals of engravings that had been in his father's house. Yet he seemed to have genuine admiration for those works. He often compared a scene to the backgrounds in early paintings.

Toward the Roman Catholic Church he was generally sympathetic, though his view of it was primarily esthetic. It had in Italy, he wrote, "all the poetry of the religion." More than once after visiting some "cool, fragrant, rich, quaint, and clerkly" monastery he had felt he could remain in that country and become a monk, though he confessed he did not believe he had been "created for vigils and fasts."

The Italian people, too, proved singularly appealing to Cooper. The lower classes he soon found "agreeably" disappointing. (He may have been prejudiced in favor of the beggars who increased from one to nearly a hundred outside his door in Sorrento to receive lire from him because they called him "the *American admiral*.") Acknowledging that he knew little of Italian society, he suggested that the institution of cicisbeism, which outraged most Anglo-Saxons, was not understood by them. He thought the Italians, compared to other peoples, supremely gifted with the capacity for enjoying the passing moment. They were more gracious than the English, more sincere than the French, more refined than the Germans, less mercenary than the Americans. There was "a grace about their minds, derived from the constant practice of contemplating the miracles of art." In this grace, "in a love, and even in a knowledge of the arts," he declared, "a large portion of the common Italians are as much superior to the Anglo-Saxon race as civilization is superior to barbarism."

Indeed, Cooper regarded Italy essentially as a great civilization in its old age, as he made clear in *Gleanings from Europe: Italy*. His conception of historic time was extended by the sight of ancient monuments of art there. He repeatedly related the age of those in Rome to the age of the American nation; referring to Paestum he exclaimed, "What a speck does the history of America become in this long vista of events—what a point the life and adventures of a single man!" The whole attitude of *dolce far niente,* he suggested, was that of a people with a venerable past. Personally he found this attitude inviting: to seem, like the Italians, "too gentlemanlike to work" suited his humor, and he felt that he could "vegetate" with them at least half his life. He thought the American nation, however, could not "afford" such an attitude:

It would check our career short of perfect civilisation. We have arts to acquire, and tastes to form, before we could enter at all into the enjoyments of these people; one half of their pleasures depending on recollections that possibly may have had their origin in the *energies* of the first of the Medici; and there are things that must be created, but which give more satisfaction in after ages than during the period of their formation.

The most distinctive element in Italian civilization to Cooper, which made him deprecate American civilization in contrast, was the recognition by Italians that the greatest values were other than pecuniary ones. Whereas in his book about England he was most conscious of the mediocrity toward which American society tended, in that about Italy he was most conscious of the dominantly commercial interests of Americans. He had been gratified to find that "the demon money" seemed forgotten in Florence, whose old merchants "truly ennobled commerce, and not commerce them"; and he fervently wished his own lot had been cast in Rome rather than in New York "or in any other mere trading town that ever existed." He conceded that the traditions of the past lay heavily on the Roman mind, and even suggested that a visit to New York might benefit the Romans by partially awakening them from their "dream of centuries." Yet he was convinced of the vitality of that past. *"Rome,* like *Troy,* was," he put it; "but it does not seem that *New York,* though accumulating annually her thousands, is ever *to be."* The difference between the residential habits of the two peoples was, he thought, significant. Whereas "we level molehills with the sagacity and zeal of speculators, they perch themselves on cliffs, and people ravines like poets," he wrote in his description of Amalfi.

We may have the best of it, considering the house as an *article* . . . but they have greatly the best of it, considering a house as a place, in which one is to indulge in his individuality, and in pleasant thoughts. I believe we make money faster than any other nation, while we spend it with less satisfaction.

Thinking of the archeological excavations sponsored by the Neapolitan government, he doubted whether "any Congress could be found sufficiently imbued with a love of learning, or sufficiently alive to its benefits even to our particular and besetting motive, gain," to act similarly. Yet a love of the fine arts and a love of learning, he insisted, were important to "general civilization, without adverting to their influence on the happiness of man, the greatest object of all just institutions." Indeed, the most distinctive feature of the civilized state as it is predicated throughout Cooper's book about Italy is the happiness or enjoyment of a people.

Perhaps because his view of the country was non-political, Cooper was not, for all his democratic sympathies, an outspoken advocate of the Italian Risorgimento. He suggested, however, that America might take warning from recent Italian history that hereditary hatreds and distrusts among sections worked against national unity.

His European years were crucial in Cooper's literary career. Before them he dealt largely in his novels with the American

Thomas Cole, THE ROMAN CAMPAGNA. Catskill, N. Y., 1843.
(Courtesy of the Wadsworth Atheneum, Hartford)

Thomas Cole, THE COURSE OF EMPIRE (THE SAVAGE
STATE, THE ARCADIAN STATE, THE CONSUMMATION OF
EMPIRE, DESTRUCTION, and DESOLATION). Catskill, N.Y.,
1836. (Begun in Florence in 1831.)
(Courtesy of The New-York Historical Society)

past, notably with the frontier scene, and held that fiction should be generally realistic. During and immediately after these years he repeatedly held up American institutions and manners for comparison with those of Europe, in both fiction and non-fiction. A social and moral critic throughout his career, he became increasingly outspoken about weaknesses in American life, partly as a result of his European experience. In a few of the novels written afterward, however, he idealized scenes and characters in a manner not before attempted. In several prefaces written afterward, moreover, he distinguished fiction from other types of writing by allowing for both moral themes and imaginative elements in it.

Cooper's Italian years more particularly marked these turns in his development. He first considered America in relation to Europe in his first non-fictional work, *Notions of the Americans* (1828), written in Paris at the instigation of Lafayette. The first two novels he wrote abroad, for the most part before he went to Italy, belong, however, in the category of those he wrote before leaving America. The third, *The Water-Witch* (1831), written in Italy, is a combination of history and fantasy which contrasts America unfavorably with Italy. The fourth, *The Bravo* (1831), inspired by Venice, is the first of three novels with European settings which Cooper wrote abroad in which American institutions are compared favorably with those of Europe. It treats history, manners, and to some extent local scene for the purpose of conveying a moral. In the prefaces to both these novels, Cooper defended all these departures from his previous practice.

The most conspicuous influence which Italy exerted on Cooper was to broaden and make more genial his concept of civilization and thus indirectly to sharpen his judgments of America. In his comparisons, both fictional and non-fictional, of America and Europe, Italy is referred to more often than any other country, almost always to the disparagement of America. Whereas in all the works he wrote abroad for the avowed purpose of making such a comparison he celebrated the superiority of American principles, in most of those he wrote after his return home he depicted American culture as essentially provincial and commercial. This picture reflects some of his later unhappy experiences in America. It first appears, however, in *The Water-Witch*. From the beginning Italy represented to Cooper the ideal civilization, to which he would have had American civilization comparable.

His experience in Italy also deepened and subtilized Cooper's imaginative vision and encouraged him in the use of non-realistic techniques. The fantasy and symbolism in his first two Italianate novels distinguish them to a great extent from the rest of his fiction. These aspects of these novels, moreover, directly reflect the impression made on him by the Italian scene, which struck him more by what it called to his mind than by what it presented to his eye, by what he termed the "ideal" as distinct from the "real."

In the eleven works Cooper wrote before he went to Italy, allusions to foreign countries are negligible. In the thirty-two he wrote afterward, this country figures far more than any other. Four of the later novels are laid respectively in Germany, Switzerland, France, and England, and references to these countries appear in a few others. Two novels are set in Italy; in another the chief characters are Italian; in seven others the characters include Americans who have been to Italy; and of the rest, thirteen contain Italian allusions. Of these later works only three—*The Two Admirals* (1842) and the two volumes on the American Navy and its officers— contain no such allusions.

The first of Cooper's novels to exhibit the influence of Italy was *The Water-Witch,* which he began in Florence, worked on in Sorrento, and finished in Rome. Laid in the city and Bay of New York in the early eighteenth century, it describes the maneuvers of a mysterious brigantine called *The Water-Witch*, operated by a free-trader, known as the Skimmer of the Seas, and his so-called brother, who is actually Eudora, daughter of the New York merchant and alderman Myndert van Beverout. Both the vessel and its chief occupants have Italian connections. The Skimmer has worked in Italian waters with Eudora's grandfather, and Eudora has been brought up in Sorrento. She describes the Bay of Naples and its shores in glowing terms at great length, in the first of Cooper's numerous treatments of this subject. The brigantine's sudden appearances and disappearances, its oracular green figurehead, and its peculiar union of the characteristics of a brig and a schooner are all described with reference to Italian phenomena; and its cargo includes wares from Lombardy, Tuscany, and Venice.

The Water-Witch is the most lighthearted and the most imaginative of all Cooper's novels. For all its echoes of *The Red Rover* (1827), which concerns a colonial American pirate, it owes both these characteristics largely to Cooper's experience in Italy. The name of the heroine, meaning "good gift," reflects his feeling for that country, and the title vessel is an embodiment of the "witchery," as Cooper often called it, of the scene at the Bay of Naples. In the preface to the London edition (1834) he accounted for the unpopularity of this novel by calling its imaginative character un-American, but he declared its fault to be "in blending too much of the real with the purely ideal." These two aspects of phenomena he said in *Gleanings from Europe: Italy* he saw uniquely "blended" at Sorrento.

The Water-Witch has, nevertheless, two thematic patterns: an international one, in which typically American and Italian ways of life are contrasted, and a metaphysical one, in which literal fact and moral truth are contrasted. In the opening paragraphs Cooper observed that Florence, Venice, and Rome had declined in accordance with natural laws, whereas America was vigorously ascendant. Yet in the novel the American way of life appears less attractive than the Italian. In the former, represented chiefly by Van Beverout, the single aim is making money. In the latter, represented by the brigantine and its chief occupants, personal freedom is unrestrained, marriage is made for love, the imagination is exercised, and the esthetic sense is gratified. Morally, moreover, the free-trader is more admirable than the alderman, who deals secretly in contraband and who has virtually abandoned his wife. A union of the two ways of life is suggested by the proposal of marriage made to Eudora by a young New York patroon. But she accepts the Skimmer instead, and the brigantine carries them out of the Bay of New York never to return—taking, significantly, the southern breeze. In metaphysical terms, the "ideal" is more substantial than the "real." For all its practicality and its anticipation of future developments in America, Van Beverout's way of life proves an empty one, and in the end the chimera-like brigantine appears to be a symbol of enduring values.

Cooper's next novel, the first in his European trilogy, was *The Bravo*. Laid in Venice at the beginning of the eighteenth century, it depicts the political corruption and the social ills of the city at that time. The hero, Jacopo Frontoni, is a bravo or professional assassin in name only, having been forced by the Venetian Senate to assume this guise in order to inform it of unrest in the city. The plot was derived from the German J. H. D. Zschokke's story of Abaellino, a Venetian bravo, which had been popularized in romances and plays a few decades earlier. (The specific sources apparently were William

Dunlap's translation of Zschokke's play, *Abaellino the Great Bandit* (1801) and M. G. Lewis' adaptation of Zschokke's novel, *Abaellino the Bravo of Venice* (1804).) From this story Cooper took five of his principal characters, the basic situation of mistaken identity, and a number of incidents. He employed a wide variety of Gothic devices. (The atmosphere of intrigue in the book probably owes something to his experience with his conniving servant Luigi in Florence.) He also, like many Gothic novelists, expounded a good deal of history, which he obtained chiefly from P. A. Daru's *Histoire de Venise*.

At the same time Cooper was at pains to give his story local color—more than he gave to any other. He did so partly, he averred, to edify Americans who had not been to Venice. Drawing on his own observations, he described the topography of the city, a typical dwelling, and part of the Feast of the Ascension; distinguished the types of vessels in the lagoon; introduced several Italian phrases into the dialogue, and referred to the "soft" Venetian accents and the "harsher dialect" of Calabria; and quoted a verse from a Venetian boat song. He was aware of his departure from the Gothic tradition in such respects. In *A Letter to his Countrymen* (1834), which contains his chief defense of *The Bravo*, he declared there was as much resemblance between Abaellino and Jacopo as between "the Lord Mortimer of an old-fashioned novel, and Tom Jones." The "most grateful compliment" he had ever received, he wrote, had come—unwittingly—from a hostile English reviewer, who said that "while Byron had seen in Venice, her palaces, her renown, and 'England's glory'," the author of *The Bravo* had seen "only her palaces and her prisons."

Cooper's aim in *The Bravo* was, however, no more realistic or historical than it was romantic. In his preface to the American edition he disclaimed any attempt to portray his-

torical characters, who were, he said, "only too fictitious in
their graver dress." It was not his object, he added in the
preface to the London edition (1834), to "illustrate manners,
except as they were connected with principles"; he had introduced local details only "to aid the verisimilitude of the
picture." In *A Letter to his Countrymen* he distinguished between the "minor plot, or narrative" and the "moral" or
theme, which was to be "inferred" from it. It was his aim in
The Bravo to convey such a "moral," as it was in his other
European novels and, indeed, in most of his subsequent ones.

In all three of Cooper's European novels the general
"moral" or theme is the same : that any government in which
the power resides in a minority conduces to oppression of the
weak and perversion of the good. During the months
immediately following his stay in Venice, Cooper was convinced by current political events in Europe that the antagon-
ism of minorities and majorities was the great political issue of
the age and determined to write about this issue a series of
novels in which "American opinion should be brought to bear
on European facts." In all these novels European institutions
are shown to be decadent yet to afford a lesson for Americans.
In *The Bravo* the parallels under consideration are closest
and the lessons made most explicit. It was "thoroughly
American," Cooper asserted, "in all that belonged to it."
Throughout he contrasted the Venetian and the American
republics, attributing the corruption of the one and the purity
of the other chiefly to the relative degrees of public influence
operating in them. "Those countries, in which public opinion
has most influence," he wrote, "are always of the purest
public practice." Apropos of the prison sub-keeper's outburst
against the mob of fishermen, he argued ingeniously that

there is more security against popular violence and popular insults
in these free States, than in any other country on earth, for there

is scarcely a citizen so debased as not to feel that, in assuming the appearance of a wish to revenge the chances of fortune, he is making an undue admission of inferiority.

In the preface to the American edition he contrasted the geographical areas of America and Italy with respect to their moral implications. "A people of diversified interests and extended territorial possessions," he conjectured, "are much less likely to be the subjects of sinister passions than the inhabitants of a single town or country."

Cooper's most telling use of the Venetian scene in *The Bravo,* however, is not realistic but symbolic. The scene of this novel is, indeed, more expressly symbolic than that of any other by him. As in *The Water-Witch,* he was evidently put in mind of this technique by the Italian scene itself. As he had been impressed by the witchlike and "ideal" view at Sorrento, his imagination and fancy had been captured in Venice.

In general the palaces of Venice in *The Bravo* symbolize tyrannous and corrupt government. Stories are said to be raised on stories

in the wanton observance of the most capricious rules of mere-tricious architecture. . . . Colonnades, medallions, and massive cornices overhung the canal, as if the art of man had taken pride in loading the superstructure in a manner to mock the unstable element which concealed its base.

Most of these edifices are built, significantly, around a "dark court." That of Senator Gradenigo, the chief representative of the ruling Council of Three, is "no bad type of the Republic itself." The Doge's palace is "a fit emblem of that mysterious power which was known to preside over the fortunes of Venice and her citizens," a "gloomy monument of the policy of the Republic, furnishing evidence, in itself, of the specious charac-ter of the prince whom it held." The proximity of this palace and the state prison, which are separated by a narrow *rio,* seems to be "eloquently proclaiming the nature of the government by the close approximation of the powers of legislation and of punishment."

Other structures in the Piazza San Marco represent the great achievements of Venice at the period when it was more truly republican. Chiefly, however, they are symbols of enduring universal values. When the body of Antonio, the innocent old fisherman whose drowning has been brought about by government agents, is brought into the Piazza,

The quaint and Oriental church, the rows of massive and rich architecture, the giddy pile of the Campanile, the columns of granite, the masts of triumph, and all those peculiar and remarkable fixtures, which had witnessed so many scenes of violence, of rejoicing, of mourning, and of gayety, were there, like landmarks of the earth, defying time; beautiful and venerable in despite of all those varying exhibitions of human passions that were daily acted around them.

The symbolic value of St. Mark's is especially significant in view of the applicability of Cooper's thesis in *The Bravo* to the Roman Catholic Church. The Venetian clergy are represented as bent to the will of the government, but the Church itself appears superior to and more enduring than all other institutions, because of the spiritual life of which it is the repository. As Antonio's funeral procession approaches St. Mark's,

The great portal of the venerable church was thrown open, and the solemn chant was heard issuing, in responses, from among the quaint columns and vaulted roofs within. The body of the lowly and sacrificed Antonio was borne beneath that arch which sustains the precious relics of Grecian art, and deposited in the nave. Candles glimmered before the altar and around the ghastly person of the dead throughout the night; and the cathedral of St. Mark was pregnant with all the imposing ceremonials of the Catholic ritual, until the day once more appeared.

Priest succeeded priest, in repeating the masses, while the attentive throng listened, as if each of its members felt that his own honor and importance were elevated by this concession to one of their number.

Most of the characters in *The Bravo,* as in Cooper's fiction generally, are depicted realistically. Gelsomina, the beloved of Jacopo, is, however, somewhat idealized. She is an innocent child of nature who knows nothing of the artificial and wicked city about her. Preserved in her journey through it by night to tell the young Don Camillo Monforte the whereabouts of his bride, she loses her reason at the execution of Jacopo.

The two other novels in Cooper's European trilogy, *The Heidenmauer* (1832) and *The Headsman* (1833), which are laid respectively in Germany and Switzerland, contain Italian elements. In the former, the Roman Catholic tradition, again sympathetically depicted, is exemplified by references to St. Peter's and to Italian cloisters. Architecture is symbolic in this novel, too, though to a lesser extent than in *The Bravo.* The main characters in *The Headsman* are en route to Italy and four of them are Italians: the Doge of Genoa, his two sons (one a bastard and an outlaw, the other supposedly the son of the headsman of Berne), and a knavish Neapolitan juggler. These Italians are mostly conventional romantic types; but in comparing the behaviour on one occasion of the "more polished and artificial" Doge with that of a German and a French nobleman, Cooper expressed his own considered estimate of Italian character. It was traceable, he wrote,

through a long line of sophisticated and politic nobles, into the consuls and patricians of Rome, and most probably through these again into the wily and ingenious Greek, a root distinguished for civilization when these patriarchs of the north lay buried in the depths of barbarism.

Setting aside the allegorical *Monikins* (1835), Cooper's next two novels were *Homeward Bound* and *Home as Found* (1838), fictional accounts of his return to America. In them the Effingham family (roughly equivalent to the Coopers) come home after several years abroad to find America deplorably vulgar in contrast to Europe. Of European countries, Italy looms largest and brightest in these novels. Eve Effingham does not hesitate to "give the palm to Italy" as the most delightful country she has seen and could even choose it as a permanent residence. When asked by one of her untravelled countrymen what Italy has that England lacks, she replies, "Its recollections, for one thing, and all that interest which time and great events throw around a region." Her cousin Paul Powis, who has been brought up in England, is dismayed by the commercial aspect of New York; he advances the argument that the Medici and Strozzi merchants were monopolists uncontaminated by trade because they dealt through agents, unlike the numerous "mere factors" who engage in trade in New York. Though in having a thousand factors for one merchant, American society is in one sense the gainer, he thinks it would be the gainer in another sense if it had one Medici for a thousand factors. At the end of *Home as Found,* the newly wed Paul and Eve embark for England, intending to go on to Italy; he especially longs to see the latter country.

Typical of the Americans with whom the Effinghams are contrasted is the aggressive, egalatarian newspaper editor Steadfast Dodge, who returns with them from abroad. His attitude to Europe is that of the culture- and status-seeker, as indicated chiefly by Italian references. He wears conspicuously a *conchiglia* and a chain, apparently from Rome and Venice, and has kept a journal of his sight-seeing in which passages such as this appear :

"I have stood, with tears, over the despair of a Niobe . . . and witnessed the contortions of the snakes in the Laocoön with a convulsive eagerness to clutch them, that has made me fancy I could hear them hiss."

In his next novel, *The Pathfinder* (1840), Cooper returned to the story of Leatherstocking, and with *The Deerslayer* (1841) he finished this story. Only minor Italian references occur in these two novels, but the idealization of Leatherstocking there is more closely related to the technique in his three novels most concerned with Italy than to any Cooper employed elsewhere. It is perhaps also significant that the last of these three—*The Wing-and-Wing* (1842)—was published the year after *The Deerslayer*. In *The Pathfinder, The Deerslayer,* and *The Wing-and-Wing,* for virtually the last time, Cooper was in complete sympathy with his material, and the prevailing mood is a buoyant one.

The Wing-and-Wing was Cooper's second novel laid in Italy. The action takes place in and around the island of Elba and the Bay of Naples, just after the French siege of Naples in 1799. The plot involves the hopeless love of Raoul Yverne, the atheistic French captain of the privateer *Le Feu-Follet,* or *The Wing-and-Wing,* for a devout Italian girl, Ghita Caroccioli (a fictitious granddaughter of the historical Neapolitan admiral Francesco Caroccioli), and propounds the thesis that freethinking and religious dogmatism are equally wrong-headed. Cooper lavished affection on descriptions of the scene, recreating some of his experiences on his voyage from Leghorn to Naples and his outings on the Bay of Naples, as described in *Gleanings from Europe: Italy.* In several respects this novel is a companion of *The Water-Witch.* Yverne long conceals from the English his own identity and that of his lugger and makes the lugger appear and disappear suddenly. In this novel, however, the setting has no relation to the theme, and the nationality of the hero and heroine is of relatively little importance.

There are, nevertheless, international contrasts in *The Wing-and-Wing*—more than in any other novel by Cooper. Among the characters are Italians, Frenchmen, Englishmen, and an American who are depicted as national types. Most prominent are the *podestà* and the *vice-governatore* of Elba, a humorous pair, who between them are excitable, fond of titles, legalistic, deferential to authority, and generally ingratiating. Cooper admitted to being regaled by them. They hardly substantiate, however, Yverne's declaration that the Italians are the "parents of modern civilization." The American is Ithuel Bolt, a shrewd, untutored, roguish seaman from New England. A dissenter, he scorns the Roman Catholic Church; a trader in contraband, he is outraged by the *vice-governatore's* offer of a bribe; he prefers cider to wine, has little emotion, speaks with a nasal twang (which sounds all the more uneuphonious among speakers of Italian), and distrusts all "Eyetalians," as he calls them.

In four other later novels by Cooper, Americans incidentally go or have been to Italy. Aunt Harding in *The Autobiography of a Pocket Handkerchief* (1843) reports that the Neapolitan Duke of Montecarbana "had the smallest ears she ever beheld on a human being" and that his family was "as old as the ruins of Paestum." In *Afloat and Ashore* (1844) the semi-autobiographical Miles Wallingford and the Brighams, who are typical tourists in a hurry, visit several Italian cities. On their tour of Europe referred to in *The Redskins* (1846), Roger and Hugh Littlepage landed at Leghorn and spent a year in Italy, in order to begin at the beginning of European civilization. At the end of that novel, ready to move to Washington in the hope of obtaining legal aid there in his case against his anti-rent tenants, Hugh consoles himself by reflecting that if he loses he has "the refuge of Florence open, where he can reside among the other victims of oppression, with the advantage of being admired as a refuge[e?] from republican tyranny." Jack Wilmington and the Europeanized mystery woman Mary Monson in *The Ways of the Hour* (1850) have also been to Italy. Most of Cooper's sophisticated Americans, in fact, have visited Europe, including Italy. Their attitudes toward their experiences there are part of their characterization, as are the attitudes of his provincial American tourists.

The other incidental references to Italy in Cooper's late novels are to its scenery, its climate, its language, its recent history, and its non-commercial atmosphere. In thirteen novels, from *The Water-Witch* to *The Oak Openings* (1848), the Italian landscape is lovingly referred to, usually to the disparagement of the American. The dissimilarity of the bays of Naples and of New York became one of Cooper's crotchets, belabored in five novels. In the prefaces to *Jack Tier* (1848) and *The Oak Openings* he referred sympathetically to the regeneration of Italy in the post-Napoleonic period. Yet in the end, as at first, he ascribed the charm of Italy largely to the age of its civilization. In the next to the last of his novels, *The Sea Lions* (1849), which contains one of the most barbaric of his aggressive Americans, he recorded that he had often observed how much more "'enjoyable,' for the intellectual and the independent, is a country on the decline, than a country on the advance." Though "the climate, and the monuments, and the recollections" contributed to its popularity with the "idle and educated," he thought that popularity largely due to the fact that

man, as a rule, is far more removed from the money-getting mania in Italy than in almost any other portion of the Christian world; and this merely because the time of her wealth and power has gone by, leaving in its train a thousand fruits that would seem to be the most savory, as the stem on which they grew would appear to be approaching its decay.

Throughout the novels written after Cooper returned from Europe, sophisticated Americans tend to supplant the unsophisticated in the protagonist's role, and the number of provincial and unprincipled antagonists increases. Leatherstocking is taken leave of, Indians are converted to Christianity, the image of the pristine wilderness fades. In a sense the image of civilization, represented generally by Europe but particularly by Italy, takes its place. In Cooper's earlier novels civilization is chiefly depicted in opposition to the wilderness, as morally superior to if less idyllic than that scene. In his later fiction the civilized state is more relaxed and enjoyable, endowed with as many esthetic values as the wilderness, and with even more intellectual ones. In his later thought and imagination, in fact, the completely instinctual and the completely civilized life were both beautiful and happy; the period between, through which America was passing too slowly to suit him, was meanly materialistic. It is perhaps significant that in the last of the novels about Leatherstocking, in which this character, who unites the best values of the frontier and the moral values of civilization, is the most fully idealized, the light of Italy figuratively penetrates the American wilderness. The blushes on the cheek of Judith Hutter when Deerslayer speaks to her are said to resemble "the wayward tints of a Neapolitan sky in November."

IV

The Language of Art:

HAWTHORNE

NATHANIEL HAWTHORNE'S APPOINTMENT IN 1853 AS AMERICAN consul at Liverpool enabled him to go abroad for the first time, to the foreign country which most attracted him and which he came to like best. Before leaving America with his family, he planned for them all to spend a year in Italy before returning. He had interest in that country, too, about which he had read sporadically and to which he had often referred in his writing. But it was his wife, prompted partly by her studies as an amateur artist, who most desired to go there. When they went, at the conclusion of Hawthorne's consular term, they stayed seventeen months : from January to June 1858 in Rome, from June to October in Florence, and from October 1858 to May 1859 in Rome again. They were some of the most stimulating, the most carefree, and the most miserable months of Hawthorne's life. He was in his fifty-fourth and fifty-fifth years. When he left Italy he had only five years more to live.

Hawthorne's first and some of his most lasting impressions of Rome were disagreeable. He arrived with his party—his wife, their three children and a young governess, Ada Shepard —late at night, after a frightening ride in a vettura from Civi-

tavecchia over a road lately visited by bandits, in the midst of
a rainy spell. For several weeks he was uncomfortably cold and
conscious chiefly of dirty streets and mean living conditions.
Throughout both his terms of residence in the city he suffered
from the effects of the climate, contracting colds in the winter
and being overcome by lassitude in the sirocco season. Other
members of his family, and the governess, were more seriously
ill. During six of the seven months of their second residence
fifteen-year-old Una Hawthorne had recurrent attacks of
malaria, including one so severe that her life was despaired of.

Chiefly on account of its unhealthiness Hawthorne often
expressed hatred for Rome. Its atmosphere had "a peculiar
quality of malignancy," he declared, was "malevolent, or, at
least, not friendly." It was "a most interesting place of residence," he wrote Franklin Pierce in October 1858, ". . . but
a very gloomy one, and I have suffered more in Rome from
low spirits than almost anywhere else." "I bitterly detest
Rome, and shall rejoice to bid it farewell forever," he wrote
the publisher James T. Fields during Una's illness;

and I fully acquiesce in all the mischief and ruin that has hap-
pened to it, from Nero's conflagration downward. In fact, I wish
the very site had been obliterated before I ever saw it.

Yet Rome also fascinated Hawthorne—more, indeed, than
any other city except perhaps his birthplace, Salem. He had
for Rome, in fact, much the same ambivalent feeling that he
had for Salem. By the time he came to leave Rome for
Florence in May 1858 he found that he had a "strange affection" for it. "It is very singular," he wrote in his journal at
that time, "the sad embrace with which Rome takes possession of the soul." Though he and his family planned to return
in a few months, they felt it "pulling at our heart strings far
more than London did." The explanation, he suggested, was
that

the intellect finds a home there, more than in any other spot in the world, and wins the heart to stay with it, in spite of a great many things strewn all about to disgust us.]

Nearing the city on his return in October, he was conscious that it drew "into itself my heart, as I think London or even little Concord itself, or old sleepy Salem, never did and never will."

Hawthorne's summer in Tuscany was a halcyon interlude between his two Roman winters. In the opinion of his son Julian it was the happiest period of his life. One of his "brightest and most uncareful" times, he called the journey from Rome to Florence. In the temperate climate and among the vivacious inhabitants of the northern region he soon felt "a sort of alacrity in my mind, and an affluence of ideas." There could hardly be a place in the world, he thought, "where life is more delicious for its own simple sake" than in Florence. It offered him an opportunity to "assuage and mollify myself a little, after that uncongenial life of the Consulate, and before going back to my own hard and dusty New-England."

For the months of August and September the Hawthornes occupied the villa of the Montauto family on the hill of Bellosguardo, where Hawthorne had at last the "pleasant" feeling that he was "really away from America." In England and even in Rome he had complained of seeing too much of his countrymen. The night before his departure he lingered on the tower of the villa, watching the sky and the lights of the city and listening to the "sweet bells of Florence . . . loth to come down into the lower world," knowing he would "never again look heavenward from an old tower-top, in such a soft, calm evening as this." Two years later, partly in memory of this tower, he had one added to his house in Concord for his use as a study.

In Siena, on his way back to Rome, Hawthorne toyed with the notion of buying the Villa Belvedere there, in which the William Wetmore Storys were staying. A "thoughtful and shy man," he felt, "might settle down . . . and spend many years in a sombre kind of happiness" in this city. He thought he would prefer it to Florence as a permanent residence. Yet only "a kind of despair," he declared, would make him "dream of finding a home in Italy; a sense that I had lost my country through absence or incongruity, and that earth, at any rate, is not an abiding place."

By this time he had seen a good many expatriates. He greatly enjoyed the company of Story in Rome and of Hiram Powers and the Brownings in Florence, but he considered foreign residence devitalizing. "It needs the native air to give life a reality," he wrote in his journal after meeting T. A. Trollope, who lived in Florence. His feelings about living abroad himself, nevertheless, were mixed. He took this truth to himself, he confessed, "regretfully . . . without feeling much inclination to go back to the reality" of his own country.

By the time of his final departure from Rome he was glad to go. He was sure that he would have "many yearnings to return hereafter, and many regrets that I did not make better use of the opportunities within my grasp," yet he felt that he had been there "long enough to be imbued with its atmosphere, and this is the essential condition of knowing a place." Analyzing his feeling about this city for the last time in his journal, he concluded that

no place ever took so strong a hold of my being, as Rome, nor ever seemed so close to me, and so strangely familiar. I seem to know it better than my birth place, and to have known it longer; and though I have been very miserable there, and languid with the effects of the atmosphere, and disgusted with a thousand things in daily life, still I cannot say I hate it—perhaps might

fairly own a love for it. But, (life being too short for such question-
able and troublesome enjoyments) I desire never to set eyes on
it again.

Toward the end of his Italian residence Hawthorne said
that he loved two countries—America and England—more
than he loved Italy. That residence made him more apprecia-
tive of England and more critical of America than he had
been previously. Whereas during his first stay in England he
had often been on the defensive as an American, in Italy he
was most conscious of the thinness of American culture. Writing to Fields a few months before he left Italy, he agreed that
"America is a country to boast of, and to get out of, and keep
away from, and that England is the only country to live in."
He had described so many Italian objects of art in *The Marble
Faun,* he wrote in the preface, partly because while preparing
the final manuscript of the novel in England,

on the broad and dreary sands of Redcar, with the gray German
Ocean tumbling in upon me, and the northern blast always
howling in my ears, the complete change of scene made these
Italian reminiscences shine out so vividly that I could not find
it in my heart to cancel them.

Together, indeed, England and Italy composed for Hawthorne twin centers of the civilized world, of which America
was a kind of outpost. The only other European country he
knew, France, made little impression on him. In *Our Old
Home* (1863), his volume of sketches about England, he
applied the figure in the title to Italy as well. He had acquired
in London "the dream-city of my youth," he wrote, "a home-
feeling . . . as nowhere else in the world." Yet afterward, he
added, he

came to have a somewhat similar sentiment in regard to Rome;
and as long as either of those two great cities shall exist, the

cities of the Past and of the Present, a man's native soil may crumble beneath his feet without leaving him altogether homeless upon earth.

Hawthorne spent most of his time in Italy sight-seeing. He constantly protested that his receptive capacity in this activity was limited, particularly (and quite correctly) that it was far less than his wife's. Yet he sought out most of the celebrated objects to be seen wherever he went and was usually deeply interested by them. He also liked to ramble about by himself, enjoying the feeling of being temporarily lost and making discoveries of his own. For upwards of "the thousandth time" he went on such rambles through the "narrow intricacies" of the streets of Rome.

Italian churches particularly attracted him. The devout attitude yet free movement of the worshippers there, the private rather than communal nature of their devotions, the religious appeal of the works of art in these churches, the system of the confessional (which he thought seemed comforting to the one who confessed though wearisome to the priest)—all commended Roman Catholicism to him. "Protestantism," he declared after a visit to the Pantheon, "needs a new Apostle to convert it into something positive." Yet he repeatedly expressed the wish that Catholic laymen and priests were more moral and the conviction that the Church, once animated by a "living spirit" which made it "a true religion," was now virtually dead.

In other aspects of contemporary Italian life Hawthorne manifested little interest. He knew few Italians personally and had slight regard for any of them. They were "loveable," "sweet (except to the sense of smell,) amiable, pleasant to encounter" except when begging or bargaining, he thought, yet possessed of "great and little faults, and no great virtues that I know of."

The principal objects of Hawthorne's attention in Italy—
and the chief subjects treated in his Italian journal—were
works of art. He began to be interested in such works in
England (where for the first time he saw a substantial number), but except for attending the Art Exhibition in Man-
chester in the summer of 1857, when he developed a taste for
painting, he afforded little time for them there. He admired
English architecture, especially Gothic specimens. The Elgin
Marbles left him cold—partly because he was fatigued by
walking through the British Museum. At the end of his stay in
England, however, he was looking forward to a more concentrated study of art in Italy.

In Italy, as in England, he approached works of art with a
characteristic skepticism : desirous of understanding them
better yet reluctant to be imposed upon. He usually hastened
through buildings and collections on his first visit; suspected
that he was "bamboozling" himself when he enjoyed them;
and felt that, since unprincipled men often had tastes for the
arts, such tastes were "artificial, the product of civilization, and
when highly developed, imply a great remove from natural
simplicity." The general arrangement of collections and his
own moods, moreover, drastically affected his impressions. Yet
in Italy Hawthorne was immediately delighted by many works
of art, applied himself diligently to studying such works, and
felt increasingly at home among them. Far from fearing their
ultimate influence, he hoped that, since "nothing elevating and
refining can be really injurious," Una would

always be the better for Rome, even if her life should be spent
where there are no pictures, no statues, nothing but the dryness
and meagreness of a New England village.

With his preference for the ornate, particularly for the
Gothic style in architecture, Hawthorne was unimpressed by
the tradition of plainness in Italian buildings. He complained

that classical architecture was "nothing but an outline," affording "no little points, or interstices, where human feelings may cling and overgrow it like ivy," and that most Florentine buildings had a "general squareness and monotony." "I do not know what," he commented after a visit to Santa Croce, "but it is in the region of the heart rather than the intellect— that Italian architecture, of whatever age or style, never seems to reach."

His architectural taste was nevertheless abundantly gratified in Italy. His first impressions, during his one day in Genoa, were of a "magnificence," "richness," and "splendor" in palaces and churches unlike anything he had ever seen before. He found the same qualities in most of the palaces and churches of Rome—notably the Barberini, Borghese, and Pamfili Doria palaces and the churches of St. Peter, St. John Lateran, and Santa Maria Maggiore. In Florence he was especially delighted by the carvings on the Campanile, the stained glass in the cathedral, and the church of Santissima Annunziata (more elaborate than most churches there). The cathedral in Siena, with its "magnificent eccentricity" and the "multitudinous richness of the ornamentation" of its façade, "bewitched" him. He particularly admired the polished variegated marbles in many of these buildings. Altogether they, like certain Italian paintings, intensified his feeling, first experienced in England, that the past had been a more splendid scene than the present.

Sculpture in Italy gave Hawthorne more pleasure in relation to the number of works which he saw than painting. He was especially taken by Praxiteles' *Faun,* the *Dying Gladiator,* the *Apollo Belvedere,* and the *Lacoön* in Rome; the *Venus de' Medici* and Michelangelo's statue for the tomb of Lorenzo de' Medici in Florence; and busts of Roman emperors in both cities. He virtually fell in love with the *Venus.* To him it was not "a senseless image" but "a being that lives to gladden the world, incapable of decay and death," and that would linger in the memory of man as "one of the treasures of spiritual existence hereafter." Indeed, it made him "more ready to believe in the high destinies of the human race, to think that this beautiful form is but Nature's plan for all womankind." All these works represented to him the Greek esthetic ideal, in relation to which he called himself "a very sturdy Goth." He felt, however, that they exerted a "refining" influence on him.

Though he vigorously objected to much of the painting which he saw in Italy, Hawthorne was most fascinated by this art and came to regard it most highly of all the arts during his sojourn there. He complained of the many darkened canvases and faded frescoes and even longed for more handsome frames, such as he had seen in England. Especially at first, he called painting an ephemeral art, of which far too many speciments had been preserved. He disapproved of voluptuous figures, notably in certain Titians, and confessed to a weakness for realistic details by "old Dutch wizards" and for minor character studies. Like his taste in architecture, however, his taste in painting was for the highly developed. He deplored the work of such primitives as Cimabue and Giotto and most admired Raphael and Guido Reni, particularly the former's *Transfiguration* and *Madonna della Seggiola* and the latter's *Beatrice Cenci* and *St. Michael Overcoming Satan*. By the time he reached Florence, moreover, he was seeing pictures "with less toil, and more pleasure" and being "more fastidious, yet more sensible of beauty where I saw none before." Without the "magnificent" Uffizi Gallery and the Pitti Palace, he wondered, "what shall we do in America?" In Florence he came to the conclusion that "the pictorial art is capable of something more like magic—more wonderful and inscrutable in its methods—than poetry, or any other mode of developing the beautiful." Above all, he recognized "the vast scope of this wonderful art," in which both Raphael and Gerard Douw excelled. He only wished the styles they represented to him— the grand and the microscopic—might be combined in a single work.

Hawthorne's comments in his journal on the works of art, particularly the paintings and sculpture, that he saw in Italy are highly personal and vary with the circumstances under which he saw them. These comments tend, nevertheless, toward a single generalization : that art forms are above all modes of intellectual communication, essentially symbolic in nature.

Michelangelo's *Lorenzo* and the *Venus de' Medici* particularly impressed him by their non-realistic character. "How wonderful!" he exclaimed of the first. "To take a block of marble and convert it wholly into thought." It had been wrought "through the efficacy of a kingly idea, which had no reference to the individual whose name it bears." Powers convinced him that the head of the *Venus* was not life-like, in which respect it was inferior to Powers' busts of Proserpine and Psyche. Hawthorne felt, however, that the sculptor of the statue had

disregarded technicalities and the imitation of actual nature, the better to produce the effect which he really does produce, in somewhat the same way as a painter works his magical illusions by touches that have no relation to the truth, if looked at from the wrong point of view.

He often contrasted the "inner soul" or "ethereal spirit" of a statue or painting with its embodiment in stone or pigment, perceived by the "grosser sense" only, and lamented the fact that the spirit was only fitfully revealed. The statues in the Vatican seemed to him to keep "for the most part, a veil about them, which they sometimes withdrew and let their beauty flow upon my sight." On such occasions he saw them as "forever new and immortally young." Often, too, he was unable to "achieve that free and generous surrender" of himself which he found essential to the estimate of excellence. Then all masterpieces were "heavily burthensome" to him. There was no middle ground. A statue was either "a celestial thing, or an old lump of stone."

At their best, Hawthorne often found paintings and sculpture in Italy not entirely comprehensible. He looked at Michelangelo's *Lorenzo* "with highest enjoyment, but also with grief and impatience, because I feel that I do not come at all [to that] which it involves, and that by-and-by I must go away and leave it forever." He was glad as well as sorry to see Guido's *Beatrice Cenci* for the last time because "it so perplexed and troubled me not to be able to get hold of its secret." The possible interpretations of such works seemed to him virtually endless, among them that of the artist's having set forth a riddle to which he had no answer.

Yet this very elusive and inconvertible quality was Hawthorne's measure of excellence in the painting and sculpture he saw in Italy. A great painting, he wrote apropos of the ambiguities he found in Michelangelo's *Three Fates,* was "a great symbol, proceeding out of a great mind; but if it means one thing, it seems to mean a thousand, and often opposite things." After a particularly enjoyable visit to the Vatican sculpture collection early in his first Roman residence he decided that

it is in vain to attempt giving the impression produced by masterpieces of art, and most in vain when we see them best. They are a language in themselves; and if they could be expressed any way except by themselves, there would have been no need of expressing those particular ideas and sentiments by sculpture.

Hawthorne knew nearly all the American artists in Italy, most of whom at that time lived in Rome. He approved of the painters as a group, acknowledging that he enjoyed the work of Cephas G. Thompson (who had painted his portrait in America) and George Loring Brown more than that of most painters in the past. But he agreed with Mrs. Anna Jameson that the sculptors in Rome (among whom were Paul Akers, E. S. Bartholomew, Harriet Hosmer, Mary Louise Lander— to whom he sat for his bust—Joseph Mozier, and Story) were, with the exception of Story, persons "with no high aims, no worthy conception of the purposes of their art, and desecrating marble by the things they wrought in it." He particularly objected to nude figures in modern sculpture because they were unrealistic. He nevertheless found the company of artists in Italy generally congenial, and his association with them stimulated his interest in and speculations about art.

Partly because of his association with American artists in Italy, Hawthorne was particularly conscious there of America's lack of interest in the arts. He wished the American republic would encourage sculpture and architecture as much as the Florentine had. But "we have the meanest government, and the shabbiest—," he declared, after hearing of Powers' failure to obtain a Congressional commission, "and, if truly represented by it, are the meanest and shabbiest people—known in history."

Hawthorne did less creative writing in Italy than he had hoped to do, partly because he found the climate debilitating and the scene distracting. Shortly after his arrival he wrote a rough draft of the work posthumously published as *The Ancestral Footstep*. In April 1858 he conceived the idea for *The Marble Faun*. He wrote a rough draft of this novel in Florence, another in Rome in the fall, and the third and last version in England in the latter part of 1859. The "Italian atmosphere," he concluded, was "not favorable to the close toil of composition, although it is a very good air to dream in."

George Inness, ST. PETER'S SEEN FROM THE CAMPAGNA. Rome? *ca.* 1872.
(Courtesy of The Detroit Institute of Arts)

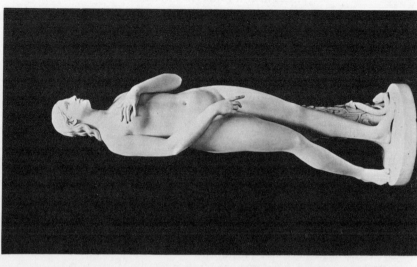

EVE TEMPTED. Florence, 1842.
(Courtesy of Roger Michahelles, Florence)

Hiram Powers

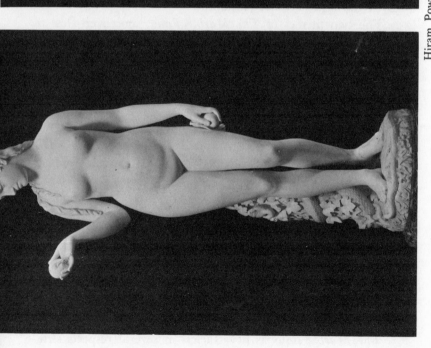

EVE DISCONSOLATE. Florence, 1871.
(Courtesy of The Cincinnati Art Museum)

The Marble Faun (1860), Hawthorne's only work inspired by his Italian residence and the last novel he completed, contains no essential elements which are radically different from those in his other fiction. References to Italy and Italian culture occur in his writing from 1831 on: in "Sights from a Steeple" (1831), "The Great Carbuncle" (1837), "Edward Randolph's Portrait" (1838), "A Virtuoso's Collection" (1842), "The Hall of Fantasy" (1843), "Egotism" (1843), "Little Daffydowndilly" (1843), "Rappaccini's Daughter" (1844), "Drowne's Wooden Image" (1846), "Passages from a Relinquished Work" (1846), "Main Street" (1849), *The Scarlet Letter* (1850), *The House of the Seven Gables* (1851), *The Blithedale Romance* (1852), *Septimius Felton* (1872), and *Dr. Grimshawe's Secret* (1882).

The two themes of *The Marble Faun,* moreover—loss of innocence or the Fall of Man, and art versus nature and society; and its two basic images—legendary Arcadia and the Garden of Eden appear throughout Hawthorne's writing. Both themes appear in "Rappaccini's Daughter," the only other of his works laid in Italy, and so do a number of the images, both major and minor, found in the novel. "The Maypole of Merry Mount" (1836) and *The Blithedale Romance* are also notable thematic and imagistic antecedents of *The Marble Faun.* Another motif in the novel—the relation of America to Europe—appears earlier and is dominant in most of the fiction written after Hawthorne went abroad. He was following his general practice when in *The Marble Faun* he introduced experiences of his own, often drawing on accounts of them in his journal; employed symbols; and purposed, as he announced in the preface, "to write a fanciful story, evolving a thoughtful moral," not to produce "a portraiture of Italian manners and character."

The Marble Faun is nevertheless in several respects strikingly different from Hawthorne's other fiction. The basic treatment of Italian material in his other works follows the Renaissance-Gothic literary tradition, but here it is derived from his experience and is more closely related to the travel or guide book tradition. Here both themes have greater scope and more optimistic implications than anywhere else in Hawthorne's fiction. In each of the four other novels undertaken after he went to Europe the American-European relationship is represented by an American claim to an estate in England— a motif reflecting Hawthorne's personal preference for that foreign country. *The Marble Faun,* however, figuratively establishes an American heritage in Italy. Of these five novels, moreover, it is the only one he was able to finish. Of all his works of fiction it is the most nearly balanced in moral vision and incomparably the richest in imagery.

For all these unusual aspects of *The Marble Faun* and for some of those which are typical of Hawthorne's fiction as well his contact with the Italian scene was responsible. He made extensive use of his Italian experiences—notably his moving from Rome to Florence and back to Rome, occupation of the Montauto villa (in which there was an alabaster skull), sight of a dead monk in the church of the Capuchins in Rome, meeting with a buffalo calf and visit to the newly excavated *Venus* on the Campagna, and acquaintance in Rome with such artists as Story, Akers, and the English sculptor John Gibson. Apparently he drew on his acquaintance with Ada Shepard, Harriet Hosmer, and Mary Louise Lander in characterizing Hilda as a young American girl abroad. (Unknown to the Hawthornes, Miss Shepard had an experience comparable to some of those had by other fictional young American girls in Italy when advances were made to her by the Italian doctor called in during Una's illness.) The only other use Hawthorne made of his Italian experiences was in the second draft of *Dr. Grimshawe's Secret,* in which the typically Gothic Dr. Ormskirk and his daughter Elsie are modelled after the English antiquarian Seymour Kirkup and the child Imogen in his house, whom Hawthorne had met in Florence.

Hawthorne's particular Italian experiences aside, the Italian scene exerted three major influences on *The Marble Faun.* It suggested the particular themes and the basic imagery, colored the views of the innocent life and of art and artists, and made possible the peculiarly elaborate symbolism in the novel.

The themes of lost innocence and of the art-nature-society relationship and the images of Arcadia and Eden were brought repeatedly to Hawthorne's mind by certain works of art, the landscape, the people, the climate, and some of the historical monuments of Italy. He got the idea of writing a story about a faun character from two statues of fauns in the Villa Borghese—one of them a copy of Praxiteles'—and from the most celebrated copy of that work in the Capitoline Museum. These creatures symbolized for him a delightful early stage of human development, and he first thought of such a story as being "funny, and philosophical, as well as poetic," "with all sorts of fun and pathos in it."

Other sculpture and certain paintings apparently exerted an equally vital influence on the gestation of *The Marble Faun* as, instead, primarily a tragedy about the conflict of good and evil resulting in loss of innocence. Chief among these works were Guido's innocent, blonde *Beatrice Cenci* and Raphael's worldly, brunette *Fornarina,* which hung near each other in the Palazzo Barberini and for which, as Hawthorne noted in his journal, this collection was famous; Guido's *St. Michael Overcoming Satan,* in the church of the Capuchins in Rome; the principal pieces of sculpture in the room of the Capitoline

Museum containing Praxiteles' *Faun* and in the one adjoining
—notably other sylvan figures, the *Dying Gladiator* and the
Girl with Dove and Snake; and the *Venus de' Medici,* in
the Uffizi Gallery in Florence. Most of these works, which
figure prominently in *The Marble Faun,* were among those
which most deeply moved Hawthorne in Italy and which are
described with unusual feeling in his journal and in that of his
wife.

A great number of other paintings and works of sculpture
which Hawthorne saw in Italy, of course, were related to the
major theme of the novel, and many of them are alluded to
in it. Notable among those of which he made no use are
several by American artists : the *Eves* of Powers and Bartholomew, Crawford's *Adam and Eve,* and Miss Hosmer's *Beatrice
Cenci.*

More generally considered, the objects of art and the contemporary artists in Italy decisively affected the development
of *The Marble Faun* as a novel concerned secondarily about
the nature of art.

Hawthorne's mental picture of Arcadia seems in effect to
have been realized in Italy. The grounds of the Villa Borghese
in Rome are said in *The Marble Faun* to be such as come to

the imagination when we read the beautiful old myths, and fancy
a brighter sky, a softer turf, a more picturesque arrangement of
venerable trees, than we find in the rude and untrained landscapes of the Western world.

Rural Tuscany is described as having "still a remote, dream-
like, Arcadian charm, which is scarcely to be found in the
daily toil of other lands." Italian peasants in the novel also
evoke this image, especially those around Rome who wear
satyr-like goatskin breeches.

Rome apparently called to Hawthorne's mind Eden after
the Fall, chiefly because of the city's unhealthiness during the

summer. Malaria is to the beautiful villas in the vicinity, he wrote in *The Marble Faun,* "what the flaming sword was to the first Eden," removing them "beyond the scope of man's actual possessions." This disease aside, the weather in Italy is said to be like none elsewhere "save in Paradise . . . certainly not in America, where it is always too strenuous on the side either of heat or cold." Corresponding in the moral sphere to the malaria is the crime of the Roman past as depicted in the novel. This crime, symbolized by many of the antique structures in the city, is often referred to as poisoning the air. It is "a contagious element, rising fog-like . . . and brooding over the dead and half-rotten city, as nowhere else on earth." Modern Rome accordingly, like the postlapsarian world, is conducive to sin. Significantly, the crime which Donatello commits is not that of Adam but that of Cain.

The same elements of the Italian scene which influenced Hawthorne's choice of themes and basic imagery also influenced his treatment of these themes in *The Marble Faun.* In this version of the loss of innocence theme certain new views of innocence are distinguishable. Here, more explicitly than elsewhere in Hawthorne's fiction, innocence is pictured as a New World characteristic, in contrast to Old World corruption. Of the five central characters, the three involved in crime are Europeans (or Europeanized), the two not involved are Americans. Urging Donatello to accompany him to America, Kenyon declares,

"In that fortunate land, each generation has only its own sins and sorrows to bear. Here, it seems as if all the weary and dreary Past were piled upon the back of the Present."

Hilda's ostensibly greatest temptation is to join the Roman Catholic Church, which is represented as largely decadent in modern times; her New England Puritan background keeps her from doing so. In the artistic sphere the same contrast obtains, with the important difference that the representatives of the New World are less able to preserve their integrity here than in the moral sphere. As the American artists linger in Italy, especially in Rome, "their originality dies out of them, or is polished away as a barbarism." It is significant that Hilda becomes a copyist.

At the same time, however, in *The Marble Faun* as nowhere else in Hawthorne, innocence is associated with the antique in contrast to the modern world. Here for the only time he depicted the prelapsarian life of man in nature directly, fully and attractively. There are weaknesses in this life—evidenced, for example, in the immaturity of the faun's character, the liability of the dancers in the Borghese grounds to accidents, and the fact that Donatello is the last of his family. Yet, especially in contrast to the pseudo-sylvan creatures at Merry Mount and the would-be Arcadians at Blithedale, the genuine primitive type represented by the early Donatello is graceful, free, innately happy, simple, harmless, and appealing. Donatello is also strikingly different from the principal Italian types of literary tradition. He was evidently drawn to some extent from life, but the major influence on his characterization was antique sculpture.

A primal innocence is depicted in *The Marble Faun*, moreover, as persisting in corrupt modern times and as being reincarnated in the character of a modern innocent. In Hawthorne's fiction generally the past exerts an altogether baneful influence on the present. In *The Marble Faun* some of the most conspicuous objects in decadent Rome represent such an innocence. The water of the Fountain of Trevi, flowing from outside the city through subterranean aqueducts, is described as still as pure as the legendary virgin who led Agrippa to its source. The Pantheon, standing symbolically "almost at the central point of the labyrinthine intricacies of the modern city," is grandly simple and has immediate access to nature through the opening in its dome. In that the Roman Catholic Church ministers to the simple, sanctifies innocence, and allows in the Carnival for a season of merry-making, it seems to carry on this strain in antique life. In this respect this institution appears to be the chief link between the ancient and modern worlds. Another example of the persistence of a delightful strain in antique life is the disinterment on the Campagna of the superior version of the *Venus de' Medici*. This statue is found near Cecilia Metella's tomb, which, Hawthorne noted, was converted in medieval times into a fortress; it thus appears emblematic of the perversion of the modern world.

Hilda is a type of the innocent young girl common in Hawthorne's fiction. (She may also have some kinship with Gelsomina in Cooper's *The Bravo*, whose journey through the streets and canals of Venice at night to Don Camillo's palace prefigures Hilda's safe wanderings about Rome.) Unlike Hawthorne's other innocent young girls, however, Hilda has vital connections with the past and with the Old World. Some such relation is suggested in *The House of the Seven Gables* by the fact that the seeds of Alice Pyncheon's "posies," which continue to flourish on the decaying roof of the Pyncheon house, came from Italy. In *The Marble Faun,* this relation is emphasized. For all her Puritanism, Hilda is devoted to the Virgin Mary, who receives credit for her preservation from harm. The greatest peril with which she is threatened is isolation from her fellows, and from it she is saved by the Roman Catholic confessional. Most striking of all, she is affiliated with the antique, pagan world. In the central myth of the novel Miriam is the faun Donatello's nymph, but it is Hilda who has the ethereal and virginal character. It is while looking for her that Kenyon discovers the buried *Venus*. Both Hilda and Kenyon admire the Pantheon, whose opening in the dome represents to their Protestant eyes a direct communication with the Deity; here, before the marble *Madonna* at Raphael's tomb, they declare their love. The image of a resurrected Arcadia is projected by Miriam's wedding gift to Hilda : a bracelet of seven gems from seven ancient Etruscan sepulchres.

Hilda, moreover, develops in Rome, though not, like Donatello, with loss of innocence. Her moral vision remains virtually unchanged, but by the end of the novel she has passed from maidenhood to womanhood and is ready to marry Kenyon. The *Venus* he discovers and the *Madonna* (as Hawthorne calls it) in the Pantheon are both in marked contrast to the statue of the Virgin on Hilda's tower as indication of her maturation.

It is Hilda's horror at Kenyon's suggestion that Donatello has been matured by his crime that brings her and Kenyon together at last, both feeling "far from home" in the moral atmosphere of Rome. They decide to return to America not because they fear the corruption of the city, however, but because "now . . . life had so much human promise in it." "The years, after all," Hawthorne here interpolated,

have a kind of emptiness, when we spend too many of them on a foreign shore. We defer the reality of life, in such cases, until a future moment, when we shall again breathe our native air; but, by and by, there are no future moments; or, if we do return, we find that the native air has lost its invigorating quality, and that life has shifted its reality to the spot where we have deemed ourselves only temporary residents. Thus, between two countries, we have none at all, or only that little space of either, in which we finally lay down our discontented bones. It is wise, therefore, to come back betimes, or never.

The greatest danger faced by Americans in any foreign country thus appears to be devitalization. It is the more remarkable, then, that Hilda is quickened with new life in Rome.

In the artistic sphere, too, Italy proves in *The Marble Faun* a vitalizing as well as a corrupting influence. As a group, the

American artists in the novel discover a simpler and happier life in Italy than they have known in America. The Fountain of Trevi, one of them suggests, might be employed in their country to operate a cotton mill. Kenyon is surely thinking of America when he says that the modern world is too utilitarian rather than wicked, as the Monte Beni butler finds it. In Kenyon's opinion, the "iron rule in our day to require an object and a purpose in life," to insist "upon everybody's adding somewhat . . . to an accumulated pile of usefulness," "makes us all parts of a complicated scheme of progress, which can only result in our arrival at a colder and drearier region than we were born in." In contrast is the "sunny, shadowy, breezy, wandering life" of the artist in Italy who travels in summer over the country, combining study of the landscape with that of art, seeking for "beauty as his treasure." (This life is also in contrast, incidentally, to that led by most artists in Rome.) It "is worth living for," Hawthorne declared, "come afterwards what may. Even if he die unrecognized, the artist has had his share of enjoyment and success." Hilda as an artist gains more than she loses in Italy, for she comes to know the works of masters whose achievements she could never have approached.

In *The Marble Faun* man's loss of innocence thus appears in the context of western history—from the time of the Etruscans to that of nineteenth-century America. No other work by Hawthorne presents such a sweeping view. No other place offered him so clear a one as did Italy, particularly Rome. There, he wrote, "barbarism and civilization" seemed "alternating with one another like actors that have prearranged their parts." No other work of his, moreover, contains so broad a vision of moral continuity, recognizing the persistent vitality as well as the baneful influence of the past. For all his love of England, that country did not give him such a vision, and for all his repugnance to certain aspects of Italian life and history,

Italy did. In this historical context, the American experience appears as an unisolable part of the experience of western man, for good as well as evil. At the same time, however, the American achievement, measured by artistic creation, is seen to be inferior to the greatest achievements of the past.

The loss of innocence also appears in *The Marble Faun* in the context of myth, to an extent unparalleled elsewhere in Hawthorne's fiction. In classical Italy, especially in the pagan and Christian capital, Rome, Hawthorne was surely made more aware of mythical conceptions. Besides the myths of the Fall and of Arcadia, which chiefly image the primary theme of the novel, two others help do so: that of the War between Heaven and Satan and the nature myth of death and rebirth. The former appears in images of towers, light, the sky, and doves alternating with those of sepulchres and subterranean areas. A death-resurrection motif appears in several imagistic sequences, notably in references to the literal disinterment of ancient Rome, but chiefly in terms of the seasons. In the summer Kenyon visits Donatello in Tuscany to escape the malaria in Rome, and in the winter (which ends, Hawthorne noted, earlier in Italy than in America) the friendship between Hilda and Kenyon deepens. In the scene on the Campagna in February, spring flowers have appeared, Kenyon encounters in the buffalo calf "a rude and healthy form of animal life," the *Venus* is excavated, and Donatello and Miriam are once again faun and nymph.

The secondary theme of *The Marble Faun*—the relation of art to nature and society—was vitally influenced by Hawthorne's contact with works of art and with artists in Italy. As a result, certain new views of art and artists are distinguishable in this version of this theme. Here more artists appear than in any other work of his; and for the only time in his fiction artist-life is depicted collectively and altogether delightfully. His American artists in Rome are in striking contrast to his other artists and artist-scientists, who are typically solitary, at odds with society, and in fatal conflict with nature.

Conflict between art and nature is pictured in *The Marble Faun*, but it is more complex and potentially more fruitful than anywhere else. Through the five central characters three aspects of this relation are projected. Donatello may represent external nature; the three artists—Kenyon, Hilda, and Miriam—have a general conception of art as the expression of inner life and experience; the Model, because of his vicious character and concealed identity, suggests the basically untruthful art of a perverted or decadent society. Nature ultimately triumphs over art that lacks moral truth or disregards natural law, as Donatello overthrows the Model and as the water in the baroque fountains of Rome maintains its flow in spite of impediments. So nature commonly triumphs over art in Hawthorne's fiction, often in fountain imagery; that in "Rappaccini's Daughter" is especially similar to that in *The Marble Faun*. Miriam, tainted by her experience with the Model, is on dangerous ground when she tells Donatello, in answer to his objection to her shutting sunlight from her studio, that artists must put themselves "at odds with Nature before trying to imitate her." Yet artists, it appears, must go beyond external nature if they would produce works of value. This relation between art and nature appears in Hawthorne only in *The Marble Faun*. The three relationships are exemplified in the novel by three groups of paintings in the Roman galleries. Most of those by Italians are pronounced too intellectual and so destined for oblivion. Those by Dutch and Flemish artists seem preferable, even under some circumstances the most satisfactory, but too much concerned with physical details. The greatest of all appear to be certain Italian religious paintings.

Most significant of all, art is depicted in *The Marble Faun* as primarily a means for the projection of experience and the greatest artists as recorders of the history of the race. In Hawthorne's other treatments of them, both artists and their works are extremely limited and distinctly mechanical in nature. The contemporary works cited in *The Marble Faun* may be called essentially organic. Miriam's sketches reveal her emotional conflicts and Kenyon's sculpture purports to embody intellectual conceptions. The most admired masterpieces of the past cited, moreover, express universal experience. Raphael, the most admired artist, is significantly the creator both of the worldly *Fornarina* and of *Madonnas*. All these new conceptions of art and artists directly reflect Hawthorne's acquisition in Italy of a broader notion of the scope of painting and sculpture and his recognition there of the achievement of some of the major artists of the western world.

To a great extent because he had arrived at these conceptions Hawthorne employed as his chief technical device in *The Marble Faun* references to specific works of art and architecture. Though such references occur in his other fiction, often in accordance with the Gothic tradition, they appear here in greater number and with further-reaching effect than anywhere else. Half apologizing for their number, he explained in the preface that "Italian objects, antique, pictorial, and statuesque . . . . fill the mind everywhere in Italy, and especially in Rome, and cannot easily be kept from flowing out upon the page." In a sense, he was giving his novel a Gothic character derived from his acquaintance with Gothic architecture rather than with Gothic romances. Yet this aspect of his work, far from being extrinsic, is an organic part of the whole. These allusions largely project the themes of the novel and show the experiences represented by them to be universal and perennial.

Most of the places in Rome visited by the characters in *The Marble Faun* have symbolic values. The novel opens, fittingly for both its themes, in the Capitoline Museum. Appropriately the Model is first seen in the Catacombs; met by Miriam at the Fountain of Trevi, a scene at once of purity and of artificiality, and in the Colosseum, a scene of suffering; and killed by a fall from the Tarpeian Rock, the traditional scene of the execution of traitors. On their ramble through the Forums, whose ruins are made to suggest fallen tyranny, these characters pause at the site of Curtius' leap. Kenyon suggests it is also the site of the murder of Virginia, and it is near that of Caesar's assassination. The struggle between the Model and Donatello thus appears to be one in a long series of historical episodes in which evil has been overthrown or thwarted at the expense of heroism or innocence. The grounds of the Villa Borghese and of the Villa Medici are fitting scenes for the exhibition of Donatello's faun-like character before and after the Model's death. The Palazzo Cenci, with which both Miriam and Hilda are associated, has the same bearing on the primary theme of the novel as has Guido's portrait of Beatrice Cenci. The Pantheon and St. Peter's are monuments respectively of primitive paganism and modern Christianity; Hilda significantly finds comfort in both.

Most of the specific paintings and pieces of sculpture alluded to in *The Marble Faun*—over thirty—concern lost innocence or the conflict of good and evil. The most prominent are Praxiteles' statue and Guido's paintings of Beatrice Cenci (whom both Miriam and Hilda are said to resemble) and of St. Michael. Among others are the *Dying Gladiator,* the *Girl with Dove and Snake* ("the Human Soul, with its choice of Innocence or Evil"), the "red" faun, the *Lycian Apollo,* a *Bacchus*, satyrs, and figures of merry-makers on a sarcophagus —all in the Capitoline Museum; the statue of the martyred St. Cecilia in the Catacomb of St. Calixtus; Bernardo Luini's painting of Herodias receiving the head of John the Baptist (which one of Miriam's sketches resembles); the figure of the Virgin on the Palazzo Scimmia (Hilda's tower); Paul Akers' statue of the dead pearl-diver and his bust of Milton, who is designated as the author of *Paradise Lost,* and Story's statue of Cleopatra (all attributed to Kenyon); Giovanni da Bologna's *Rape of the Sabines;* the profane nudes of John Gibson (the unnamed English sculptor); the statue of Marcus Aurelius on the Campidoglio; the figure of the virgin at the Fountain of Trevi; the frescoes and alabaster skull at the Montauto (Monte Beni) villa (one of the frescoes contains a figure resembling Donatello); the statue of Pope Julius in Perugia; Leonardo's painting of the supposed murderess Joanna of Aragon (who resembles Miriam); Raphael's *Madonna da Foligno, Fornarina,* and *Transfiguration;* Sodoma's fresco in Siena of Christ at the pillar; Guercino's painting of the dead St. Petronilla; Michelangelo's bust of Brutus (to which Kenyon's bust of Donatello is likened); the *Laocoön* ("a type of the long, fierce struggle of man, involved in the knotted entanglements of Error and Evil"); the version of the *Venus de' Medici* discovered on the Campagna; the *Madonna* at Raphael's tomb.

To this list certain imaginary works might be added: Miriam's sketches of a rustic dance and of episodes which convey "the idea of woman, acting the part of a revengeful mischief towards man"; the supposed drawing by Guido for his painting of *St. Michael Overcoming Satan* (in which Satan resembles the Model); the nymph at the Monte Beni fountain; Panini's portrait (entitled "Innocence, dying of a bloodstain") of Hilda looking at Leonardo's painting of Joanna of Aragon; Kenyon's bust of Donatello.

By their very number these allusions make *The Marble Faun* extraordinarily rich in imagery. Their multiple significations, moreover, give it an imagistic complexity which no other work by Hawthorne has. His technique, which generally tends to allegory, is here most sustainedly symbolic.

Although the immediate end served by allusions to works of art in *The Marble Faun* is thematic, ultimately these allusions create the distinctive atmosphere of the novel. Italy was chiefly valuable to him, he wrote in his preface, as a site "affording a sort of poetic or fairy precinct, where actualities would not be so terribly insisted upon as they are, and must needs be in America."

Such a precinct is established in *The Marble Faun* partly by references to Roman ruins. They endow the Roman past with a "massiveness" that makes the present have a "dreamy character" and living persons seem thinner than ghosts of the dead. On the contrary, Hawthorne often gave the American past romantic values and the American present realistic ones, most explicitly in the preface to *The House of the Seven Gables*.

Chiefly, however, references to works of art and descriptions of the daily lives of artists create a non-realistic atmosphere in *The Marble Faun*. As a class, artists are said to be "lifted by the ideality of their pursuits a little way off the earth." Miriam's studio, described as a typical one, hardly seems "to belong to the actual world, but rather to be the outward type of a poet's haunted imagination." Yet the creations of such an imagination are represented as more substantial and longer-lived than anything in that world. The antique statues in the Capitoline Museum are "still shining in the undiminished majesty and beauty of their ideal life," and when the head is restored to the newly discovered *Venus*, "the beautiful Idea at once asserted its Immortality." Most of the figures in the paintings and sculpture cited also seem to come to life. Their actions, moreover, seem to constitute the central story of the novel. Indeed, so long, complex, and often violent a sequence is represented by these actions—from the War in Heaven to the fall of the pagan gods, and from the assassination of Julius Caesar to the worship of the Virgin Mary—that a timeless drama about the crucial experiences of mankind seems to be taking place. For this drama, nineteenth-century Rome, with its Italians and its American and other foreign visitors, composes an artificial backdrop.

The kind of reality depicted in *The Marble Faun* thus

differs from that in most of Hawthorne's other fiction. Whereas in *The Scarlet Letter,* for example, he was at pains to give his story the reality of history, in *The Marble Faun* he was equally at pains to give it that of the imagination. In America, indeed—as he more than once complained in the prefaces to his novels—flights of the imagination required apology or a realistic explanation. In Italy, they were part of the fabric of civilization. As neither America nor England did, Italy sanctioned his belief in the validity of imaginative experience.

It appears, indeed, that Italy afforded the writer of romance even more of a "fairy precinct" than Hawthorne realized. His reluctance to come to grips with his meaning in the conclusion of *The Marble Faun* perhaps reflects his pondering the theory, in connection with certain works of art in Italy, of the ultimately ambiguous nature of art. The most damaging flaws in the novel—the episode of Hilda's disappearance and the failure to dispose satisfactorily of Miriam and Donatello—seem, however, to be primarily the result of Hawthorne's desire to insure an atmosphere of romantic mystery. Such an atmosphere in this novel, haunted by presences from history and from the realm of art, is to say the least supererogatory.

In Italy Hawthorne found abundant confirmation of his conception of the moral weakness and the limited powers of man. Yet his stay there gave him a more hopeful view of human nature than he ever before entertained. There, as nowhere else, he saw its weaknesses and limitations in perspective : beside a long series of catastrophes survived by the spirit, as recorded in beautiful and enduring works of the imagination.

V

The Enigmatic Past:

HOWELLS

IN 1861, AT THE AGE OF TWENTY-FOUR, WILLIAM DEAN Howells became, somewhat by chance, the American consul in Venice. Unsuccessful in his attempts to launch a literary career, he had applied for a diplomatic position abroad, specifying the city of Munich so that he might pursue his interest in German literature. He was also interested in Spanish literature —the first of all his "literary passions." Italy had no particular attraction for him. The city to which he was appointed, however, was Rome. Learning that the stipend there was only $500 in fees, he negotiated and got instead the post in Venice, with a salary of $1500. Italy proved to be the European country with which he had most connections throughout his life and which most influenced his writing.

En route to take up his consular duties Howells stopped briefly in England and Germany. He was offended in the first country by criticism of America and in the second by nude statuary and the stratification of society. Venice, which he reached in December 1861, fascinated him immediately. "This wonder city," he called it in his first letter to his family. His heart, he added, "if beauty could satisfy it, would be at peace."

There could be "nothing else in the world," he declared in *Venetian Life* (1866), his first volume of Italian sketches, "so full of glittering and exquisite surprise" as one's first glimpse at night of this city in its "peerless strangeness." Compared to other cities, it was "like the pleasant improbability of the theatre to everyday, commonplace life," never losing "its claim upon constant surprise and regard" though he was able to see behind the scenes. After his marriage, in Paris in December 1862, to the American Elinor Mead, he lived on the Grand Canal, first in Casa Falier and then in the Palazzo Giustiniani. Eventually he felt more "intensely at home" in Venice than in any other city, "even Boston itself." He remained until July 1865—longer than he was ever again out of America.

Though he traveled a good deal in Italy during these years, no other Italian city impressed Howells so much. In addition to excursions in the neighborhood of Venice, he made brief trips to most of the northern cities, and, during his last few months in the country, to Rome and Naples. He preferred the north to the south, though he was delighted by Pompeii, with its memorials of the common life of the past. Rome he thoroughly disliked. It was "the least interesting town in Italy," he thought. Its architecture was "hopelessly ugly," its streets filthy, its ruins "rubbish," he wrote in *Italian Journeys* (1867), his second volume of Italian sketches. On some of these journeys he followed the footsteps of Hawthorne, whom he admired and had met in America. (He had written a review of *The Marble Faun*.) He sought out the Tarpeian Rock in memory of Miriam and Donatello, noted Hawthorne's residence on Bellosguardo, and thought of Dr. Rappaccini in Padua. (In Venice he was reminded of scenes in both *The Marble Faun* and Cooper's *Bravo*.)

For all its charm, however, Venice gradually palled on

Howells. Its decayed aspect, in which he first "rioted sentimentally," finally depressed him. Because of the Austrian occupation of the city at the time, its social life was curtailed and its citizens were suspicious of strangers. Howells' acquaintances were few, chief among them G. A. Tortorini, the retired apothecary who was mayor of nearby Monselice; the young Paduan student Eugenio Brunetta; and Padre Giacomo Issaverdenz, an Armenian in the monastery on the island of San Lazzaro. American visitors were rare. Among the number were Mrs. Howells' sister Mary and her brother Larkin Mead, the sculptor, who married a Venetian and remained in Italy.

The duties of the American consulate in Venice at this time, moreover, were slight. Only four American ships appeared during Howells' first year in office, and throughout his term most of his time was his own. He devoted himself chiefly to learning Italian, reading Italian literature and history, and writing. Yet even in these generally congenial projects he felt that "I had forsaken wholesome struggle in the currents where I felt the motion of the age, only to drift into a lifeless eddy of the world, remote from incentive and sensation." Such was Venice, he concluded,

that the will must be strong and the faith indomitable in him who can long retain, amid the influences of her stagnant quiet, a practical belief in God's purpose of a moving, anxious, toiling, aspiring world outside. . . . The charm of the place sweetens your temper, but corrupts you.

What Howells saw of "uncountryed Americans" convinced him, too, that prolonged residence abroad had a bad effect on character. By leaving it, Americans should chiefly discover, he felt, "what a dear country" they had.

By the spring of 1864 he had decided not to apply for reappointment to his post. When the time came to leave Venice, however, he had mixed emotions. He was going, he wrote

James Russell Lowell, with "unspeakable regret," explaining, "I am too fond of Italy already; and in a year or two more of lotus-eating, I shouldn't want to go home at all." Yet there was perhaps another element in his regret. As early as the spring of 1862 Howells began to have a recurring dream in which he had returned to America too soon—before knowing "perfectly all the glorious and beautiful things" in Venice. That he felt he did leave under some such circumstances is suggested in a letter he wrote in 1872 to Henry James, who was then in Europe. "O my lagoons of Venice, and the sea-weedy smell of the shallows!" he exclaimed. ". . . *Ricordati di me*—when you lie there in your boat, and at least say, Poor Howells, he liked Venice, though perhaps he didn't understand her."

Howell's ambivalent attitude toward Italy is expressed throughout the sketches and in other non-fiction concerning it which he wrote during and immediately after his consular years. These works reveal what most engaged him there. They also reveal that certain aspects of his nature—his Puritanically moral view, his lack of interest in the past, and his slight esthetic sense—made him hostile or cut off his approach to much of Italian civilization. He seems to have distrusted some of his feelings, however, as well as to have feared rendering unpopular judgments. With his characteristic reluctance to come to grips with terminology, he often expressed conflicting opinions of that civilization. Most significantly of all, he often implied that he wished that he could appreciate certain aspects of it more.

Italy's chief appeal to Howells, indicated especially in his sketches, was twofold : the novelty yet the universally human quality of its common life. He was less interested in "proper Objects of Interest" than in "dark and secret little courts," "remote and noisome canals," street scenes, and humble characters. "Singular," "marvelous," "quaint" as these scenes and the activities in them so often were, especially in Venice, these characters seemed to Howells essentially universal types. An old man roasting coffee he thought might have been "some dread supernatural agency, turning the wheel of fortune, and doing men instead of coffee"; a ruffian boy dancing in wooden shoes embodied for him the spirit of the builders of Venice, overcoming the difficulties of the site. "Simple, abstract humanity, wholly unrelated to individuality, has its own grandeur in Italy," he wrote, "so that it is not hard here for the artist to find the primitive types with which genius loves best to deal." Italians had "so transparent a civilization," so thin a "conventional coating, however showy," he wrote in his article on contemporary Italian drama, that "all the impulses of human nature in action . . . are constantly visible." The histrionic disposition of Italians particularly made Howells see them in this light. He thought this their chief characteristic, noting manifestations of it in early Italian painting and in the *commedia dell' arte tradition*. Indeed, Italy at its most appealing was to Howells, as he suggested in his description of Venice, supremely a theatre, where the novel and the common, the particular and the universal complemented each other.

Howells defended Italians against many of the common judgments of them, partly in opposition to the romantic literary tradition which fostered these judgments. Hawthorne's Donatello, different as that character was from the stock Italian bandit, he pronounced "a copy in great part from Italian nature." He held up for emulation the kindness and courtesy which he felt characterized most Italians and put great faith in an "equality in Italian fibre" which he thought fit this people for democratic institutions. "The citizen of every free country loves Italy next to his own land," he went so far as to say apropos of Italian unification, "and feels her prosperous fortune to be the advantage of civilization."

Yet essentially Howells considered Italian character unreliable and Italian civilization immoral. Referring to Venetian conventions in courtship he wrote his sister Victoria a few months after his arrival that "the young men are beasts, and the young women what you might expect them" and adjured her, "O Vic, Vic! prize America all you can. Try not to think of the Americans' faults—they are a people so much purer and nobler than any other, that I think they will be pardoned the wrong they do." The uneducated Anglo-Saxon, he conceded in *Venetian Life,* was "a savage," whereas "the Italian, though born to utter ignorance, poverty, and depravity, is a civilized man." But he would not call the Italian's a civilization "of a high order." The education of the Italian, he wrote, "has left his passions undisciplined, while it has carefully polished his manner; he yields lightly to temptation, he loses his self-control, he blasphemes habitually; his gentleness is conventional, his civilization is not individual." In an article on Italian brigandage written after his trip to Naples, he deplored more than any particular vices of Italians in certain parts of the country the "complaisant indifference with regard to abominable things all over Italy." He condemned certain practices of the Roman Catholic Church, though not very heatedly. (In revising *Venetian Life* for the edition of 1907, Howells omitted his severest strictures on Italian morality, chiefly in deference to the objections of his friend Eugenio Brunetta, and in later descriptions represented Brunetta as being typically Italian in his admirable traits.)

Howells also devoted a good deal of attention in his sketches to Italian history. Yet he confessed that he "made use of rather than found pleasure in" his reading of that history, and it constantly offended him. "One learns in these old lands," he declared, "to hate and execrate the past." For the decay of the Pisani villa at Stra he had no regret. "How can you feel sympathy for those dull and wicked ghosts of eighteenth century corruption?" he inquired. "There is rottenness enough in the world without digging up old putridity and sentimentalizing on it."

In later years Howells said that when he went to Venice in 1861 he had intended to write a history of the city. In 1874, 1882, and 1899 he broached this project with publishers, proposing on the last two occasions to relate Venetian to American history. Nothing, however, came of the project.

To Italian art Howells was frankly insensitive—as indeed he was to art in general. Under the influence of his wife, an amateur artist, he tried soon after their marriage to become interested in art history, but without much success. He found Venice as a whole and all Gothic architecture beautiful, but he did not care for more distinctively Italian architectural styles and had little interest in painting and sculpture. In churches he was often less impressed by the paintings than by persons who would have been subjects for genre painters : an old woman warming her hands at a *scaldino*, a boy descending by a rope from a roof-opening and receiving a cuff from a good-natured priest. He sweepingly condemned art criticism and was inclined to satirize estheticism. After reading Ruskin's description of St. Mark's, which he had seen every day for three years, he "began to have dreadful doubts of its existence." Yet though he repeatedly disclaimed the intention of discussing works of art in *Venetian Life* and *Italian Journeys,* he was— especially in the former—on the defensive about the matter.

The aspect of Italian civilization with which Howells was most in sympathy was its contemporary literature. In Venice he read *La Divina Commedia, Il Pastor Fido,* and *Aminta*— all of which he treated in *My Literary Passions* (1895)— but he found Dante often "dull and dry" and was disappointed in the Italian historical romance because it bore little relation to Italian life. (His attitude toward Dante changed several times, but it was never altogether one of admiration.) Modern Italian literature pleased him because it did reflect Italian life. He praised modern Italian poets, despite his growing aversion to the romantic school which they represented, chiefly for their dedication to the cause of Italian nationalism. Eventually he wrote several essays about them, which were collected in *Modern Italian Poets* (1887), his only critical volume devoted exclusively to a foreign literature. He was especially attracted by the realistic modern Italian drama, and above all Italian authors he admired the father of that drama, Carlo Goldoni. What Goldoni had seen in the Venice of the eighteenth century was "so true," he thought, "that it was the very life of Venice in my own day," and for that "truth in art" he fell in love with that writer. Goldoni also appealed to him for being "almost English, almost American, indeed, in his observance of the proprieties." Howell's interest in modern Italian literature, however, subsequently gave place to his interest in the modern literatures of England and of Russia.

In later years Howells made three visits to Italy. All were short, the second and third were disappointing, and none materially altered his views of the country. His second, which lasted from December 1882 to June 1883, was made with his family chiefly to benefit his daughter Winifred's health and to enable him to write a series of articles on several north Italian cities. En route, the party stopped in England and in Switzerland. They spent some four and a half months in Tuscany— most of the time in Florence—four weeks in Venice, and two weeks in Verona, where they visited Eugenio Brunetta. Howells also renewed his acquaintance with G. A. Tortorini and Padre Issaverdenz. He found Florence less desirable than Switzerland as a residence and Venice "forlorner and shabbier than ever." As for living there again for four years, he wrote his father, he would do so "on hardly any conditions short of ownership of the city—and then I should be afraid it would fall on my hands." In the preparation of his sketches he consulted books to put himself "in rapport with Italy again," but he wasn't sure that it paid. "After all," he boasted, "*we* have the country of the present and the future." He abandoned a plan to write a novel laid in Venice at the time of its decadence and ultimately reduced from a proposed thirteen to seven the number of cities treated in his sketches. Most of them were evidently written after his return to America. With him part of the time in Italy was the young American painter Joseph Pennell, who, with a few others, provided illustrations for the sketches. First appearing in the *Century Magazine,* they were collected in *Tuscan Cities* in 1886.

These sketches reflect less of Howells' prevailing mood during his second Italian visit, however, than of the pattern of his earlier ones. He gave historical accounts of all the cities —Florence, Siena, Pisa, Lucca, Pistoia, Prato, and Fiesole— lavishing especial care on the account of Florence; yet again he expressed thankfulness to be living in the nineteenth century. Of Italian character he was less critical than before, declaring that "union of grace with sympathy" formed the "true expression of Italian civilization"; yet there was irony in his remark that "when the Italian makes up his mind to be just, it is in no ungracious spirit." Again he half-apologetically slighted the subject of art and ridiculed certain works. The cathedral of Siena, with its black and white marble, he thought worthy the name of the Church of the Holy Zebra. (His introduction and comments for *A Little Girl among the Old Masters* (1884)—a book of drawings by his ten-year-old daughter Mildred in imitation of paintings in Florence and Venice—implied that such works might be best understood by the young.) As before, he was interested most of all in Italian life—in the piazzas, the churches, even the Florentine police court. Italy was, he decided once more, "above all lands the home of human nature."

Between 1894 and 1913 Howells made eight trips to Europe, but though he several times talked of going to Italy he got there only twice during that time. In October 1905, for the sake of Mrs. Howells' health, he took her from England to San Remo, where they stayed until the following March. At first delighted by the tropical atmosphere, he soon found the society dull. He occupied himself by working on *London Films* (1906) and *Certain Delightful English Towns* (1906).

Nevertheless as he was revising *Venetian Life* in 1907, "the old wine got into my brain," Howells wrote Lowell, "and I began to dream of Italy, with such effect that I babbled in my sleep to Harpers of it." With arrangements made for the publication of another series of travel sketches, he made with his wife his last visit to Italy. They were there from January to April 1908, about a week in and around Naples, two months in Rome, and the rest of the time in Leghorn, Pisa, and Genoa.

On this trip, at the age of seventy-one and decidedly mellower than on any other, Howells was most successful in renewing his early enthusiasm. Yet he retained his early moral, esthetic, and historical-political prejudices and adopted in his sketches "the old point of view helplessly." The chief new impression he received was in Rome, now the national capital, whose program of cleaning and building pleased him. "I am a Newer-Roman to the core," he declared, aligning himself against the sentimentalists who deplored this program, "perhaps because I knew the Older Rome and what it was like." In Genoa he sensed "something businesslike which agrees with your American mood if you are true to America, and recalls you to duty if you are not." (He hoped that he was not being "untrue" to his country in calling Mediterranean scenery the most beautiful in the world, and as if to redress the matter entitled his chapter on Monte Carlo "Eden after the Fall.")

Chiefly because of their achievements as a nation he now called the Italians "a great people," perhaps "destined to their old primacy." Yet he also suggested that that primacy held them back in the modern world and concluded that it was "better to have too little past, as we have, than too much, as they have." His sketches, which were first published in the New York *Sun,* appeared as *Roman Holidays and Others* later in the year.

Howell's attitude to the other European countries he visited is revealed chiefly in his five other travel books—one about Switzerland, three about England, and one about Spain—and in *Their Silver Wedding Journey* (1899), his fictional account of his and his wife's sojourn in Germany in 1897. Most of these travels were made, however, in his later years, when he was both more tolerant of and less excited by the foreign scene, and these travel books follow the general pattern established in those about Italy. Of them all, indeed, the first— *Venetian Life*—is unique in its freshness, sharpness, and intense interest in that scene.

Howell's first years in Venice had a multiple influence on his career. They gave him, he said, "almost uninterrupted leisure for study and literary work" and "a wider outlook on the world." More specifically, they turned him from poetry to prose and led him into three literary genres: criticism, fiction, and drama. They also turned him from the romantic to the realistic technique and largely determined some of the principal themes in his fiction. Indirectly they were responsible for the auspicious beginning of his career.

Before he left America in 1861 Howells had tried his hand at several kinds of writing, but he aspired at first to be a poet. His first compositions in Venice were poems of a generally romantic nature, as his earlier ones had been, and of prose travel letters for newspapers such as he had written in

America. As the former proved difficult to get published and the latter successful, he virtually gave up writing poetry. The collections of his letters or sketches, *Venetian Life* and *Italian Journeys*, were his first two books, both of which were widely praised. The year before he left Venice he wrote his first piece of literary criticism, "Recent Italian Comedy." Lowell's acceptance of it for the *North American Review* he called the "turning point" of his life—the decisive factor in his giving up poetry for prose. The year after his return to America, he began—as assistant editor—his long term on the staff of the *Atlantic Monthly,* chiefly on the strength of his prose writings about Italy.

Two Italian influences turned Howells toward realism in Venice : the plays of Goldoni and the Venetian scene. In later years he gave the chief credit to Goldoni. When he went to Venice, he said, he was an "idealist" who "had a notion that in literature, persons and things should be nobler and better than they are in the sordid reality" and who was kept by "this romantic glamour . . . from seeing things as they are." In "the lanes and alleys of Venice," however, he "found Goldoni everywhere." He believed that this was the beginning of his "revolt," although it was a good while before he found his own bearings. In his own short comedies of manners, which began to appear in 1876, he was more particularly indebted to the Italian playwright.

The Venetian "lanes and alleys," nevertheless, were at least as influential as Goldoni on Howells' development as a realist. Whereas certain aspects of common life in America had seemed sordid to him as a newspaper-reporter, he found such life in Venice picturesque. It was also newsworthy, since most previous descriptions of the city, concentrating on its famous monuments and works of art, had ignored this aspect of it. Howell's primary aim in his sketches of Venice was, accordingly, to tell "as much as possible of the every-day life of a people whose habits are so different from ours." At the same time he found that Venice belied the chief traditions about it, being neither altogether dream-like ("the Venice of Byron, of Rogers, and Cooper") nor totally unsafe. Accordingly he also aimed in his sketches to correct "sentimental errors" about people, customs, and places there, as, indeed, he did in his sketches of other parts of Italy. He adopted a point of view midway between both traditional extremes and emphasized the average, universal aspects of Italian life.

From this kind of travel account it was but a step to fiction of a realistic sort, and indeed Howells' fiction grew directly out of his travel books. His first piece was the local-color story, "Tonelli's Marriage" (1869), laid in Venice. His first four novels involve journeys made by the central characters, play up the local scene, and contrast romantic preconceptions with reality. The third and fourth—*A Foregone Conclusion* (1875) and *The Lady of the Aroostook* (1879)—are laid in Venice.

Most of Howells' novels, in fact, are distinguished as realistic by several technical devices which were originally suggested by his early Italian experience. Chief among them are local color, the structural pattern of a journey, a median point of view, extensive use of dialogue, and the itemization of scenic minutiae. The last two devices, essentially dramatic as they are, were apparently derived from the dramatic tradition which impressed Howells in Venice as being prominent in Italian life, art, and literature. The novelty of the Italian scene sharpened his eye, too, for minute, property-like details.

The major issues in Howells' novels also emerged from his first experience in Italy. In much of his subsequent fiction, as in his first, the theme of realism versus romanticism appears. His major concern, however, was with American character types confronted by moral problems. The universal patterns of life in Italy drew his attention to basic human emotions and actions. The "wider view of the world" which he had in

Venice, moreover, heightened his nationalistic sense and deepened his moral consciousness. It convinced him of the superiority of American moral standards to those of Europe and of the danger of isolation from society, and it posed for him the problems of preserving those standards and of avoiding that isolation. These problems were first clearly presented in Howells' fiction in his first three novels laid in Italy. They were touched upon, however, in nearly all his others. Insofar as he was speaking from experience in Europe when he declared that "the more smiling aspects of life" were "the more American," that experience was predominantly Italian. His theory, moreover, of "complicity," of the responsibilities of all members of society to each other—which was his chief contribution to the solution of the problems of both immorality and isolation—had roots in his first, extended residence in Italy.

Howells' residences in Italy inspired for the most part six poems, four travel books, two stories, five novels, a volume of literary criticism, some eighteen uncollected sketches, and half a dozen uncollected articles on literary, social, political, and religious topics. Except for one travel book, one novel, one story, and half a dozen sketches, all these works were published by 1887. They belong, roughly speaking, to the first period of his literary career, the period of his first "psychological romances" and his chief use of the international theme. To some extent they represent his exploitation of subject matter which had proved popular. (He also manifested his interest in Italian literature during the first few years after his return to America by his lectures on this subject at Harvard and the Lowell Institute and by his membership in the Dante Club in Cambridge and the Dante Society of America.)

In the 1880's Howells turned his attention in fiction to American social problems, partly in acknowledgment of James'

Albert Bierstadt, THE PORTICO OF OCTAVIUS, ROME, 1858.

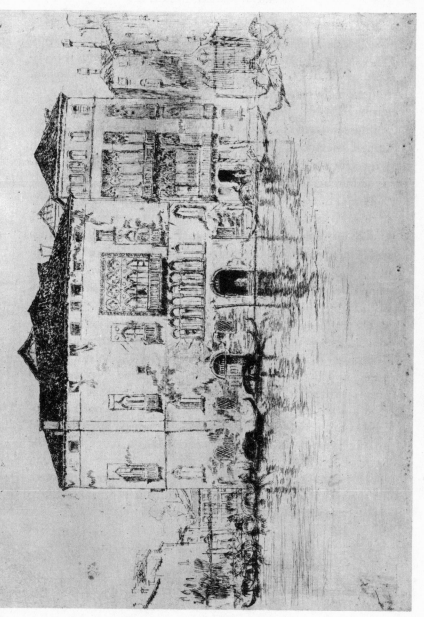

James Abbott McNeill Whistler, THE PALACES. Venice? *ca* 1880.
(Courtesy of The Metropolitan Museum of Art)

mastery of the international novel, and found another literary passion in contemporary Russian fiction. "Italian I care nothing for," he wrote T. B. Aldrich in 1885, "but my Russian I am proud of." In later years he returned to the psychological romance, but only incidentally to the international theme or setting. During the last two years of his life, however, in a reminiscent mood, he wrote five sketches drawing on his Italian memories, mostly of his first years in Venice, and projected a volume of autobiography which would have included an account of those years.

Throughout his career, moreover, Howells referred to Italy in poems, sketches, fiction, criticism, plays, and reminiscences and often reviewed books by or about Italian authors. Altogether he utilized his knowledge of Italy and Italian culture in about half his one hundred separately published works and in some three dozen other pieces, in all the types of writing which he did.

The influence of Italy was most pronounced on Howells' imaginative writing. In his plays, modelled as they are after Goldoni's, that influence is almost entirely implicit. In his poems and fiction it is explicit and widespread. Nearly all his poems written in Venice contain references to that city. The most ambitious—*No Love Lost,* written in 1863 but not published until 1869—is a notable anticipation of his novels laid in Italy and of his fiction in general. It is a narrative in the form of letters written by American travellers in Venice, in which romantic and realistic views of the city are contrasted. To the romantic heroine, Bertha, Venice is a veritable Eden, where, she writes of her lover and herself,

> . . . in our paradise of love we reigned, newcreated,
> As in the youth of the world, in the days before evil
>   and conscience.

To the more realistic Fanny, "palaces and mosquitoes rise

from the water together" in Venice. Her brother and aunt are humorous tourist types.

Four other poems of this period were inspired by Howells' experiences in Venice : "Saint Christopher," a description of a figure on a Venetian gate; "The Faithful of the Gonzago," a ballad about an episode in Mantuan history; "Pordone," recounting an episode in the life of that artist; an epithalamium for an Italian couple; and a poem in *terza rima* ("the first fruits and the last," he said, of his reading of Dante). Five others contain references to the Venetian scene : "Louis Lebeau's Conversion," "Sweet Clover," "By the Sea," "Elegy on John Butler Howells," and "The Mulberries."

Of Howells' works of fiction laid (substantially if not wholly) in Italy, "Tonelli's Marriage," *A Foregone Conclusion, The Lady of the Aroostook,* and *A Fearful Responsibility* (1881) were inspired by his first trip there; *Indian Summer* (1886), by his second; *Ragged Lady* (1899) by his recollections of both these trips; and "A Sleep and a Forgetting" (1907–08) by his third. Twenty-two of his other thirty-eight volumes of fiction —including the first and the last—either involve characters who have been or who go to Italy or contain other references to that country.

Howells' first prose narrative to be published—the Venice-laid, local-color "Tonelli's Marriage"—is unique in his fiction in having no American elements. All the characters are Italian. Most of them, however, are drawn from friends of his in Venice. Eugenio Brunetta, his friend Signorina Perisenotti, her mother and uncle, and the uncle's employer are the originals of Pennellini, the Cenatorri, and Tonelli.

In much of Howells' subsequent fiction about Italy (as in his fiction generally) he drew on his own experiences. Ferris, the consul, in *A Foregone Conclusion* (who lives in a house corresponding in location to Casa Falier), the historian Elmore in *A Fearful Responsibility*, and Colville, the disillusioned journalist in *Indian Summer,* are all drawn from Howells himself; Don Ippolito and Padre Girolamo in *A Foregone Conclusion* from Padre Libera (with whom Howells read Dante in the 1860's) and Padre Issaverdenz; Lily Mayhew in *A Fearful Responsibility* from Mary Mead; Clay Hoskins in the same novel from the type of American sculptor in Italy best represented by Hiram Powers (if not from Powers himself, with whom Larkin Mead studied); the Inglehart boys in *Indian Summer* from students of Frank Duveneck and possibly Waters in this novel from a clergyman whom Howells met in Florence in 1882. The experiences of vice-consul Bennam in *Ragged Lady* are based on those of Howells as consul. The heroine in "A Sleep and a Forgetting" is ill at San Remo, as was Mrs. Howells. Italian references in *The Minister's Charge* (1887), *Annie Kilburn* (1889), *An Imperative Duty* (1893), and the novels in which Basil and Isabel March appear also reflect experiences of Howells in Italy.

His chief use of Italian material in his fiction, however, was not primarily in the interest of local color or realism. Except in "Tonelli's Marriage" and in "A Sleep and a Forgetting" (where San Remo has no particular bearing on the action), he employed this material primarily to raise a moral issue : that of pernicious European influences on American society.

Two such influences may be distinguished : that, derived from general European social conventions, which promotes immoral practices and stiff behavior, and that, peculiarly operative in Italy, which undermines ambition and encourages idleness. The first of these influences, with which Howells was concerned somewhat more at the beginning of his career than later, is seen chiefly in the experience of American girls who are courted in Italy by foreigners (not necessarily Italians). The second, which is present in a greater number of novels, is seen chiefly in the experience of American men who are artists or writers in Italy. The Americans, incidentally, are often unsophisticated types and often have associations with the western part of their country. In no instance, however, does either of these foreign influences wholly triumph.

Howells' first three novels set in Italy—all of them in Venice—primarily concern the love affairs of American girls. Florida Vervain, Lydia Blood, and Lily Mayhew all receive attention—and two of them proposals of marriage—from foreigners, but all eventually marry Americans. In the first two of these novels the foreign suitors are weak or reprehensible, but in the third the Austrian Captain Von Ehrhardt is a romantic character and Lily seems to fall in love with him. Yet Professor Elmore is said to have "acted the part of a prudent and conscientious man" in advising her against marrying a foreigner, and his pronouncement on international marriages goes unchallenged:

"Sometimes they succeed; but generally they're wretched failures. The barriers of different race, language, education, religion,— they're terrible barriers."

In all these novels Americans are confronted with demoralizing influences in Italy. In *A Foregone Conclusion* the chief such influence is the Roman Catholic priesthood. An effort is made to distinguish between unfavorable romantic conceptions of this institution and the facts about it in particular cases. Padre Girolamo and the monastery on San Lazzaro are admirable, and Don Ippolito, who seems modelled in part after Hawthorne's Donatello, arouses sympathy. Yet Ferris, an avowed enemy of all "theatricalization," finds a priest at best "under sentence of death to the natural ties between himself and the human race." Don Ippolito's skepticism and erotic susceptibility make him, moreover, a version of the traditional Italian villain-priest. Yet he is too weak a character to influence Florida. Instead, her truthfulness—such as he has never known before—leads to his conversion and reconciliation to the church.

It is also suggested in *A Foregone Conclusion* that Venice in the past was generally corrupt. To both Ferris and Florida the villas on the Brenta represent a wicked society; they make her glad that she is an American and that there is no past for her.

The first glimpse which the rural New Englander Lydia Blood, in *The Lady of the Aroostook,* has of Italy, at Messina, vividly animates her and makes her seem to have "found a world within herself as well as without." Her admirer, Staniford, imagines her splendor when she will blossom "in that fervid air of art and beauty," yet he wonders what will happen to her ideals "in that depraved Old World—so long past trouble for its sins as to have got a sort of sweetness and innocence in them." Both his hopes and his fears prove groundless. Lydia is shocked by almost every aspect of society that she sees in Venice—marital infidelity, profanity, and opera-going on Sundays—and is momentarily led to doubt her own innocence. In the end, however, her character is unchanged.

The other American female character in Italy in this novel, Lydia's aunt, Mrs. Erwin, has become a socialite of the worst order during nearly twenty years abroad. At first a typical uninhibited American girl, she has come not only to observe rigid European conventions but to condone immoral ones. Yet she is essentially motivated by a perverse Americanism, snubbing Americans in the English manner in the hope of proving that an American can be more European than a European. Finding in Lydia a simpler and stronger Americanism than her own, she gives up trying to Europeanize her niece, and with her husband follows the Stanifords to California. She finds there the life "for which she had really been adapted after all" and in the climate of Santa Barbara "all that she had left in Italy."

Lily Mayhew in *A Fearful Responsibility* is also inhibited

by European social conventions. In deference to the convention of strictly formal behavior between the sexes before marriage, she breaks off her enjoyable informal association with Von Ehrhardt. Whether she eventually falls in love with him or not, she is "greatly sobered" after her return to America and does not marry for many years. When she does, she is living in the west.

It is, significantly, the American Elmore through whom this European convention is transmitted. After eighteen months in Venice, whither he has come to gather material for a history of the city, Elmore is more sensitive to some of the values there than to some American ones. Convinced that

The only good that Europe can do American girls who travel here is to keep them in total exile from what they call a good time,—from parties and attentions and flirtations; to force them, through the hard discipline of social deprivation, to take some interest in the things that make for civilization—in history, in art, in humanity,

he conducts Lily to the chief historical sites in the city. She is unimpressed by them, however, and Mrs. Elmore, who has become increasingly bored with Venice and Venetians, delivers the final verdict on her husband's notion when she tells him:

"American girls are the nicest girls in the world, just as they are. . . . You've lived so long here among your manuscripts that you've forgotten there is any such time as the present. If you're getting so Europeanized, I think the sooner we go home the better."

In these three novels another, peculiarly Italian influence operates adversely on American men in Italy, tending to keep them from professional achievement. Ferris asks for a consulate in Italy so that he may pursue his career as a painter there, but during his residence in Venice he loafs a good deal and produces only some half-finished sketches and a portrait of

Don Ippolito. His life there is in particular contrast to his participation in the Civil War after his return to America. Staniford, in his role of dilettante and snob at the beginning of *The Lady of the Aroostook,* has been twice to Italy, on his third trip thinks that "art may fall in love" with him there and proposes setting up a studio in Florence. Though it is a temporary political situation in each country which is responsible, the Elmores feel cut off from both American and Italian life during their stay in Venice. For whatever reason (Mrs. Elmore is sure no book about so uninteresting a people could be popular) Elmore's history is not a success.

In contrast to these characters, Clay Hoskins, the folksy California sculptor acting as American consul in Venice in *A Fearful Responsibility,* achieves professional success in Italy, largely by resisting Italian influences. His "indomitable hopefulness" about the outcome of the Civil War is embodied in his bas-relief, *Westward the Star of Empire.* An Italian sculptor, Elmore thinks, would have expressed instead the anxiety of the times. Hoskin's conception of the work is essentially Greek, but in modelling the central figure from Lily he gives that conception "the purest American expression." The other piece on which he is at work—an allegorical figure entitled *The Pacific Slope*—is also America-inspired. The implication is that he will take Lily's advice and remain in Italy only long enough to finish both pieces before returning to America.

Indian Summer, Howells' fourth novel laid in Italy, reflects his disillusion during his second visit there. The major theme is the conflict of romanticism with reality. Again an American girl has a love affair in Italy, but this time no foreigners are involved and European social conventions do not figure prominently. Imogene Graham falls prey instead to the traditional romanticization of this country.

The Italian scene has a more direct effect on Colville than on Imogene and is more functional in connection with the minor theme of this novel: that of expatriation. This scene fosters romantic conceptions and discourages practical activity, particularly on the part of certain types of character. The passively-inclined Colville is such a character. At the time of his first visit he had been a young architect with literary aspirations, whom the combined influence of Italian Gothic architecture and the writing of Ruskin had encouraged to be a dilettante. He had also failed, because of being too great a "mixture," to win the American girl with whom he had fallen in love in Italy at that time. On his second visit he is disappointed in Florence (chiefly because the sights are no longer novel), yet is still susceptible to the same influences there. He fails to write the short history of the city which he has projected; carries on an abortive romance with Imogene, who is much younger than he; and almost loses Mrs. Bowen, a widow of his own age, whom he finally marries.

Most of the Americans in *Indian Summer* are expatriates: Mrs. Bowen, the Reverend Mr. Waters, Mme Uccelli, Mrs. Armsden, and several artists. All manage to maintain their national character and some are very happy. The artists lead "simple and innocent lives in a world of the ideal." Waters, an amateur historian with a special interest in Savonarola, is the "most delightfully expatriated compatriot" whom Colville sees—and indeed the only ardent admirer of Italian civilization and Italians in all Howells' fiction.

Yet all these Americans are cut off from the main currents of life, both in their own and in their adopted country. The "alien life" they and the English residents of Florence lead strikes Colville as "one of the phases of modern civilisation worthy of note, if not particular study," for he thinks it destined to spread throughout Europe "as the conditions in England and America grow more tiresome and more onerous." It was, Howells commented, a doubly artificial life that such nationals led abroad, especially in Italy and most particularly in Florence. In that city it was not the real Englishman or American who was catered to but "a *forestière* conventionalised from the Florentine's observation of many Anglo Saxons." Colville is inclined to reproach "feeble-minded fellow-citizens who abandon their native climate and come to live in Italy," and Waters tends to agree with him about those who do so "in the heyday of life."

It is significant that Waters is an old man who has completed one career before settling in Florence. At first encouraged about his own historical project by Waters' example, Colville decides as he watches Waters secure from a library a book on early Florentine history and give him "the scholar's far-off look" that

he did not wish to come to just that yet, either. Life, active life, life of his own day, called to him; he had been one of its busiest children : could he turn his back upon it for any charm or use that was in the past?

He is tempted to

curse the day in which he had returned to this outworn Old World. Idler on its modern surface, or delver in its deep-hearted past, could he reconcile himself to it? What did he care for the Italians of to-day, or the history of the Florentines as expressed in their architectural monuments? It was the problems of the vast, tumultuous American life, which he had turned his back on, that really concerned him.

Later, he thinks, he may take up some historical study. Presumably he and Mrs. Bowen will eventually return to America.

In two novels of the late 1890's Howells returned briefly to the international theme and depicted American girls exposed to danger in society in Italy. In *The Landlord at Lion's Head* (1897) Genevieve Vostrand, whose mother has had a salon in Florence, marries there an Italian officer, Count Luigi de' Popalani Grassi. He mistreats her, and she leaves him. After his death she is happily married to the self-made Jeff Durgin, and the entire family leave for their native land, as Mrs. Vostrand puts it, "to live and die true Americans." Another character in this novel who has lived in Italy is the painter Westover, one of the few artists in Howells' fiction who benefit from going abroad.

The heroine of *Ragged Lady,* Clementina Claxon, is a phlegmatic version of Lydia Blood. Her trip to Italy brings her, too, to maturity, not only without changing her character but without making any considerable impression on her. At the gatherings of Miss Milray in Florence, Clementina becomes, though not "less American" or even "sophisticated," more conventionalized. The knowledge of good and evil in things that had all seemed indifferently good to her once, had crept upon her, and she distinguished in her actions. . . . She put on the world, but she wore it simply and in most matters unconsciously.

But in Venice—where, after the death of her companion, Mrs. Lander, she sees almost no one except the American vice-consul—she allows "the world . . . or so much of it as she had seen at Florence" to fall from her and lives as much as possible as she did in her New England village home. In Venice she is given occasion for coveting Mrs. Lander's fortune—which is bequeathed to her though it turns out to have been already expended—but to this temptation, too, she is impervious. She rejects the proposal of marriage of the American expatriate in Florence, Dr. Welwright, and after her return home marries, successively, the two other suitors (both Americans) whom she has in Italy.

The Italian scene is not directly responsible for any of these developments. Many of the Americans in Italy in this novel are, in fact, pointedly detached from that scene. Miss Milray has inherited a weak character rather than been corrupted by exile; Mrs. Lander is content with looking from her hotel window and going for short drives about Florence; the Reverend Mr. Orson hardly leaves his hotel room in Venice; vice-consul Bennam in Venice thinks only of going home; Clementina discovers there are famous objects to be seen in Florence from overhearing the conversation of tourists, but apparently sees few such objects either there or in Venice. This very detachment, however, makes the most damaging point about this scene. It lacks the power not only of strongly influencing character but even of attracting much attention.

The issue of expatriation is raised in two other novels of Howells' later career in connection with Americans who have lived in Italy. The heroine of *Annie Kilburn,* who has spent eleven winters in Rome with her father, returns to America after his death because she wishes to be of use in the world. Though some of her altruistic efforts have tragic results, she finds her place in society with her marriage. In contrast to the social reforms in which she is interested after her return is the project for the soldiers' monument in Hatboro' which she had sponsored before going abroad. This work has been executed in Rome by a Kansas girl, who has produced, instead of the originally planned realistic figure of a soldier, a winged Victory, whose "involuntary frivolity insulted the solemn memory of the slain." In itself this episode is another example of the deleterious effect of foreign residence on an American artist.

Dr. Edward Olney, in *An Imperative Duty,* is forced for financial reasons to give up his residence in Florence, where he has practiced medicine "among the nervous Americans who came increasingly abroad every year," but back in America he finds himself homesick for Italy. The sympathy he feels for the Negro race and his marriage to the part-Negro Rhoda Aldgate (who has travelled in Italy) suggest that he is profoundly attracted to non-Anglo-Saxon cultures, as no other character in Howells' fiction is. Rhoda, however, proves to be a nervous patient herself, and the Olneys' permanent removal to Rome (where she is thought to look Italian) represents less a triumph over American racial prejudice than a retreat from society.

The principal other characters in Howells' later novels who have been in Italy are the ineffectual Ben Halleck in *A Modern Instance* (1882); the amiable but dilettantish Bromfield Corey, who first appears in *The Rise of Silas Lapham* (1885); the sailor Williams in *The Minister's Charge,* who thinks Venice is "a kind of a hole of a place"; the Passmer family—with its flighty daughter Alice—and the artist Dan Mavering in *April Hopes* (1888); the Marches, who in *Their Wedding Journey* (1871) and *A Hazard of New Fortunes* (1890) remember Italy chiefly for its food and wine, and who in *Their Silver Wedding Journey* talk of revisiting it but do not do so; the more conservative members of the Hilary family in *The Quality of Mercy* (1892); the would-be bohemian Charmian Maybaugh in *The Coast of Bohemia* (1893); the Reverend Hugh Brichon in *The Kentons* (1902), who says it is "the most interesting country"; Mrs. Strange in *Through the Eye of the Needle* (1907); Parthenope Brook in *The Vacation of the Kelwyns* (1920), who was born in Naples. None of these characters, however, has an experience in Italy significantly different from that of other characters which Howells treats more extensively.

Italian immigrants to America appear in Howells' *Suburban Sketches* (1871) and in five of his later novels : *April Hopes, A Hazard of New Fortunes, The World of Chance* (1893), *Their Silver Wedding Journey,* and *The Vacation of the Kelwyns.* All, however, are minor characters, who are representative less of their own country than of the American melting pot. In

Howells' opinion such Italians showed to little advantage in their new home. "A malign chance," he wrote in *Impressions and Experiences* (1896), had transformed those in New York from

the friendly folk they are at home to the surly race they mostly show themselves here : shrewd for their advancement in material things, which seem the only good things to the Americanized aliens of all races, and fierce for their full share of the political pottage.

In his middle years Howells became to some extent disillusioned about the ethics of American social and business practices. Yet he never lost his faith in the vitality of American moral standards, and he never thought that any answer to American problems might be found abroad. Only in the recognition by individual Americans of their involvement in these problems was there, he felt, hope for their resolution. His theory of "complicity" was conceived of in national terms, though it had international implications.

Yet Howells never quite got over the feeling that Italy had more meaning, particularly for Americans, than he was able to comprehend. The very persistence of Italian references in his later fiction suggests some such feeling. His periodic consideration of writing a history of Venice, with the idea of relating it to American history, and his return at the end of his life to his earliest memories of Venice are significant in this connection. In the fright, revulsion, and frustration of some of his American characters in Italy and in the superficial tribute paid to it by others, moreover, there is the implication of a disappointing quest, a limited exploration.

The last cluster of Italian references in Howells' fiction, in *The Vacation of the Kelwyns,* is especially wistful. Parthenope Brook, the daughter of a sculptor and a painter who had gone to Italy "in those simple days when living in Italy was almost a brevet of genius," bears the antique name of her birthplace, the name of the siren who threw herself into the sea after failing to bring Ulysses to shipwreck. The parents having died of the Roman fever soon after her birth, Parthenope has been brought up in America and has no recollection of Italy. She, too, is artistic. The gracefulness of an Italian organ-grinder and his family makes her "sigh aloud" at "the contrast they offered to the mannerless uncouthness of the Yankee country-folks." At the end of her session at an art school she thinks of going to Europe, but instead, for "a fresh point of view," visits her cousins the Kelwyns, who have taken a house from a New England community of Shakers. There she meets the pragmatic teacher-playwright Elihu Emerance, whom she marries.

Thus again, as in the major pattern of Howells' Italianate fiction, an American experience in Italy faces fatality yet is ultimately absorbed in main currents of American life. This time, however, there is no glimpse of a corrupt or even an idle Italian society. There is instead an echo of an antique song, beautiful yet dangerous, haunting the mind like a recurrent, enigmatic dream.

VI

The Moral Field:

JAMES

DURING THE EUROPEAN SOJOURN OF THE ELDER HENRY JAMES and his family in the late 1850's only the youngest son, Robertson, went to Italy. Only he, his brother Henry wrote over fifty years later, had been "the subject of what seemed to me even then a privilege of the highest intensity," and on this account Henry had thought throughout these years with particular regret of Robertson's unsuccessful career. Robertson "had been dipped as a boy into the sacred stream," and the experience might have proved his salvation. For Henry, Italy was, from his first to his last years, the sacred, the life-stored land.

In the "solutional Europe" of which Henry dreamed as a boy—it was natural enough in the household of his cosmopolitan father—the strongest ingredient was Italy. He could think that the James home—with a view of Florence by Thomas Cole, a Tuscan landscape by Lefebvre, and a Bacchante bust by an American sculptor in Rome—contained "a great abundance of Italy." When he wrote a review, for publication early in 1868, of Howells' *Italian Journeys,* he was already analyzing the appeal of that country for writers as well as mere travellers, even though he had not been there. So long as it stood in its unique relation "aesthetically and intellectually, to the rest of civilization," he thought the world would no more weary of reading about than of visiting it. "We go to Italy," he wrote, "to gaze upon certain of the highest achievements of human power," representing "to the imagination the *maximum* of man's creative force." With its long history of glories and sufferings, its art, its nature, and its Church, it had indeed so complex an appeal that, he concluded, "betwixt admiration and longing and pity and reverence, it is little wonder that we are charmed and touched beyond healing."

Before James went to Italy he knew and admired the work of two American writers who had been there : Hawthorne and Howells. A few years afterward he was calling Hawthorne's treatment of the country old-fashionedly romantic and approving Howells' as realistic; but he regarded the point of view of both writers as above all peculiarly American. After their example as well as in expression of depths of his own consciousness, he made Italian references in nearly half the stories he wrote in America between 1864 and 1869.

Thus when in the latter year, at the age of twenty-six, James went to Italy for the first time, he was not only gratifying an intense personal desire but consciously following an American literary tradition. He had preconceptions, too, not only of the great achievements of the past to be seen but of a stimulus to the creative impulse operative there.

James' first European trip made alone, for the purpose of improving his education and his health, lasted some fifteen months, of which five—between August 1869 and January 1870—were spent in Italy. He travelled almost the length of the peninsula, from Cadenabbia to Paestum and back to Genoa, having all his expectations realized, as he wrote in ecstatic letters to his family. In contrast to the "good married matron" England and the "magnificent man" Switzerland, Italy was, he promptly reported, "a beautiful dishevelled nymph." Venice, the first city he visited, made him feel as though he had been "born in Boston" and was thus unable to surrender himself to "the genius of Italy—or the Spirit of the South," but not for long. The charm of Italy, he decided a few weeks later, was "inexpressible, indefinable," but it was one which, "once deeply felt, leaves forever its mark upon the sensitive mind & fastens it to the Italian soil thro' all its future wanderings by a delicate chain of longings & regrets." This, in short, was the "land of the immortal gods." Leaving it, he thought most of Florence—the "pearl of cities," "the most feminine of cities," the city with "an immortal soul," the "one thing" he intended to talk of when he reached home. Yet it was Rome which made the greatest impression on him, then and during his next several visits. "At last—for the first time— I live!" he wrote his brother William on the day he arrived. He "went reeling and moaning thro' the streets, in a fever of enjoyment," traversed almost the whole of the city in four or five hours, and by night felt that already he had "caught the keynote of its operation on the senses." He was least pleased by Naples—"glorious" in situation but "a barbarous city," with a "shiny varnish of civilization," which made him conceive a "loathing" for the "hideous heritage of the past." "Decidedly I go in for Northern Italy," he wrote his mother. Not until eleven years later did he return to Naples, and altogether he made only four visits there. In later years—after his stay of two months in 1881—be became much fonder of Venice.

On his first visit, as on subsequent ones, James took relatively little interest in Italian scenery, though he was fascinated from the first by "the great violet Campagna . . . a wilderness of sunny decay & vacancy." The few Italians—mostly servants— with whom he had dealings only inspired him to say of the English that "in the midst of these false and beautiful Italians they glow with the light of the great fact, that after all they love a bath-tub and they hate a lie." For Italian painting, sculpture, architecture, and gardens, however, he had a seemingly insatiable appetite. He systematically visited galleries and churches, conscientiously consulting Murray's guidebooks about them. His highest praise for painting and sculpture went to the work of Tintoretto (whose pictures he wished he could imitate in "prose of corresponding force & color") and Giotto, portraits by Raphael and Leonardo, and Michelangelo's figures for the Medici tombs. He was most impressed, however, by architecture. Half the merit of the pictures he saw in Rome was, in his estimation, their being "in their delightful princely shabby old Palaces—with their great names." He felt his lack of historical and especially of architectural knowledge, and he talked of spending the winter in Florence studying Italian art. But he came closest to expressing his own peculiar apprehension of art and history in Italy when he wrote William, trying to put in a formula "the *Italian feeling*," that "one is conscious here of the esthetic presence of the past."

By the time he reached London after leaving Italy—having bewailed his departure the entire way—he doubted that he would seriously study Italian history or art, but already he foresaw the nature and the depth of the influence which Italy was to exert on him. He wished he could "exorcise this Italian ghost that haunts me" by writing a series of sketches about the country, but decided not to do so. "I had far rather," he wrote William, "let Italy slumber in my mind untouched as a perpetual capital, whereof for my literary needs I shall draw simply the income—let it lie warm & nutritive at the base of my mind, manuring & enriching its roots."

No continental country besides Italy made a major impression on James during his 1869–70 European trip, and after it even England seemed "dull." Back in America he had "the wish—the absolute sense of need—to see Italy again" and promised himself when he returned it would be "not for months but years."

When James next went abroad, ostensibly as a writer of travel sketches for the *Nation,* he stayed some twenty-eight months : from the summer of 1872 to the fall of 1874, nearly half this period in Italy. He conducted his sister Alice and his Aunt Kate Walsh on a brief tour through northern Italy early in September 1872; spent from December 1872 to May 1873 chiefly in Rome; and lived, most of the time with his brother William, from October to December 1873 and from January to June 1874, chiefly in Florence, during December in Rome.

Again he was captivated by the "unanalyzable *loveableness*" of the country. Partly because of the changes introduced at Rome since it had become the national capital, he found that city "Much less simply & sensuously & satisfyingly picturesque" and regarded it "far less gushingly" than in 1869–70. Yet even more than before he was aware of the *"muchness"* there, "the importunate presence of tradition of *every* kind—the influence of an atmosphere electrically charged with historic intimations and whisperings." He stayed on to give himself "a chance to react," gathering "impressions"—"priceless ones"— to use later. He especially enjoyed the coming of spring in Rome, with more vegetation in its midst than Florence.

The second of these two sojourns was, however, the longest James ever made in Italy. Its climate in the summer proved enervating for him. Both times he had to leave in June, envious of "lethargic" Luther Terry, the painter, and "tough" William Wetmore Story, who could stay in Rome until the first of July. The Italian scene, moreover, proved too distracting at all times for him to write or even read very much. He spent far less time studying Italian and reading Tasso than he had planned, and his writing consisted chiefly of some travel sketches (republished in *Transatlantic Sketches*), "The Last of the Valerii," "Adina," and part of *Roderick Hudson*—begun in the spring of 1874 in his "high, charming, shabby old room" on the Piazza Santa Maria Novella in Florence. On later visits to Italy he wrote chiefly part of *The Portrait of a Lady* (begun in Florence in 1880 and finished in Venice in 1881), most of "The Aspern Papers" (at the Villa Brichieri-Colombi in Florence in 1887), and the beginning of *A London Life* (in "one of the wonderful faded back rooms" of the Palazzo Barbaro in Venice, also in 1887).

Nor did James find congenial society in Italy. There was, he reported early in 1873, no "interesting or 'cultivated' native society" in Rome as there was in Paris and London. The next year he confessed that he did not find "an easy initiation" into what lay behind the "whole *mise en scene* of Italian life" and that he was sometimes "overwhelmed with the pitifulness of this absurd want of reciprocity between Italy itself and all my rhapsodies about it." More particularly, there were in Italy no writers of significance, like those with whom James later associated fruitfully in Paris and London.

During his 1872–74 visits he became well acquainted among the Americans living in Florence and Rome, and with a few—chiefly the Storys in Rome and Frank and Elizabeth Boott in Florence—he was on intimate terms throughout the years he and they were in Italy. (The Edmund Tweedys, in Rome, were old friends of the James family.) Yet he found most of this group, with the exception of a few women, dull. The work of the American artists in Rome—the most celebrated of whom were Story, Terry, and John Tilton—did not impress him. The best he could say of all whom he met in that city was, as he put it in his biography of Story, that they constituted a kind of symphony, in which none mattered individually but in which, as part of a whole—under the conductorship of the "spirit of the place," "the enclosing fact of Rome"—none could be discordant. In later years he became intimately acquainted in Italy with Constance Fenimore Woolson (whom he met in Florence in 1880), Mrs. Katherine DeKay Bronson (whom he first visited in Venice in 1881), and the D. S. Curtises (whom he first visited in Venice in 1887).

Yet if most of the Americans whom James knew in Italy were not stimulating to him socially, they proved to be so imaginatively. They directed his attention to the subject of the American in that country and to the theme of limited achievement in a highly cultivated environment. Many of them exerted influence on specific characterizations: the artists in Rome on those in *Roderick Hudson* (most notably Story on Roderick and Gloriani); the Bootts on Osmond and Pansy in *The Portrait of a Lady* and the Ververs in *The Golden Bowl;* Elena Lowe on Christina Light in *Roderick Hudson* and *The Princess Casamassima;* Mrs. Sarah Butler Wister on Mrs. Rushback in "The Solution"; Miss Woolson on Tita (or Tina) Bordereau in "The Aspern Papers," May Bartram in "The Beast in the Jungle," and both Milly Theale and Kate Croy in *The Wings of the Dove;* Mrs. Bronson on Mrs. Prest in "The Aspern Papers"; Curtis on old Mr. Probert in *The Reverberator.*

James' visits, moreover, to Americans living in Italian palaces and villas—the Storys in the Barberini, the Terrys in the Odescalchi, the Bootts in the Belvedere al Saracino (or Castellani), Miss Woolson in the Brichieri-Colombi, the Curtises in the Barbaro—familiarized him with such places, which inspired not only some of his most memorable settings but much of his symbolism. Two of these residences appear with especial effectiveness in his fiction: the Villa Belvedere al Saracino (the Pandolfini in *Roderick Hudson* and Osmond's villa in *The Portrait of a Lady*) and the Palazzo Barbaro (the Leporelli in *The Wings of the Dove*). The Palazzo Capello in Venice, where the English writer Constance Fletcher lived, is described as the residence of the Misses Bordereau in "The

Aspern Papers" (whose setting was shifted from Florence, where the original events involving Claire Clairmont and Captain Silsbee occurred and where James heard about them in 1887). The drawing room of the Tweedys in Via Gregoriana in Rome is described as that of Mrs. Walker in "Daisy Miller" (based on a story James heard in Rome in 1877). Mrs. Bronson's Casa Alvisi and her apartments in the adjoining Palazzo Giustiniani are commemorated in an essay which was reprinted in James' volume of Italian sketches, *Italian Hours*.

After James established his residence abroad, first in Paris in 1875 and the next year in London, he went to Italy every few years until nearly the end of his travelling days, usually for about three months of the spring or early summer: in 1877, 1880, 1881, 1886–87, 1888, 1889, 1892, 1894, 1899, and 1907. Altogether he made fourteen visits. (He had gone only "a few times," he plaintively wrote William shortly before his last visit, "—so much fewer than I've wanted.") The most notable later one was that from December 1886 to July 1887, when he spent about four months in Florence, three of them in the Villa Brichieri-Colombi (then leased by Miss Woolson and during part of this time occupied by her), and about three in Venice, the guest first of Mrs. Bronson and then, for five weeks, of the Curtises. His trip in 1894 was made primarily to go over Miss Woolson's literary effects in Venice, where she had died earlier in the year, with her sister from America, Mrs. Clara Woolson Benedict.

Increasingly he deplored the vulgarization and "cockney-fication" of the country—"utterly the prey of the Barbarian now"—by English and American tourists and the new regime, and nostalgically he recalled the "less blighted and dishonoured time." Yet his "unspeakably tender passion" for "the Italy *of* Italy," "quella terra santa," "that Paradise" from which "one returns but to Purgatories at the best," never diminished. "Never has the whole place seemed to me sweeter, dearer, diviner," he wrote of Venice on his last visit. Driving from Rome to Naples and back at this time he felt

with an intimacy and a penetration unprecedented how incomparably the old *coquine* of an Italy is the most beautiful country in the world—of a beauty (and an interest and complexity of beauty) so far beyond any other that none other is worth talking about.

Though changes came with the years, he found, "the spell, the charm, the magic" of Italy remained. It was "always Italy —and the only thing really to be depended on quand même." It was "a refuge from . . . the hardness & haste, of the Northern world," though it "wouldn't do" alone, without that world.

In later years James philosophized a good deal along this line. The southern, pagan world of Italy represented, he suggested, the whole early experience of man, as the northern, Christian, particularly the Anglo-Saxon world represented man's recent experience. As he travelled south in any longitude, he wrote in his account of his trip to the southeastern United States in 1905, he was always struck with "that most charming of all watchable processes, the gradual soft, the distinctly demoralized, conversion of the soul of Nature," its return "from a comparatively grim Theistic faith to the ineradicable principle of Paganism." He felt he was travelling in time rather than in space. Yet these two worlds of experience as he saw them made up the life of man. The English, he came to believe, were "the great race," the Italians, "eternal children"; yet he thought the English might have been improved by an infusion of the Florentine spirit. On the other hand, he found it significant that the "dream of Italy" which Axel Munthe's villa on Capri embodied was that of a "sophisticated Norseman," nurtured in *"ultima Thule."*

As he became more productive, James said he enjoyed Italy "more reasonably & profitably." Yet as his apprehension of it became more complex, he found it harder to write about to his satisfaction. "The loved Italy was the scene of my fiction," he wrote in his preface to *Roderick Hudson,* "—so much more loved than one has ever been able, even after fifty efforts, to say!" There was an "infirm side" of the felicity of the Italian experience, he wrote in his preface to the New York Edition volume containing "The Aspern Papers"—namely "the sense . . . of things too numerous, too deep, too obscure, too strange or simply too beautiful, for any ease of intellectual relation." One had to "induce almost any 'Italian subject' to *make believe* it gives up its secret, in order to keep at all on working —or call them perhaps rather playing—terms with the general impression." For

right and left in Italy—before the great historic complexity at least—penetration fails; we scratch at the extensive surface, we meet the perfunctory smile, we hang about in the golden air. But we exaggerate our gathered values only if we are eminently witless. It is fortunately the exhibition in all the world before which, as admirers, we can most remain superficial without feeling silly.

No wonder James was appalled at Emile Zola's plan, before he had ever been to Rome, of "working up" a treatment of that city for inclusion in *Les Trois Villes.* "One thought of one's own frequentations, saturations," James commented, ". . . and of how the effect of them had somehow been but to make the subject too august." At the same time he realized in his later years that "no Rome of reality" had been concerned in his experience, "that the whole thing was a rare state of the imagination, dosed and drugged . . . by the effectual Borgia cup."

Italian references are scattered through much of James' non-fictional works : in several of his essays, his biographies of Hawthorne and Story, his autobiographical volumes, and his travel accounts. His major treatment of the Italian scene outside his fiction was in his Italian travel sketches.

These sketches were composed between 1872 and 1909. Most of them appeared first in book form in *Transatlantic Sketches* (1875), others in *Portraits of Places* (1883), and all but one ("Very Modern Rome," published posthumously) in *Italian Hours* (1909). The last volume, in which many were revised, was illustrated by Joseph Pennell. Of the twenty-two in this collection six are devoted to Rome and its neighborhoods, five to Venice, two and part of another to Florence, two to other Tuscan cities, two to northern entrances to Italy, and one each to Siena, Ravenna, the towns between Rome and Florence, and Munthe's villa on Capri. As he prepared the final volume, he had misgivings about how his reactions "in presence of all the unutterable old Rome I originally found and adored" would appear in the light of the modern city. Yet the essays he wrote at this time are chiefly notable for emphasizing the characteristics he always ascribed to Italy as its most salient : an inexhaustible complexity, an infinite capacity for absorbing the shocks of history.

James' Italian sketches bear out his repeated statements in letters that it was "impressions" above everything else which he got from Italy—more, he often said, than he knew what to do with. There was, nevertheless, a single overwhelming one. It was the impression of what might be called the *lived life*—of a greater "mixture," "diversity of sensation," "wealth of consciousness" than was to be found elsewhere. Of impressions themselves there seemed to him to be an "unbroken continuity" —an example of the "intellectual background" of enjoyment in Italy, which prevented "pleasure from becoming vulgar." One's sensation, he noted, "rarely begins and ends with itself;

it reverberates—it recalls, commemorates, resuscitates something else." His characterization of London as "the particular spot in the world which communicates the greatest sense of life" referred by implication to the present. It was cumulative life which he sensed in Italy. Everywhere he found "the deep interfusion of the present with the past," the grain of "that wondrous mill of history which during so many years ground finer than any other on earth." Yet, like Ralph Pendrel in *The Sense of the Past,* he coveted such a "sense," "still more than historic records can give it," rather than the knowledge to be obtained from such records. He did not see the Sienese archives until 1892, and then he chose, rather than descend into that "deep, dark mine," to stroll on the Lizza. There a "general aftertaste of experience" seemed "to breathe . . . from the very stones and to make a thick strong liquor of the very air," which was "more the indestructible mixture of lived things." The "deep stain of experience" lingering around a place like the Boboli Gardens gave it eventually, to his sensibility, a "human soul." Though such an atmosphere might be slow in coming, "there is nothing like it," he declared, "when it *has* come."

Closely associated with this sense of place through which James received much of his impression of the life of the past in Italy was his apprehension of the principle of style or form operative there. This principle was the essence of the "aesthetic" which he met on every hand, "so intense that you feel you should live on the taste of it." Everywhere he saw "composition," "picture," "scene." Even in desolate places he detected "that especial form of Roman faith, the fine aesthetic conscience in things, that is never, never broken." The "Genius of Style" seemed to him to haunt the Villa d'Este, "amid a conception and order of things all mossed over from disuse, but still without a form abandoned or a principle disowned." The whole secret of Italy, he more than once suggested, was "style." In his essay on D'Annunzio, printed in 1902, he returned to this idea. "Does it not really all come back to style?" he inquired.

It was to the Latin spirit that the Renaissance was primarily vouchsafed . . . . and when the Latin spirit after many misadventures again clears itself we shall see how all the while this treasure has been in its keeping.

It was, in the last analysis, an impression of life not only lived but *formed* which James had in Italy. It was an impression not so much of a "mixture" as of a "fusion." The "incomparable wrought *fusion* . . . of human history and mortal passion with the elements of earth and air, of colour, composition and form," he wrote of the country in his last Italian essay, ". . . constitute her appeal and give it the supreme heroic grace." It was, he thought, a unique appeal. Describing his feeling as he looked across the Bay of Naples from Munthe's villa, he wrote,

The way in which the Italian scene on such occasions as this seems to purify itself to the transcendent and perfect *idea* alone — idea of beauty, of dignity, of comprehensive grace, with all accidents merged, all defects disowned, all experience outlived, and to gather itself up into the mere mute eloquence of what has just incalculably *been,* remains forever the secret and the lesson of the subtlest daughter of history.

The chief images for James of lived life in Italy were the most massive forms of art there : the great buildings, especially the palaces and churches. They seemed to him supremely stages, where, as in the Boboli Gardens, "something was once done . . . done or meant to be done." In places such as the Palazzo Corsini in Florence, "that have been lived in so long and so much and in such a fine old way," the past seemed to have left "a sensible deposit, an aroma, an atmosphere," prompting one to speculate on what had been done, thought.

and said there. Deeper even than the esthetic charm of such a church as Santa Maria Maggiore went the effect on him of its "social or historic note or tone," the impression it gave of "having been prayed in for several centuries by an endlessly curious and complex society." In general, the Italian were, he he thought, "the *churchiest* churches in Europe—the fullest of gathered memories, of the experience of their office."

These buildings, especially the palaces, were also to James images of life lived greatly. In Italy one felt oneself, he wrote, "among the traditions of the grand style in architecture"; one had to go there "to recover the sense of the domiciliary mass," since "a good specimen of an old Italian palazzo" had a "nobleness" not matched by houses in northern countries. "If the Italians at bottom despise the rest of mankind and regard them as barbarians, disinherited of the tradition of form," he decided, "the idea proceeds largely, no doubt, from our living in comparative molehills. They alone were really to build their civilization." Tuscan palaces seemed to him "the most dignified dwellings in the world," their ground floors serving as pedestals for the habitated parts, as though "people weren't properly housed unless . . . they should be lifted fifty feet above the pavement." He imagined that apartments decorated like those at the ruined Villa Madama near Rome could "have been meant only for the recreation of people greater than any we know, people for whom life was impudent ease and success." If they had fewer diversions than later generations, "the old generations built and arranged greatly for the simple reason that they liked it, and they could bore themselves . . . better in noble conditions than in mean ones." It was as "one of the greatest of human achievements" that St. Peter's chiefly impressed him, as an assurance about man rather than an aspiration toward God. It was a refuge for the human spirit as a place which made one "still believe in the heroic will and the heroic act," if not a place in which to pray.

Of all the arts, indeed, architecture was to James most symbolic of moral values. Its concern with mass made it a "supreme embodiment of vigorous effort" and a great building "the greatest conceivable work of art." More than any other art, it represented "difficulties mastered, resources combined, labour, courage and patience." In ecclesiastical architecture he required "absolute felicity of proportion," since "strictly formal beauty seems best to express our conception of spiritual beauty."

For all the impression of vitality which James received in Italy, he often had, in the same places, a feeling of sadness and even of apprehension. A sinister atmosphere lurked for him "wherever the terrible game of the life of the Renaissance was played as the Italians played it." Above all, in the palaces and churches whose great size was out of proportion to their current use, which were virtually empty of people, he received an "almost aching vision, more frequent in the Italy of to-day than anywhere in the world, of the uncalculated waste of a myriad forms of piety, forces of labour, beautiful fruits of genius."

James was also conscious in Italy of powerful counterforces to great life, to the fusion of experience. In his view such counterforces dominated the whole post-Renaissance era, most devastatingly the nineteenth century. The best of modern manners he esteemed too poor for "many of the great places," and the "poor stupid little red-faced brother" who showed him the fresco by Leonardo in the church of St. Onofrio in Rome (where Tasso spent his last months) made him certain there was "more intellect" in that work "than under all the monkish tonsures it has seen coming and going these three hundred years." Yet he did not find the attitude of the new Italian state to the Roman Catholic Church, which was of a piece with its business-like attitude to ruins and works of art, any more promising : it was intrinsically "hostile to the elements of picture and colour and 'style.' " With political unity, Italy had achieved at last a virtual separation of art and life which he regarded as damaging to both. Disconnected "from the present and future of the place, from the actual life and manners, the native ideal," the great productions of the Renaissance had been left in "spiritual solitude."

Yet the romantic attitude of foreigners who praised the Italian past at the expense of the present was to James another delimiting, divisive force. He himself freely applied to Italy the epithets of "romantic," "picturesque," "charming," "enchanting," "magical," "quaint." There was an "amenity" in almost any experience in that country, he thought; there one saw "charm" in things that seemed vulgar elsewhere. The "old" Italy, which he chiefly associated with the landscapes of Claude and Rosa, and to some extent with Gothic romances, was still to be seen in places like the Benedictine Convent at Subiaco. Yet appearances could be deceiving, as he learned when an "operatic" young Italian turned out to be a political radical and the lamp in a wayside shrine to be "nourished with the essence of Pennsylvania." It behooved the rest of the world to give up its "insufferable aesthetic patronage" of Italy, he declared, not only because she might at last resent it but because, as a gratification of sensibility alone, it meant as fatal a separation of life and art as did the denial of sensibility. James himself struggled hard with his distaste for denuded ruins and new buildings in Rome in 1877, he recalled in "Very Modern Rome." As a result, however, he became more interested in the city's increasingly complex history.

Notwithstanding James' hostility to stock romanticism, part of his tolerance of "new" Italy rested on a typically romantic conception : namely, that his earliest experiences in Italy constituted a great personal revelation, of the sort vouchsafed a person once only, ideally in youth. "It is a sad truth," he reflected during his second visit to Venice, "that one can stand in the Ducal Palace for the first time but once, with the deliciously ponderous sense of that particular half-hour's being an era in one's mental history." On later visits to Italy he heard appeals that seemed "to have been uttered first in the sonorous chambers of youth" and had the sense of the Rome of his "particular infatuated prime." That city of "his first unpremeditated rapture" shone, indeed, "to memory . . . in the manner of a lost paradise." More than once he declared that he could imagine no happier situation than to be a young artist in Italy. When he wrote Percy Lubbock in 1902, as Lubbock, then twenty-three, prepared to go to Italy for the first time, he offered congratulations on "the great event of your young, your first, your never to be surpassed or effaced prime Italiänische Reise. It's a great event (*the* revelation) at any time of life, but it's altogether immeasurable at *your* lucky one."

This note of personal destiny in James' essays on Italy is absent from his three other travel books: *A Little Tour in France* (1884), *English Hours* (1905), and *The American Scene* (1907). The last, however, his account of his visit in several eastern and southern states in 1905, calls for attention in this connection. The most personally revealing of the three, it abounds in Italian references. The mountains in New England, he wrote, had reminded him of the Apennines; he compared the skyscrapers in New York to Giotto's campanile in Florence, New York to Venice, and the Capitol in Washington to St. Peter's; in South Carolina and Florida, he said, he had felt the atmosphere of southern Italy. A half-submerged image of Italy accompanies his entire account of his American visit. The fact is significant. In this his most concentrated and last attempt to identify himself with his native land, he was met everywhere by memories of the land which from boyhood had engaged him more emotionally and more imaginatively than any other.

John Singer Sargent, THE INTERIOR OF A PALACE IN VENICE. London? 1899. (The Palazzo Barbaro. Mr. and Mrs. Ralph W. Curtis at left, Mr. and Mrs. Daniel S. Curtis at right.)

(Courtesy of the Royal Academy of Arts, London)

William Wetmore Story

CLEOPATRA. Rome ca. 1858.

(Courtesy of The Metropolitan Museum of Art.)

THE LIBYAN SIBYL. Rome, 1861.

(Courtesy of the Smithsonian Institution, Washington, D.C.)

The influence of Italy on James' fiction was pervasive. Of his twenty-two novels and one hundred twelve shorter pieces all but two novels and fifty-one stories contain some reference to that country. Six novels and eighteen stories are laid there, partly if not entirely, and in most of the other works characters go or have been there. Though James had launched upon a literary career before he went abroad in 1869, it was as a result of his visits to Italy then and during the next few years that he became established in that career. Italy was a scene, directly or indirectly, in nearly all the fiction of his first mature period; of all he wrote between 1869 and 1884, only four stories have no Italian reference. He made least use of this scene between 1891 and 1901, but he returned to it in his last period. Except in the dramatization of "Daisy Miller," he made no use of it in his plays. All his specific Italian settings are places he had visited, and those most often used—Rome, Florence, and Venice, in that order—were his personal favorites.

Throughout James' career, Italy figured more often than any other country in his fiction dealing with the international theme, the theme which concerned him chiefly early and late, only slightly in his middle period. Some ten or fifteen works dealing with this theme are laid for the most part in other countries, but many of these works contain characters who have a meaningful connection with Italy. The narrator of "A Passionate Pilgrim," for example, is as enthusiastic about Italy as about England; Christopher Newman in *The American* is characterized partly in terms of his enjoyment of Venice; it was Italy that Caroline Spencer in "Four Meetings" most wanted to see; the father of Felix and Eugenia Young in *The Europeans* was born in Sicily; in "The Modern Warning" Agatha Grice and Sir Rufus Chasemore meet at Cadenabbia. Of James' major treatments of the international theme—*The Portrait of a Lady, The Wings of the Dove, The Ambassadors,* and *The Golden Bowl*—all except *The Ambassadors* are either laid mainly in Italy or continue action begun there.

The international theme as James treated it was a version of the broader, essentially moral theme which preoccupied him from his earliest writing in America through his middle period to the end : the theme of self-realization, achieved through initiation, the enlargement of experience, or the meeting of doom. As James conceived it, the process of self-realization has a negative as well as a positive aspect, for limitations are imposed on it by the nature of the characters involved, by antecedent events in the lives of other characters, and by social conventions. He predicated it, however, exclusively in terms of sensitive natures; his insensitive characters do not develop. The theme of self-realization in his fiction thus involves a conflict between romantic preconceptions and reality or between innocence, conceived of as the assumption that one is free to do as he pleases, and experience, conceived of as the recognition of inevitability, limitation, and convention.

James projected this theme most clearly and fully in international terms : most often in terms of a young American going to Europe (usually to Italy)—often in fulfillment of a long-cherished desire, falling in love there (not necessarily with a foreigner), and often marrying. The central characters in Italy who are not American are most often English. Other symbolic acts which may be performed on the foreign scene are renunciation, dying, and the creation or collection of works of art. Whatever the outcome, the action and the characterization are commensurate with the scope of the scene, and all have heroic or epic qualities. In the fiction of James' middle period these elements are generally demeaned. The impulse toward self-realization is corrupted to a will to power, the artist fights a losing battle with society, the moral sense is found chiefly in the immature, and means are devised to escape life altogether. The scene is circumscribed and, so far as it is national, is most often English.

Italy, then, is pre-eminently the scene of self-realization in James' fiction. For this fact, certain peculiarities of the country are largely responsible. As James depicted it, the Italian environment represents chiefly the nonintellectual-esthetic-pagan component in human history, largely unrepresented in Anglo-Saxon environments, which he distinguished above all for their nurture of the moral sense. In going to Italy, Anglo-Saxons in James' fiction are thus potentially completing their experience, developing all their faculties. For those not prepared to enlarge their lives, however—those who only substitute an Italian for an Anglo-Saxon environment—Italy may prove too heady. In any case, the Italian scene, as James depicted it, dignifies the lives of all these characters.

Works of art, especially churches and private residences, constitute the most important single element in this scene. In the self-realization process in Italy, as James treated it, these works are highly symbolic and singularly influential agents, since in themselves they represent the unity of experience : the interfusion of past and present, of the esthetic and the erotic. In most of his non-Italian pieces of fiction, works of art are relatively few and unimportant. Two of the chief exceptions among these pieces—*The American* and *The Ambassadors*—are, however, treatments of the international theme.

Before he went to Italy in 1869 some such pattern as this was beginning to appear in James' fiction. In three of the stories written before that time one character retires to that country after two blighted love affairs (in "Poor Richard"), another falls in love with a false woman there (in "The Story of a Masterpiece"), and a third there marries his first love and loses her by death (in "De Grey").

The first story James wrote after going abroad in 1869—"Travelling Companions," which was printed the next year,

constitutes a full introduction to his treatment of the international theme. Though perhaps most romantic of all his
treatments, it contains some of his chief character types and
exhibits the general use he made of Italian art. The narrator,
the American Mr. Brooke, the first of James' "passionate pil-
grims," visits the chief Italian cities from Milan to Naples
(virtually following James' route of 1869–79 and receiving
most of the same impressions). His great expectations are
largely met, though he is highly analytical of his impressions
and his romantic tendency is curbed—chiefly by a woman em-
bittered by misfortune whom he meets in the cathedral in
Milan. In Italy he gets his deepest impression—deeper than
that he had gotten in England—of "the social secrets of mankind," of "the unapplied, spontaneous moral life of society";
yet he also has "an overwhelming sense of the sadness of man's
spiritual history," which makes conventionally romantic pil-
grimages seem foolish and vulgar. His greatest emotion comes
from feeling himself among scenes where "art had ranged so
freely," where at every turn appears "a vital principle of grace,
—from the smile of a chambermaid to the curve of an arch."
His "perception" seems "for the first time to live a sturdy
creative life of its own."

In Italy Brooke meets and successfully woos an American
girl, Miss Evans, who also feels deeply but who is more
realistic than he is. Her father is an admirable type of
American aristocrat, though without taste and generally un-
responsive to Italy. The lovers' chief meetings occur in a series
of churches (their romance encounters its one impediment
when they remain so long in the Giotto chapel in Padua
that they have to spend the night in the city, scandalizing Mr.
Evans), and their whole relationship is reflected in a series of
paintings. The most notable of these paintings are Leonardo's
Cenacolo, before which Miss Evans exhibits the feeling which
first attracts Brooke; a pseudo-Correggio, whose subject she

resembles; the Giotto frescoes, which move her to exclaim, "We ought to learn from all this to be *real* . . . to discriminate between . . . sentiment and sentimentality"; and Titian's *Sacred and Profane Love* in the Borghese Gallery in Rome, in which Brooke says the nude woman represents "love as a sentiment" and the other woman "love as an experience," and before which he and Miss Evans come to their final understanding.

Among other characters in James' fiction who have successful love affairs in Italy are the heroine of "Adina," Martha Valerio in "The Last of the Valerii," Stanmer in "The Diary of a Man of Fifty," Bernard Longueville in *Confidence* (who first sees Angela Vivian outside a church in Siena), Jeffrey Aspern, Henry Wilmerding in "The Solution," and Rose Tramore and Captain Jay in "The Chaperon" (who are reunited at the entrance to the cathedral in Milan). The narrator of "At Isella," who from the time he could use his wits has "done little else than fancy dramas and romances and love-tales, and lodge them in Italy," is to join his fiancée in Florence and probably to marry her in Rome; though the Italian woman whom he meets fleeing from her cruel husband causes him to revise some of his preconceptions of the country, he helps her on her way to her lover in Switzerland. James' only great story of married love, *The Golden Bowl,* begins in Italy. In Venice Merton Densher's love for Kate Croy is consummated (he makes the proposal in front of St. Mark's) and his idealization of Milly Theale is begun.

The association of romantic love with Italy also occurs obliquely in several of James' works. From Florence, on his honeymoon, Owen Gereth writes Fleda Vetch offering her something from Poynton. In *The Tragic Muse* Nick Dormer proposes to Julia Dallow in a structure on her estate resembling the Temple of Vesta at Rome. In *The Bostonians,* Cape Cod, where Basil Ransom most ardently woos Verena Tarrant, is called "the Italy . . . of Massachusetts."

Other successful ventures or enlargements of experience are had in Italy by artists and writers (such as the narrators of "The Last of the Valerii" and "The Impressions of a Cousin," Sam Singleton in *Roderick Hudson,* Aspern, the author of *Beltraffio,* and Paul Overt in "The Lesson of the Master"); retired spinsters (Jane Rimmle in "'Europe'" as well as Gertrude Whittaker in "Poor Richard"); adolescents approaching maturity (Nora in *Watch and Ward* and Morgan Moreen in "The Pupil"); and guardians who take their protégés (notably Rowland Mallet in *Roderick Hudson* and Mrs. Touchett in *The Portrait of a Lady;* Mrs. Gereth's plans to take Fleda Vetch to Florence, in *The Spoils of Poynton,* do not materialize). In Italy the sweetheart of M. Brisieux acquires and then loses a fiancé, but the latter experience prepares her for one larger. Here too, for all the tragic consequences, Hyacinth Robinson in *The Princess Casamassima* and John Marcher in "The Beast in the Jungle" receive their deepest insights into their own natures. It is significant that certain features of the Great Good Place of Refuge remind George Dane of Italian places and paintings and that Ralph Pendrel, in *The Sense of the Past,* compares the paintings of the ancestor with whom he has identified himself to paintings he has seen in Italy. To the extent their aspirations are realized in Italy, Roderick Hudson, Isabel Archer, and Milly Theale also belong to this group.

Many of James' characters who go to Italy, on the other hand, become disappointed in love, fail in artistic undertakings, or are corrupted, and some die there. He was more interested in the complexities of such experiences than in simply positive ones, and he made major studies of some of these characters. The general cause of the undoing of them all is the denial or perversion of esthetic-erotic values—a major threat to self—

realization in much of James' fiction, but one most often depicted in the environment of Italy. The effects of the disappointments in love, of course, extend to innocent persons, notably Mary Garland, Isabel Archer, and Maggie Verver.

All those who are guilty of the violation of these values are well described by Gilbert Osmond in *The Portrait of a Lady* as "the people who couldn't 'realise' . . . on their sensibility." There are two general types, of which Roderick Hudson and Osmond are the most fully developed exemplars. Roderick is sensitive, creative, but undisciplined, having impossibly ideal conceptions (both in art and in love) and no concern with form, and tending to separate art from life. After initial ecstasy he becomes virtually paralyzed both artistically and sexually in Italy. Another character of this type is Theobald in "The Madonna of the Future" (whose "high aesthetic fever" is proof of his American origin). Without Scholastica to turn to, the playwright Benvolio cannot fully benefit from his visit to Italy with the social Countess; and the author of *Beltraffio,* "impregnated—even to morbidity—with the spirit of Italy," is weaker than his moralistic wife in their conflict over their son. Harold Staines in "The Sweetheart of M. Brisieux" (who lectures to his sweetheart about the Claudian aqueduct before proposing to her and prefers copying Leonardo's *Mona Lisa* to painting his sweetheart's portrait), though limited in sensibility, also denies the vitality of art, to the detriment of his paintings and the loss of his fiancée.

Even more insidious is the effect of the Italian environment on the type of character represented by Gilbert Osmond, who is sensitive but immoral. He devotes himself to the gratification of his own taste, as distinct from esthetic or erotic enjoyment, and of possessive or collective instincts, rather than creative ones, valuing forms and conventions for their own sake. (The other collector in *The Portrait of a Lady,* Edward

Rosier, who may be regarded as a foil of Osmond's, has lived longer in France than in Italy and sells part of his collection in his attempt to win Pansy.) Adam Verver in *The Golden Bowl* also exemplifies this type, though he is at worst amoral. Temporarily he influences his daughter. Temporarily Martha Valerio also exhibits these characteristics. (It is significant that it is a Minerva which she hopes to have excavated and instead a Juno—not a Venus, the narrator comments—which comes to light.) Sam Scrope, who makes the initial mistake of denying his own sensitivity, is intemperate in all his dealings about the gem he acquires; significantly, the image on it is of the sensual emperor Tiberius, and on this account Adina refuses Scrope's offer of it. Mrs. Light in *Roderick Hudson* first takes an interest in Christina on discovering her to be beautiful, but educates her to take her place in a rigidly conventional society. Charlotte Stant and Prince Amerigo in *The Golden Bowl* subordinate love to money during their early relationship in Italy, and Miss Gunston of Poughkeepsie falls in love with her prince's heritage rather than with him. James' two chief novels dealing with collectors in England have Italian echoes : Poynton is "all France and Italy," and the picture under consideration in *The Outcry* is by an Italian.

To both these groups of characters undone by experience in Italy Christina Light, in *Roderick Hudson* and *The Princess Casamassima,* is related. From one point of view she is James' prime example of the Anglo-Saxon-Italian relationship, since —though she passes for an American—she had an Italian father and a half-American, half-English mother. (Her supposed resemblance to a goddess taken with her name suggests a pagan-Christian combination.) The issue of this union, however, is both illegitimate and psychologically unstable. An embodiment rather than a devotee of beauty, Christina has more form than feeling. Despite her "corrupt" education, she harbors high intellectual and moral ideals—which make her reject Roderick and which her Italian husband is unable to comprehend; but they are too abstract to be effectually opposed to society or projected in a lover.

Madame Merle, the remaining major corrupted character of James' living in Italy, is, like Christina, not esthetically sensitive, and it is not clear to what extent the Italian environment has directly affected her. Osmond has largely made her what she is. Yet, like Christina, she is essentially in love with an ideal—that of greatness—rather than with a man, and to her infatuation with this ideal her residence in Italy has probably contributed.

Another explanation for esthetic-erotic failure in Italy besides that of unrealized sensibility is suggested in a few stories of James' as being the denial of the values of "old" Italy—supremely those of making love and enjoying or producing art—by later generations, who are chiefly in pursuit of social position, valued objects, or money. Both Daisy Miller and Winterbourne are diverted from romantic tendencies by their esteem of social values, with the ironic result that Daisy falls victim to one of the chief romantic adventures of Rome : seeing the Colosseum by moonlight. In the greatest contrast to the relation between Jeffrey Aspern and the young Juliana is that between the old Juliana, her niece, and the rapacious young publisher-narrator. The narrator of "The Diary of a Man of Fifty" is more influenced by the tradition of Italian violence (perhaps partly encouraged by the associations of the name of Via Ghilbellina, on which the woman he loves resides) than by that of romantic love—or by his heart.

James also suggested that prolonged expatriation in Italy tended to corrupt the next generation. Gilbert and Amy Osmond and Charlotte Stant are the children and Christina

Light is a grandchild of Anglo-Saxons who had settled there permanently. The elder Mrs. Osmond had pretended to an intellectual career and approved of political marriages. The elder Stants had been "'of a corrupt generation, demoralised, falsified, polyglot." About Charlotte, who has a "strange sense for tongues" and seems to Amerigo to have the blood of "every race" in her veins, there is a suggestion of mongrelization.

In his studies of contracted or negative experience in Italy James made most use of Italian art and architecture, with the result that his artistic references as a whole have limiting or conditioning values. Of the lovers who meet in churches, more are destined to disappointment than to success: Roderick, Christina, and Mary; Daisy and Winterbourne (though Daisy doesn't see him); Longstaff and Diana; Isabel, Warburton, and Osmond—all meet in St. Peter's. Roderick and Christina also meet in the church at Engelberg in Switzerland. Churches are also visited (though not for religious aid) by persons passing through crises or facing decisions: the Pantheon by Count Valerio, St. Cecilia's (with its association with female martyrdom) by Christina, St. Mark's by Morgan Moreen and Pemberton. Mallet goes to the Franciscan convent at Fiesole under such circumstances. Historic palaces reflect flaws in their fictitious inhabitants: the Falconieri, with the suggestion in its name of predacity, which Mrs. Light occupies (the name is added in the New York Edition of *Roderick Hudson,* though the falcons surmounting the building are not mentioned); the blank-faced villa (the Belvedere al Saracino) in Florence and the ominously named Palazzo Roccanera ("Blackstone"), with its mutilated statues, in Rome, both of which are occupied by Osmond. The old, generally shabby palaces in which Diana Belfield dies and the penniless Misses Bordereau and the Moreen family, with their dying son, live are also appropriate residences for these characters. The Colosseum, with its tragic associations, is the scene of the mental anguish of Angelo (in "Adina"), Roderick Hudson, and Edward Rosier; and of Daisy Miller's contraction of her fatal fever. Amid the ruins of the Forum Isabel rejects Warburton, and amid those of Pompeii John Marcher has his first premonition about "the beast in the jungle." The subjects of particular paintings and pieces of statuary, too, are thematic. Roderick is drawing the antique head of Juno when he first sees Christina, whom he regards more as a goddess than as a woman. The only painting which the "innocent" Daisy Miller is specified to have seen in Rome is Velasquez' portrait of Innocent X. When Isabel sees Warburton next after refusing him in the Forum, they are before the statue of the *Dying Gladiator*.

James' greatest characterizations, however, are neither of persons whose dreams are largely realized nor of failures, but of those who achieve self-realization through a measure of renunciation, by arresting the forces of limitation. These characters are both sensitive and moral. They are endowed also with a strength of will which chiefly distinguishes them from certain characters in James' fiction of the middle period who maintain their moral sense (conceived on a much smaller scale) in the face of opposition but are relatively powerless.

Of these great characterizations, the chief examples are Isabel Archer, Milly Theale, and Maggie Verver, all of whom have the climactic experiences of their lives in Italy or in consequence of having been there. All are victims of corruption in others (Isabel and Maggie of Italy-induced corruption), yet all achieve a kind of victory—Maggie a virtually complete one. That they do so is owing fundamentally to their moral sense, which is part of their cultural inheritance. Yet in the last analysis, they achieve this victory by exercising a sense of form, which is developed through their acquaintance with works of art in Italy. Art appeals to them all finally and pre-eminently as form, composition, the resolution of conflict by the disposition of parts into a whole. In *The Portrait of a Lady, The Wings of the Dove,* and *The Golden Bowl,* moreover, in which the number of artistic images increases, these images tend to produce the effect of character itself as composition or form. In *The Portrait of a Lady* and *The Golden Bowl* the image of an art collection is dominant.

Isabel's first request the day she arrives at Gardencourt is to be shown the paintings, and Ralph Touchett's first impression of her is that she has a character finer than a work of art, that he has received "a Titian, by the post, to hang on my wall—a Greek bas-relief . . . the key to a beautiful edifice." After Isabel learns of her inheritance from Mr. Touchett she looks as solemn, Mrs. Touchett says, as a Cimabue Madonna. Osmond thinks Mrs. Touchett (whom he calls "an old Florentine . . . a contemporary of the Medici") resembles a portrait in a fresco by Ghirlandaio. Osmond himself is described as being "as fine as one of the drawings in the long gallery above the bridge, at the Uffizi." Ralph's ideal of a regular occupation is that of the young man in the Lancret painting at Gardencourt, leaning against the pedestal of the statue of a nymph and playing the guitar for two ladies. The image, with its multiple implications, comes to life when Ralph subsequently sits at the base of the statue of Terpsichore, done in the manner of Bernini, in the garden of the Palazzo Crescentini, while Isabel tells him of her engagement to Osmond.

For Isabel, Italy is to a great extent a land of art, but not entirely so. At San Remo it "stretched before her as a land of promise, a land in which a love of the beautiful might be comforted by endless knowledge." It is above all a land of the life of the past. Isabel's prototype in this respect is Nora in *Watch and Ward,* who writes home that she never tires of visiting the churches in Rome because "they are so picturesque and historic; so redolent of memories, so rich with traditions, so haunted with the past." Going into most of them for her "is like reading some novel, better than I find most novels." It seems to Isabel that in the storied Palazzo Crescentini "the spirit of the past was shut up . . . like a refugee from the outer world." The name of the palace, a fictitious one which means "slight growth," may be allegorical. Having always been fond of history and having an imagination "that kindled at the mention of great deeds," Isabel responds most to Rome, where there is "history in the stones of the street and the atoms of the sunshine" and "wherever she turned some great deed had been acted." The

sense of the mighty human past was heavy upon her but it was interfused in the strangest, suddenest, most capricious way, with the fresh, cool breath of the future.

On her first visit to St. Peter's, "her conception of greatness received an extension. After this it never lacked space to soar."

Broad as her sensitivity is, Isabel is immune to the more constricting Italian influences. She falls, nevertheless, like Roderick Hudson and others of his type, into the error of idealizing Italy—of regarding it as a place apart from the common, from evil, from responsibility. It seems to her a completed composition or scene. So does the career of Osmond, whom she also idealizes. Devoted to study and connoisseurship, that career appears to her "in the disposed vistas and with the ranges of steps and terraces and fountains of a formal Italian garden." Isabel thus tends to disallow freedom of action in Osmond, as he at first does in judging her. In a sense he idealizes her too, seeing only her taste and her money, regarding her as property belonging in a collection such as his. "Italy," as James put it, "had been a party to their first impressions of each other."

When Isabel elects, like Osmond, to preserve the appearance

of their marriage, Italy is again an involved party. Osmond's appeal "in the name of something sacred and precious—the observance of a magnificent form" is, like his appeal in general, to her imagination rather than her judgment. Her return to him from England is, indeed, in one sense a flight from Caspar Goodwood's uncontrolled passion, which emphasizes at a significant point her tendency to sexual coldness. Yet the formal ideal to which she is at last committed has greater scope and vitality than Osmond's, chiefly on account of her acquaintance with some of the greatest monuments of the past in Rome. In the "glorious room among the shining antique marbles" of the Capitoline Museum (where, before her marriage, she bade Warburton farewell), looking at "their beautiful blank faces; listening, as it were, to their eternal silence," she feels the effect of their "noble quietude; which, as with a high door closed for the ceremony, slowly drops on the spirit the large white mantle of peace." She even, "under the charm of their motionless grace," fancies them alive—the best company she could have, she tells Osmond. After her rupture with him it is "old Rome" which means most to her, since "in a world of ruins the ruin of her happiness seemed a less unnatural catastrophe," and she comes to think of the city chiefly as "the place where people had suffered." But this world also offers her "companionship in endurance" and the spectacle of a "splendid" sadness.

She rested her weariness upon things that had crumbled for centuries and were still upright; she dropped her secret sadness into the silence of lonely places, where its very modern quality detached itself and grew objective, so that as she sat in a sun-warmed angle on a winter's day, or stood in a mouldy church to which no one came, she could almost smile at it and think of its smallness.

Through her "haunting sense of the continuity of the human lot," imaged in the forms of enduring art and architecture, she escapes, as Osmond does not, the spiritual death attending the operation of great limiting, centripetal forces.

To Milly Theale, Italy represents first "learning" as opposed to "life" (she and Mrs. Stringham go immediately to Italy from America) and last the triumph of art over the limits of life. In England, between her two visits to Italy, she feels caught up in life, in company with the entire human race, yet she also has her first acute sense both of death and of art as other than academic. At Lancaster Gate she sees the house as the center of a "Watteau-composition" and its contents as achieving a "largeness of style" which is a "great containing vessel"; and she sees her own likeness in the Bronzino portrait. The moments she spends before this painting constitute "the high-watermark of her security" yet also mark "her consciously . . . rounding her protective promontory, quitting the blue gulf of comparative ignorance and reaching her view of the troubled sea." When she ambiguously exclaims, "I shall never be better than this," she is recognizing the beauty that may be brought out of sorrow and even death by art.

Yet in these terms Milly does become not only more effective than she is on this occasion but a kind of artist herself when in Venice she is established in the Palazzo Leporelli. Here, because of its beauty and its seclusion, she wishes to die, and here she does die. In this respect it has an antecedent in the tapestry-hung Roman palace, ornamented with papal arms, in which Diana Belfield chooses to die. The image of death in Venice is prefigured in "The Aspern Papers" and "The Pupil" (though Morgan Moreen actually dies in Paris); in the latter story the description of Venice's mean aspect in November anticipates that of the city during a storm in *The Wings of the Dove*.

But the Palazzo Leporelli is also the place where Milly lives, both more securely and more expansively than anywhere else.

Its name, substituted by James for that of the Barbaro, is presumably the diminutive of *lepore,* which may be translated "gracefulness" or "sprightliness." If she succeeds in buying it, Milly says, "It will be my life—paid for as that." Here she is lodged, as Mrs. Stringham puts it, "for the first time as she ought, from her type, to be." Before going to Venice she is repeatedly referred to as a princess. Considering her physical limitations, her compact establishment there is more her "form," as she recognizes, than anything in England. It is "the ark of her deluge." On one of the upper floors she has the fancy of "never going down, of remaining aloft in the divine dustless air, where she would hear but the plash of water against stone." If one owned and cherished such a house, she thinks, "it would pay one back in kind, would close one in from harm."

It is, however, above all enlargement of life which Milly experiences in the Palazzo Leporelli. With its artistic furnishings and its historic background (she had asked that it have both), it "set up round her a whirlwind of suggestion that never dropped for an hour." Within its walls is not confinement but "the freedom of all the centuries." She herself, though dying, infuses it with new life. She brings out "all its glory." It gains from her, "for effect and harmony," as much as it gives. She also brings others into relation with it, arranging all the elements into a kind of composition, which is likened to a Veronese painting. When she is said to have candles lighted in increasing number in the great saloon, to illumine "the pervasive mystery of Style," the reference is surely as much to this composition of hers as to the palace.

This composition encompasses—it is part of the stylistic "mystery" that it does—anomalous elements, both apparent and real. Mrs. Stringham is the "inevitable dwarf" of Veronese, but she belongs to Milly's entourage. Kate Croy and—at first—Merton Densher do not. Like Isabel, Milly tends to idealize, especially in the Italian environment, and to disallow the operation of such forces as Kate and Densher represent. Because of her illness she has less personal resistance than Isabel, but with more creative power she has a greater triumph. This power at last transforms Densher. Plastic as he is, he is most impressed by a large design. Conscious that his attitude "lacked the highest style, in a cómposition" in which everything else had it, he is drawn to the Palazzo Leporelli by the very scope of that composition. When he considers disengaging himself from Kate's project and leaving Venice, he has only to cross the threshold "to see all the elements of the business compose, as painters called it, differently," making him out a "gentleman" instead of a "brute." It is the whole "spectacle" which is at work—as on the night of Milly's entertainment to welcome Sir Luke Strett Densher feels it transform everyone present—and which finally takes him in, spirit as well as body. In keeping with it, Milly herself engages in duplicity, telling Lord Mark that Densher is in love with her rather than with Kate. In the end her lie is transformed into the truth.

Like Isabel Archer, Maggie Verver tends in the beginning to romanticize her husband and to conceive of her marriage in static terms. She has a more definite prototype in Martha Valerio, who seems as much in love with her husband's villa as with him, hopes to convert him and refurnish it, and saves her marriage finally by acknowledging that the world in which she made believe is real.

Maggie has been attracted to Amerigo on account of the history of his family, especially the crimes and wicked persons in it and its connection with the Vespuccis. Yet she is unable to recognize either evil when faced with it or Amerigo's American-like desire to be occupied. In the beginning she tends, like her father, to regard Amerigo as part of Mr.

Verver's collection, chiefly formed in Italy, yet to be unwilling to pay for him or to test his value. (At the time Mr. Verver announced his daughter's engagement, he was negotiating for a painting by Bernadino Luini.) In a sense Maggie is also part of her father's collection. She has to him the appearance of an antique statue or figure on a vase, with a mythological or nymph-like air, in the Vatican or the Capitoline Museum. Because of her "long association with nobleness in art," she wears her hair plain regardless of fashion. Father and daughter have, Amerigo thinks, a peculiarly Anglo-Saxon as distinguished from Italian romanticism, theirs being compounded of childlike innocence, excessive imagination, and an undemanding laxity.

Maggie, however, unlike her father, is not ruled by her esthetic sense, and ultimately she makes this sense serve erotic values. She reunites both separated couples by making, after the manner of Milly Theale, large assumptions about them as parts of a beautiful whole. The chief symbol of this relationship in the novel is the golden bowl, which has a vague Italian association. The foreign dealer from whom it comes understands and speaks Italian, though he denies being an Italian. (Like Milly Theale's Eugenio talking to Densher, he speaks English when addressed in Italian and Italian when addressed in English). Maggie's conception of ideal relationships as well as of nobility of character, however, is derived chiefly from her father's collection, and in terms of it the two marriages are reconstituted at her hands. Giving him up for Amerigo, she keeps as if in his place the early Florentine painting which he gave her at the time of her marriage. When on their last afternoon together at Fawns they survey the treasures in the drawing-room, with its "old lustres of Venice," "the whole nobleness" includes the "two noble persons" seated there—Charlotte and Amerigo. The pair fairly "placed" themselves . . . as high expressions of the kind of human furniture required, esthetically, by such a scene. The fusion of their presence with the decorative elements, their contribution to the triumph of selection, was complete and admirable . . . .

When they turn their attention to Maggie and her father, it is "like an ampler submission to the general duty of magnificence." The Ververs' agreements that, as they look at the Florentine painting, "It's all right" and that Maggie has "some good things" are ambiguous in the same way as Milly Theale's exclamation in front of the Bronzino. Like Milly, too, Maggie makes even duplicity serve her vision of beauty and morality, denying to Charlotte her suspicions about Charlotte and Amerigo.

Throughout *The Golden Bowl* a series of figures of speech further link the characters with works of art and architecture —to a greater extent than in any other novel by James. The cinquecento "at its most golden hour" wouldn't have been ashamed of Maggie, Amerigo tells her; he thinks it would have been ashamed of him. To him Charlotte's arms are of the "completely rounded, the polished slimness that Florentine sculptors, in the great time, had loved." The relations between himself, Maggie, and Amerigo, Mr. Verver thinks, may be represented by a public square into which a Palladian church has suddenly been dropped; he is glad Amerigo is not angular, like the Ducal Palace in Venice. Amerigo is most elaborately described in such figures. His eyes are said to resemble "the high windows of a Roman palace, of an historic front by one of the great old designers, thrown open on a feast-day to the golden air," and his look itself is called "some very noble personage who, expected, acclaimed by the crowd in the street and with old precious stuffs falling over the sill for his support, had gaily and gallantly come to show himself," "lighting up brave architecture and diffusing the sense of a function." For his part in the restitution of the marriages, he remains fixed, like a statue of one of his ancestors.

Such images as these tend at first to point up Mr. Verver's static sense, by presenting the chief characters in the novel, as he sees them, as collectors' items. But in the end these images help substantiate Maggie's deeper conception of these characters as superior creations in fact as well as fancy.

Among James' Americans who go to Italy there are, finally, some who have neither positive nor negative experiences of note; who, having little or no sensibility, are not destined to develop radically in any process of self-realization. A few, notably Mrs. Hudson, are frightened in what seems to them a sinister place; but more, like Mr. Leavenworth in *Roderick Hudson* and Randolph Miller, are most impressed by the inferiority of Italian to American culture. Catherine Sloper and Caspar Goodwood are totally unimpressed. Mr. Evans in "Travelling Companions" is most admirable. Mary Garland in *Roderick Hudson* and Henrietta Stackpole in *The Portrait of a Lady* develop to a degree. But Mary, whose pleasure in Rome is chiefly intellectual, shrinks from its "old and complex civilization"; and Henrietta (whose response to the Correggio painting of the Virgin and Child in the Uffizi Gallery is in pointed contrast to Goodwood's and indirectly reflects her growing affection for Mr. Bantling) remains a largely un-Europeanized American. Most of these characters, moreover, appear in James' early fiction. His major, increasing interest was not in depicting the responses of a variety of American types to the Italian environment, but in probing the conflict provoked by the deep involvement of a few.

In his treatment of the international theme in Italian terms, James made relatively slight use of Italian characters. Though the episode which was the source of *The Reverberator* occurred in Venice, he decided against setting his novel either there, in Florence, or in Rome for the reason that the feelings of inhabitants of these cities "are not interesting enough—the race is poor and represents today too little." Yet it is equally significant that he changed his original plan and made the young husband in *The Golden Bowl* an Italian instead of a Frenchman.

Italians appear in some fifteen pieces of his fiction, all in key roles. All—the aristocratic Count Valerio and the Princes Casamassima and Amerigo as well as peasant types like the model Sarafina in "The Madonna of the Future" and Angelo in "Adina"—are intellectually simple. Though there is an air of duplicity about most of them (the pathological liar Mr. Capedose and his wife, significantly, are said to resemble Italian types), it is, rather, an inscrutable neutrality, a histrionic and instrumental character which they have. Miriam Rooth in *The Tragic Muse* studies acting in Italy with an Italian, and the medium-like Verena Tarrant reminds Basil Ransom in *The Bostonians* of an Italian *improvisatrice*. The reference in *The Awkward Age* to the duchess' "old operatic days at Naples" suggests part of the background of the highly trained Agnesina, whose name and manner are belied by her subsequent behavior. Oronte in "The Real Thing" proves to be so good a model because he has "in a wonderful degree the *sentiment de la pose* . . . uncultivated, instinctive." The literal role of instrument or agent is played chiefly by the Cavaliere in *Roderick Hudson,* by Giovanelli in "Daisy Miller," and by Eugenio in *The Wings of the Dove.* Yet in a sense, nearly all James' Italians are agents of the Italian experience itself, allowing it to operate with the greatest effect upon outsiders. The adaptability of these Italians also often makes them foils of those outsiders who become caught between the possibilities and the limits of that experience.

In his late period James was less interested in the social and more in the moral aspects of the international theme than he was in his first treatment of it. The nationality of the characters in *The Wings of the Dove* and *The Golden Bowl* was, he declared, incidental to the subjects of these novels, which were concerned with

the conquests of civilization, the multiplied symptoms among educated people, from wherever drawn, of a common intelligence and a social fusion tending to abridge old rigours of separation . : . . Behind all the small comedies and tragedies of the international . . . has exquisitely lurked for me the idea of some eventually sublime consensus of the educated . . . the personal drama of the future.

Even so, it is significant that the civilization projected in both novels is largely a fusion of Anglo-Saxon and Italian elements, whose relation in all James' Italianate fiction, in fact, adumbrates some such future.

Indeed, when the major pieces of this fiction and a few minor ones are taken as a group, they may be considered a drama of even greater scope, one which follows the progress of man from his dreams of an ideal existence, through his downfall to a redemption of his spirit. Essentially they project the myth of the Fall of Adam and Eve in the Garden of Eden. Equally important, however, are certain motifs—the exaltation of woman, a purgatorial center, and a tendency toward reconciliation—which seem echoes from the account of man's moral development in *La Divina Commedia*.

This Jamesian drama may be said to consist of a prologue and five acts. "Travelling Companions" (1870), "At Isella" (1871), part of *Watch and Ward* (1871), "The Last of the Valerii" (1874), part of *Confidence* (1879), "The Impressions of a Cousin" (1883), "The Solution" (1889–90), and "The Chaperon" (1891) chiefly form the prologue. In it lovers are

united and life is spent contemplating or creating works of art
in an idyllic scene.

In *Roderick Hudson* (1875), which may be regarded as
Act I, the scene, superficially glorious but deeply decayed and
corrupting, is a fallen world. (In this novel the influence of
The Marble Faun on James' treatment of Italian material is
particularly evident.) It is specifically associated with the myths
of man's Fall and Redemption by the subjects of Roderick's
first two statues made in Rome—Adam and Eve—and by the
name of Christina Light. In this novel, James' chief study of
the negative aspects of experience in Italy, the Italian past
looms large and baleful—for almost the only time in his fiction.
An ominous atmosphere is created by descriptions of the ruins
and the old parts of Rome—"weighted with a crushing past,
blighted with the melancholy of things that have had their
day." It is the city of "the artificial element in life and the
infinite superpositions of history," "the immemorial city of
convention." In such a world, the man of the senses is doomed
to fall speedily, and the woman—as the case is—with immature regard for the intellect is fated to support lost causes.
Though less vicious in action or influence than many of James'
characters, Christina is more often than any of them called
"corrupt." Her chief flaw seems to be, like Eve's, her attitude
toward knowledge. Yet detachment from this world, to which
Mary Garland is inclined and which Rowland Mallet at last
urges upon her, does not appear as the solution to the problem
which it poses.

The sequel to Christina's story as told in *Roderick Hudson,
The Princess Casamassima* (1886), involves two futile attempts
at atonement on behalf of a fallen world. In this novel the
modern age is distinguished for its social and political ferment
(as seen in London) and its betrayal of the sensuous nature of
man (represented by the art of Paris and Venice). Convinced
that the Italian race and European society in general are

decadent, Christina seeks to make amends for the "frivolity" of her marriage to Prince Casamassima by being "serious" the rest of her life and so joins the revolutionary movement. On the other hand, Hyacinth Robinson (who, like Christina, is the offspring of an illegitimate union and who has a nature warped by the age) comes to regard the cultures which produce great art as the superior ones and to defect from that movement. His "demoralization" begins when he meets Christina and is completed in Venice, where he writes her his long account of the illumination he has there and in Paris. In these places he is happier than ever in his life except at Medley, Christina's estate. They show him how misery can be redeemed by art, by "the great achievements of which man has been capable," by

the conquest of learning and taste, the general fabric of civilization as we know it, based if you will, upon all the despotisms, the cruelties, the exclusion, the monopolies and the rapacities of the past, but thanks to which, all the same, the world is less impracticable and life more tolerable.

His suicide is a gesture toward the preservation of this redeeming force in the world.

The Portrait of a Lady (1881), James' chief study of temptation and purgation, forms the central act of his drama about man's moral history. Whereas the atmosphere of Italy goes to Roderick's head immediately, Isabel Archer takes it in slowly, goes away and returns before finally succumbing, in the general pattern of Eve's experience in *Paradise Lost*. Isabel's temptation, moreover, like that of Adam and Eve, involves the issues of knowledge and freedom. In the novel, however, the Italian scene most resembles Dante's Earthly Paradise, for though the corruption lurking there is compound (in the natures of Osmand and Madame Merle), the means of redemption are at hand. Isabel does not so much atone for that corruption as expiate her own mistake. Its venial nature, the fact that she not only assents to but assumes her punishment, and her sense that life—not renunciation—"would be her business for a long time to come," all give her experience an association with Purgatory, the great middle, terrestrial estate. Ground as she is "in the very mill of the conventional," as Ralph puts it, she chooses, in the light of the knowledge disseminated by the scene around her, even less freedom than she can have. It is the only choice possible if the Tree of Knowledge is to prove the Tree of Life.

In James' last two Italian novels, acts of atonement or reconciliation are again performed in a corrupt world, this time efficaciously. In *The Wings of the Dove* (1902) Milly Theale is cast particularly in the role of intercessor or mediator for the delinquent Densher. She not only saves his reputation, most importantly with Mrs. Lowder, by her assertion that he is in love with her, but by her death and bequest she removes temptation from him. At the same time her death is in effect a penalty exacted by his sin. The image of a dove, to which she is persistently compared, suggests the Paraclete of the Trinity, sent from Heaven after the death of the Son. The fact that her letter to Densher announcing her gift to him arrives on Christmas Eve (by which time she is dead) further associates her with Christian mythology and also contributes to the image of her—remote, elevated, clad in white as she is during the last weeks of her life—as removed from earth, exalted, transfigured. Without her, the Venetian scene means nothing; the storm breaks with her knowledge of her betrayal and her turn for the worse. At this point in the Jamesian drama, indeed, the scene seems about to shift to another world altogether, as Dante's does at the end of the *Purgatorio*.

In *The Golden Bowl* (1904)—the final act of James' drama of human destiny—the scene does shift from the Eden of Italy but not in the direction of Paradise. Amerigo, a "modern

Roman" who finds in London "a more convincing image of the truth of the ancient state" than in Rome, is a postlapsarian Adam. His Italian palace, villa, and castle, encumbered though they are with mortgages, are the "brightest spots of his lost paradise," "the ever-to-be-loved Italy." He seeks in his marriage to Maggie Verver, however, not so much financial security as the means of achieving a "new history," without the vices and superstitions of his race. The Ververs (Adam's name is noteworthy) are, on the other hand, prelapsarian in their ignorance of evil and in their idleness, and they exert a retrogressive influence on Amerigo. He blushes at the thought of accompanying Charlotte, as they seem to assume that he does, in a state of "childlike innocence, the state of our primitive parents before the Fall." In this pattern, Charlotte corresponds to Lilith. Maggie rises, however, to the role of a new Eve. The discovery of evil has almost exclusively beneficent effects on her. It makes her, in Mrs. Assingham's words, "decide to live"—precisely the opposite of the way it affects Milly Theale. It leads her to make overdue breaks with the past, takes her into the world, and, most important of all, arouses both her passion for her husband and his for her. The conclusion of James' drama about man's moral development is not the regaining of Paradise but the beginning of another cycle of life on another stage, played out by characters of moral sensibility and intellect, representing the best elements in the Old and the New worlds.

Italy thus remained for James supremely the scene of man's crucial moral conflict, the turning point in his history. There he was confronted in fullest measure with the ambiguities of experience—of freedom and discipline, innocence and knowledge, good and evil—and with mortal choices. For all its resemblance to the Earthly Paradise, it was not an ideal abode, and even at best it was one for man in his maturity to pass beyond. It was the Eden of his history.

The experience of Americans, especially artists and writers, in Europe, particularly in Italy, occupied James' attention to a considerable degree in his non-fiction : in his biographies of Hawthorne and Story, a few reviews of books by Hawthorne and Howells, and several prefaces to his own works. As an American abroad, he was highly conscious of belonging to a group. As one of the first Americans to go to Europe after the Civil War, particularly to go to Italy after the unification of that country, he thought of himself as a late comer. He often referred wistfully to the "old" Italy which he had not seen and half-envied the pre-1860 travellers, the "precursors," who lived at the "pure and precious time," "the dawn of the American consciousness of the complicated world it was so persistently to annex." His *William Wetmore Story and his Friends* (1904) is in effect a biography of them all. Among those he treated most substantially were Allston, Thomas Gold Appleton, Christopher Pearse Cranch, Thomas Crawford, Jasper Cropsey, George William Curtis, the Greenoughs, Hawthorne, Miss Hosmer, Longfellow, Lowell, William Page, Powers, and Margaret Fuller Ossoli.

These writers and artists interested James most of all as representing different types of American experience abroad, as "cases," as he often called them. As he depicted it, the Italian experience of most of them was not altogether fructifying. This fact itself, in view of the glamour with which he invested this experience in the abstract, invited inquiry into the "case" of the whole group. Though he did not front this fact, he provided a general explanation of it. Many of those mentioned in his life of Story, he several times intimated, had minor talents, which perhaps no environment would have developed. Cranch was typical of them, one of the "precursors of the purest water, whose portion was ever to tread the path rather than arrive at the goal."

Yet such was Italy, James declared, that not since Claude

had any northerner there achieved "the grand style." Though it was "the aesthetic antidote to the ugliness of the rest of the world—that is, of Anglo-Saxondom in especial," it was also a "Borgia cup concocted for the strenuous mind," offering so many stimuli that the mind could not withdraw into its own life. Rare ones like the German historian Gregorovius managed merely to taste "the insidious liquor," but "the sensitive soul in general drained" the cup, with fatal results. Indeed, a certain "too much . . . constituted precisely, and most characteristically and gracefully, the amusement of the wanton Italy at the expense of her victim." (In his life of Story James also described this combined charm and fatality in Italy by references to the Garden of Eden.)

To James, Story was the prime example among the Americans of the "consenting victim of Italy," of the "old-time victim . . . not of any mere colourless fugitive from the Philistines." Going to Italy in mid-life to begin the profession of sculpture without any formal training, Story tried to substitute for the discipline of such training, as James saw it, the multitude of "impressions" there. The result was that he failed to concentrate his talent and became "the prey of mere beguilement." His career was

a sort of beautiful sacrifice to a noble mistake . . . that of the frank consent to be beguiled. It is for all the world, as if there were always, for however earnest a man, some seed of danger in consciously planning for happiness, and a seed quite capable of sprouting even when the plan has succeeded. To have said "No— I give up everything else for a lifetime of the golden air; the golden air is *the* thing, no matter what others may be, and to have had it, all there is of it, that alone, for me, won't have been failure" : to have expressed one's self in that sense, which was practically what Story did, was to make one's bid for felicity about as straight as possible.

Yet this very "golden air" of Italy was in James' analysis

ultimately responsible for Story's fate. It tended, James felt, to undermine the writer's whole "relation to his subject," especially if that subject were a "picturesque" one. Such a subject was best treated outside a "picturesque" country like Italy, "in some air unfriendly to the element at large." Judging Story's poetic talent as greater than his talent for sculpture, James thought Story might have been a better poet had he remained in America. He should have written a better "Ginevra da Siena," for example, in Boston or even in London, because there "he would have *had* to live with his conception, there being nothing else about him of the same color or quality." Excepting Browning in this discussion, James suggested that partly because this poet was the practitioner of only one art, he had an unusually "stout and single" relation to his subject. Another American artist in Italy who, James thought, suffered there from lack of discipline was the painter William Page.

James puzzled for years over his own difficulty with literary composition in Italy. Recalling his "divided, frustrated mind" while working on *The Portrait of a Lady* in Venice, he concluded in his preface that such "romantic and historic sites" as this country abounded in "are too rich in their own life and too charged with their own meanings" to help the writer in a particular way. The "presence of the moderate and the neutral, to which we may lend something of the light of our vision," he thought was more likely to do so. The "strong Venetian voice, full of history and humanity and waking perpetual echoes," which came to him from a neighboring court while he worked on *A London Life,* "seemed to say more in ten warm words, of whatever tone, than twenty pages of one's cold pale prose." Of necessity, he wrote most of his Italianate fiction outside Italy.

James credited Longfellow with more success than other Americans in harmonizing his American and European experience—to such an extent, in fact, that the effect was a "fine

. . . ambiguity." One could hardly tell whether his "liberal existence" was a piece of the Old World fitted into the New or a piece of the New fitted into the Old.

Of all these early Americans abroad, Hawthorne interested James most and pleased him best with work inspired by Italy. With his "provincial" quality, the limitations of his esthetic sense, his painful discomfort on account of "the usual accidents of Italian life," Hawthorne was "the last of the old-fashioned Americans," he declared. Yet this very provincialism constituted for him Hawthorne's peculiar appeal. "We seem to see him," James wrote, reviewing Hawthorne's *French and Italian Note-Books,*

strolling through churches and galleries as the last pure American — attesting by his shy responses to dark canvas and cold marble his loyalty to a simpler and less encumbered civilization.

Considering the age at which Hawthorne went abroad, James thought "the striking thing" was "not what he missed but what he so ingeniously and vividly made out." For all the flaws in *The Marble Faun,* James declared that

Nothing is more striking than the awkward grace with which the author utters . . . the message, the mystery of the medium in which his actors move . . . the breath of old Rome, the sense of old Italy, still meet us as we turn the page, and the book will long, on the great sentimental journey, continue to peep out of most pockets.

The whole episode in which Miriam first sees Kenyon's *Cleopatra* and Kenyon describes his conception of this work was apparently more evocative for James, as he intimated in *William Wetmore Story and his Friends,* than Story's statue itself.

James wrote complimentarily about Howells' Italian novels and travel books—both in printed essays and in letters to Howells himself. He left it significantly open, however, to what extent Howells was affected by his Italian experience. Praising *A Foregone Conclusion* for its departure from the romantic and the Gothic traditions and for its American quality, James wrote in his review of this work for the *Nation,* with perhaps unintentional irony, that the author "takes Italy as no Italian surely ever took it—as your enterprising Yankee alone is at pains to take it." Again with a suggestion of double-entendre, in an essay in *Harper's Weekly* in 1886, James deplored the fact that there was nothing in Howells' recent fiction— *The Rise of Silas Lapham, Dr. Breen's Practice, A Modern Instance,* and *The Undiscovered Country*—

to suggest that its author had at one time either wooed the lyric Muse or surrendered himself to those Italian initiations without which we of other countries remain always, after all, more or less barbarians.

Apparently James recognized in Howells another type of American provincial in Italy, with far less capability than Hawthorne for transcending his limitations.

The "case" of Allston was that of the American artist frustrated by his return to America, "the American who has bitten deep into the apple, as we may figure it, of 'Europe,' " James wrote in his life of Story, "and then has been obliged to take his lips from the fruit." Prompted by Story's statement in a letter to Lowell that

Allston starved spiritually in Cambridgeport; he fed upon himself. There was nothing congenial without, and he turned all his powers inward and drained his memory dry,

James recollected the impression made on him by Allston's unfinished painting *Belshazzar's Feast,* which he saw during the early 1870's at the Boston Athenaeum. It was, he thought, both "the mask of some impenetrable inward strain" and "the fact of Italy." Afterward as he had walked home through Cambridgeport, he had engaged himself "with the remorseless analysis of the quiet painter's nostalgia" and the thought of how much finer Allston's experience—in the older Italy— must have been than his own. "To have seen," he speculated, what in his divine *Wanderjahre,* he had seen, and to see, that period ended, what he did see—verily the intensity of the latter experience on one's own part acted creatively in one's own mind, in respect to the former.

In the winter of 1869–70, as James debated with himself in Cambridge whether or not to return to Europe, he thought of himself as following in Story's footsteps rather than Allston's. So he was, in making his permanent residence abroad. Yet it was Allston's Italian experience which his own came to resemble more closely. Like Allston—and like Hawthorne— he produced his Italy-inspired work for the most part in a more northerly land, assisted largely by memory.

This long-distance, retrospective engagement with the Italian scene was, indeed, the one which proved most fruitful for early American writers and artists alike. Of all the works inspired by this scene during the period of its discovery by both these groups, the most beautiful and original were the paintings of Allston and the fiction of Hawthorne and James.

VII

The Young American in the Italian Life School

THE INFLUENCE OF *The Marble Faun* ON SUBSEQUENT American novels and stories laid in Italy has been powerful and long-lasting. Preceded by six such novels in four decades, it was followed by four in six years, and early in the next decade by the first Italian fiction of Howells and James. Most of the authors of these later works were indebted to Hawthorne's. Indeed, Americans writing novels laid in Italy have continued down to the present to take his work as something of a model.

Yet *The Marble Faun* crystallized rather than originated a pattern. This pattern began to emerge in the first American fiction inspired by Italy—Allston's. First fully apparent in that of Tuckerman (though not fully in a single work), it was most elaborated in that of James. Except in Howells and James, it largely gave place to other patterns in this fiction after 1870.

The central character in nearly all the Italianate fiction of the American literary discoverers of Italy is either an artist—usually a youth—or a young girl, nearly always from America. In the earliest of these works—Allston's and Irving's—the central characters are Italian or French artists. A young girl is first given experience in Italy in Cooper's *Water-Witch* and first depicted there in Tuckerman's *Isabel*. An American artist

249

in Italy, appearing first in a story by Tuckerman, is first treated fully by Willis in *Paul Fane*. The two types are combined only once, in Hawthorne's Hilda. Most of the central characters after her are young American girls.

Both these character types are engaged in the same general process : that of learning, either in connection with a profession or in coming to maturity. The Americans are almost uniformly cast in the role of learners. The artists have gone to Italy to study art. Most of the girls are in effect finishing their education by taking the Grand Tour, and many of them marry at the conclusion of their Italian visits. Both groups are to a considerable extent amateur students of history, chiefly as it is commemorated in art and architecture. A general emphasis on semi-formal education, in fact, distinguishes all this fiction from most other American fiction based on travels, at home or abroad.

To a great extent this whole pattern represents the experience which the writers of this Italianate fiction had in Italy. All but four—Cooper, Hawthorne, Mrs. Stowe, and Miss Brewster—were in their twenties when they first went there. Tuckerman, Howells, and James definitely entered the profession of letters in consequence of their first visit, and the literary careers of nearly all the others were vitally affected by their Italian experience.

The chief acquaintances of these writers in Italy were American artists, most of whom had gone there to study. Nearly half the writers themselves—Allston, Irving, Willis, Henry Greenough, and Leland—either were art students or considered becoming artists while in Italy. Three others— Hawthorne, Mrs. Greenough, and Howells—were married to professional or amateur artists.

Young American girls in Italy were also familiar to these writers. Several were members of their own parties : the daughters of Cooper and of Mrs. Stowe, the Hawthorne children's governess, Howells' sister-in-law.

The fictional young learners depicted by these writers are, however, not so much drawn from life as symbolic of intellectual and moral experience. The American artists, who are most obviously students, learn most in Italy about matters other than art. Paul Fane finds out about society, Ernest Carroll enjoys congenial company, James Caper explores unconventional life, Roderick Hudson experiences extremes of sensation. Only Hilda devotes much time to art, and what she learns most about is the nature of evil. For them all, Italy is more of a life school than an academy.

The young girls in Italy, whatever their nationality, are even more clearly symbolic than the artists. Most of them are natural, innocent types, confronted for the first time with high civilization and with evil. It is particularly significant that in two of the three historical novels in this body of fiction prominent roles are played by young Italian girls who are comparable to the American girls in Italy: Gelsomina in Cooper's *Bravo* and Agnes in Mrs. Stowe's *Agnes of Sorrento*.

The chief literary progenitor of all these young girls is the romantic child of nature, brought up without knowledge of the world of men. But whereas the typical child of nature is fatally affected by contact with the world, the young girls are generally matured by it. The chief intellectual influence on this aspect of their characterization, evidenced in numerous allusions to the Garden of Eden story, seems to have been the myth of the Fortunate Fall. Two other influences were also formative: the Italian landscape, where nature is intergrown with the works of men to an exceptional degree, and the professional activities of art students. It is noteworthy that the landscape is more prominent in connection with the young girls than with the artists. Its historical associations, moreover, receive more emphasis than its purely naturalistic aspect. Cooper's Eudora van Beverout and Eve Effingham are particularly impressed by it. The learning experience which the young girls as a group have in Italy, however, is most distinctively patterned after that of art students. As a group, they are, in fact, more interested in the works of art there than are the artists. The greatest growth of the girls comes about through the agency of these works or is described in figures of speech drawn from them.

The chief function of works of art in the education of these young girls is to lead them fruitfully beyond nature, offering interpretations of human experience in general and in particular compensating for the existence of evil. The young girls of Howells, who are least reconciled to their moral discoveries in Italy, have hardly any interest in such works, and those of James, who develop most as a result of their Italian experience, have the closest association with them. Isabel Otley, first to be conscious of a disparity between nature and society in Italy, hopes the triumph of the Risorgimento will make the latter as agreeable as the former, apparently judging Italians chiefly by what she sees of their past artistic and architectural achievements. Even Hawthorne's Hilda, who in her deepest disillusionment is not consoled by the paintings in the Roman galleries, has access through them to a realm superior to sin and sorrow.

In the last analysis, works of art appear in this fiction as witnesses to a life beyond both nature and the world, though not in conflict with nature. It is noteworthy that sculpture is somewhat more prominent than painting. Particular statues in Italian collections are of key importance in the stories of Hilda, Agnes, Lilian, Venitia Howard, and Isabel Archer. The emphasis probably reflects the great vogue for sculpture at this period, exemplified by the greater number of American sculptors than painters living in Italy. Nevertheless this art's realistic three-dimensional character, the human nature of most of its subjects, and the heroic subjects of most of the antique specimens made it peculiarly useful to the writers of this fiction. Here statues and busts in effect connect the realms of physical and of intellectual or spiritual life, of the temporary and the permanent.

A third character type, in contrast to both the artist and the young girl, appears in much of the first body of Italy-inspired American fiction : the practical American Yankee, at best intelligent and tolerant though unimaginative, at worst aggressive, mercenary, and chauvinistic. First seen in the character of Cooper's Steadfast Dodge, who is drawn after his visit to Italy, the type is first depicted there in Tuckerman's Clifford Frazier. Other representatives of it are Cooper's Ithuel Bolt, Leland's William Browne and sculptor Chapin, and several characters of Howells and James, notably Howells' Clay Hoskins and James' Caspar Goodwood and Adam Verver. Most of these characters are men, and a few, ironically, are artists. Generally unchanged by their contact with the Italian scene, they tend to be highly critical of it. It should be noted, moreover, that several of the novels in which this type does not appear contain references to it or to the set of values it embodies.

The nationality of all these fictional Americans in Italy is an important aspect of their characterization. Theirs is pointedly an American experience. Collectively they represent the consciousness of the youthful nation as it seeks both to take its place among the mature nations of the world and to maintain an individuality of its own. By means of these characters, in fact, the authors of this fiction to a great extent analyzed the American national character, pointing out what in their opinion were its chief faults and its greatest strength, and criticized the general pattern of American life, finding in it certain large vacuities.

The chief faults of the American national character appear in the Yankee types. Their worst trait is their satisfaction with themselves, both as individuals and as Americans, which cuts off their development altogether. The most obviously American of all the American characters, they are as a group isolationists at heart.

The greatest strength attributed to the American character is that embodied in the young girls: an innocence compounded with knowledge. Their sex is in this connection especially appropriate. The Christian name of Eve Effingham —the first American-bred young person of either sex said to have visited Italy—is significant. She is a new Eve, uncorrupted by what she learns of the world abroad. She is also the first of a new species in American fiction—the American who is a citizen of the world.

At the same time, one of the chief criticisms made of American life is a moral one. It is significant that the knowledge which is joined to the innocence of the young girls is acquired abroad and that for the most part their strength of character is developed there. Many arrive on foreign soil with a naïve disregard for the operation of evil which is patently American and which proves not only unrealistic but painfully misleading. For Daisy Miller and Milly Theale it proves fatal. The pattern of life in America, it would seem, fails to provide adequate exercise of the moral faculty.

The pattern of American life as seen in this fiction consists, in fact, almost exclusively of activities related to commercial enterprises. The Yankee types miss such enterprises most in Italy and disparage that country chiefly because of their absence there. On the other hand, the artists and young girls are supremely delighted in Italy to find open before them virtually every realm of human activity except commercialism —society, history, religion, art—all interrelated. In Italy both groups of characters acquire above everything else a sense of life—of a palpable, exciting, complex whole—unavailable to them in America.

The particular foreign scene visited by all these Americans has an important bearing on both their characterization and their learning experience. The philosophy of *dolce far niente* and the prevailing esthetic standard of values in Italy are the antitheses of the aggressiveness and the mercenary interests characterizing American culture. In contrast to the scene about them, the Yankee types in Italy appear joyless and their professional activities fruitless.

For the American learners, Italy would seem to be a uniquely instructive school. Its civilization is the oldest that is still vigorous in the western world, whereas theirs is the youngest. Its art collections are the largest, as the artists had known before they went. Its moral atmosphere, as the young girls especially discover, is exceptionally dense, on account of the pervasive influence of the Roman Catholic Church and the acute conflict between ethical ideals and practices.

The greatest distinction of Italy as a school of instruction seems to be the unparalelled extent to which human experience has been objectified there. The chief examples given of this objectification are the ruins, the works of art, and the institution of the Church. It is also exemplified by certain behavior patterns of Italians, who in their ready expression of feeling are seen as types of human nature rather than as nationals and whose genius for pantomime is displayed even in everyday situations. It is indeed almost entirely a visual education which the American learners receive in Italy, cut off as they are from much of Italian life by the barrier of language. Yet this education is one which meets them on every hand and which transcends national boundaries. Italy is for them above all a school of life.

The education which they receive in Italy does not, however, denationalize these Americans. Delightful as they find this country, few decide to remain there. Though many regard Italians romantically, few American-Italian marriages are made; the most notable are the first, that of Isabel Otley to Count Vittorio, and the last, that of Maggie Verver to Prince Amerigo. The ultimate knowledge which these Americans obtain in Italy is self-knowledge. It is knowledge which is clearly applicable, moreover, to the collective American experience, particularly in its attempt to define itself.

All these visitors to Italy are, in the last analysis, part of the large group of Americans in nineteenth-century American fiction who travel both within and outside their country. Prominent among the others are Poe's A. Gordon Pym, Melville's sailors, and Clemens' boys on the Mississippi. As a group they all are, in effect, in search of knowledge that may illumine the American situation, isolated as it is both geographically and psychically. The destination most often sought among them is Italy. The experiences of Americans there, moreover, is on the whole more widely illuminating and more deeply satisfying than it is elsewhere. Whereas many of the other travellers are motivated by a desire to escape and disturbed by a sense of alienation, nearly all those who go to Italy engage themselves with history or society, often painfully but most of the time to their edification and their pleasure. As American Adams and Eves, they emerge at the end of their travels with not only an enlightened innocence but the sense of a delightfulness in human experience that is commensurate with its pain.

The experience of most of these fictional American travel-

Elihu Vedder, KATE FIELD. Florence, 1860.
(*From Vedder's* The Digressions of V.)

William Page, SOPHIE CANDACE STEVENS PAGE. Rome, *ca.*
1860.
(Courtesy of The Detroit Institute of Arts)

Frank Duveneck and Clement Barnhorn, MEMORIAL TO ELIZABETH BOOTT
DUVENECK. Cincinnati? *ca.* 1891.
Allori Cemetery, Florence.

William James Hubard, HORATIO GREENOUGH, THE AMERI-
CAN SCULPTOR, IN HIS STUDIO IN FLORENCE. Florence,
1839.
(Courtesy of The Valentine Museum, Richmond, Virginia)

John Gadsby Chapman, J. G. C. IN HIS STUDIO. Rome, 1881.
(Courtesy of The Valentine Museum, Richmond, Virginia)

lers in Italy largely reflects that of their creators. These writers, too, were representatives of young America at school in Italy. Probably the student status of many of their friends among the artists there made them conscious of their own similar status. In any event, what they learned in Italy vitally affected their development as literary artists, particularly as American literary artists.

In Italy the imagination of these writers was stimulated chiefly by complexities of human experience, the like of which did not exist in America. Had he been interested only in nature, Irving wrote in *The Sketch-Book,* he might never have gone abroad, since no country equalled America in scenic richness. "But Europe," he added,

held forth all the charms of storied and poetical association. There were to be seen the masterpieces of art, the refinements of highly cultivated society, the quaint peculiarities of ancient and local custom. My native country was full of youthful promise; Europe was rich in the accumulated treasures of age. Her very ruins told the history of times gone by and every mouldering stone was a chronicle. I longed to wander over the scenes of renowned achievement—to tread, as it were, in the footsteps of antiquity— to loiter about the ruined castle—to meditate on the falling tower—to escape, in short, from the commonplace realities of the present, and lose myself among the shadowy grandeurs of the past.

He was describing to a great extent what all these writers found abroad, for the most part in Italy. When Hawthorne complained, in his preface to *The Marble Faun,* of

the difficulty of writing a romance about a country where there is no shadow, no antiquity, no mystery, no picturesque and gloomy wrong, nor anything but a commonplace prosperity, in broad and simple daylight, as is happily the case with my dear native land, he implied that he had found in Italy a country satisfactory to his purpose. James, commenting on this passage in his life of Hawthorne, declared:

It takes so many things, as Hawthorne must have felt later in life, when he made the acquaintance of the denser, richer, warmer European spectacle—it takes such an accumulation of history and custom, such a complexity of manners and types to form a fund of suggestion for a novelist.

He, too, found the richest such fund in Italy.

More particularly the imagination of these writers was stimulated by the visual arts, of which there were few specimens in America. Those they saw in Italy proved richly "procreative," as Allston put it. The experience of these writers, in fact, suggests that the development of a vigorous literature in America waited in part on the availablity of a variety of visual as well as of intellectual stimuli.

Most of these writers were convinced or reassured in Italy, moreover, that a work of art was essentially ideal in nature. With all their respect for observed phenomena and their interest in the novelties of the foreign scene, they went ultimately beyond these externals in their Italianate fiction. A few, notably Cooper, were permanently influenced in this direction. It is particularly interesting that the two who wrote historical novels laid in Italy—Cooper and Mrs. Stowe—as well as Hawthorne, disavowed any intention of dealing strictly with fact, and that both Hawthorne and Mrs. Stowe declared that they had sought to create a "fairy" or ideal realm in their Italianate works. It is notable, too, that though most of these writers were sympathetic with the contemporaneous movement for Italian independence, none treated it directly in fiction.

Herman Melville spoke for most of these writers in his lecture "Statues in Rome," based on his sight-seeing in that city in 1857, when he emphasized the ideality of art as represented by those works. They were, he said, "the true and undying population" of Rome, the chief "representatives of the mighty past," which often supplied information wanting in histories. Milton, he thought, must have been inspired by some of them in his descriptions of the fallen angels in *Paradise Lost*. "These marbles," he declared,

the works of the dreamers and idealists of old, live on, leading and pointing to good. They are the representation of the ideal. They are grand, beautiful, and true, and they speak with a voice that echoes through the ages. Governments have changed; empires have fallen; nations have passed away; but these mute marbles remain — the oracles of time, the perfection of art. They were formed by those who had yearnings for something better, and strove to attain it by embodiments in cold stone. We can ourselves judge with what success they have worked. How well in the Apollo is expressed the idea of the perfect man. Who could better it? Can art, not life, make the ideal?

He thought that all the "triumphs" of the modern world, scientific as most of them were, could not "equal those of the heroes and divinities that stand there silent, the incarnation of grandeur and of beauty." "The ancients of the ideal description," he concluded,

instead of trying to turn their impracticable chimeras, as does the modern dreamer, into social and political prodigies, deposited them in great works of art, which still live while states and constitutions have perished, bequeathing to posterity not shameful defects but triumphant successes.

In Italy most of these writers learned, too, the peculiar usefulness of symbolism for transmitting both complex and inner experience. Natural as this technique apparently was to them as Americans and inclined as some of them were to employ it before they went to Italy, they found the greatest use for it in their Italianate fiction. There, too, they found art objects most useful as symbols. In the other fiction of some of these writers—notably Cooper and Hawthorne—and in that of other Americans of this period, symbols are derived to a great extent from nature. As a group the Americans who came under Italian influence learned, in effect, to carry on a conversation about the nature and the history of man by using some of his artistic achievements as locutions. At its best, it was a conversation of economy and sophistication.

In the last analysis, these writers belong to the company of all other American writers of the period who were travellers, in their own country or abroad, and who projected their travels in their writing. Most of the others and some of these— notably Melville, Clemens, Parkman, and Whitman—moved generally in the opposite direction from Europe : westward with the frontier and even as far as the Pacific islands. All these writers, however, had a common impulse. They sought both knowledge and the material of art in geographical exploration. A smaller number of writers of this period— Irving, Cooper, Simms, Hawthorne, Longfellow, and several of the "literary" historians, for example—explored the past with the same ends in view, and endeavored to make their country's history at once more substantial and more legendary. To those who went to Italy, both dimensions were available. They made a journey in space and in time—almost as far in time as it was possible to go among historical remains. They returned with a greater comprehension of the habitable scene and of history, of that which their country possessed most abundantly and that which it most notably lacked. They returned, in short, with knowledge of the scope of a fully civilized society.

Sources of Quotations

PRELIMINARY PAGES

15: *The Writings of James Russell Lowell* (Boston, 1893), I, 123–25.

CHAPTER II

WASHINGTON ALLSTON

38: William Dunlap, *A History of the Rise and Progress of the Arts of Design in the United States* (N. Y., 1834), II, 156, 163.

38–39: Jared B. Flagg, *The Life and Letters of Washington Allston* (N. Y., 1892), pp. 292, 319.

39–40: *Lectures on Art, and Poems* (N. Y., 1850), pp. 158, 327, 377–79.

41–43: *Monaldi* (Boston, 1841), pp. [7], 23, 24, 29, 65, 19–21, 82-84, 177.

WASHINGTON IRVING

45: Evert A. Duyckinck, *Cyclopaedia of American Literature* (N. Y., 1855), II, 14–15.

45–47: *Notes and Journal of Travel in Europe, 1804–1805* (N. Y., 1921), II, 19–21, 24–25, 10–11, 4, 60, 26.

48–50: *The Works of Washington Irving* (N.Y., 1860–61), XIV, 317–18, 111, 378; XIII, 19.

HENRY T. TUCKERMAN

53: *Maga Papers about Paris* (N. Y., 1854), p. 159; *A Month in England* (N. Y., 1854), p. 159; *Poems* (Boston, 1851), p. 171.

53–54: *The Italian Sketch Book* (Philadelphia, 1835), pp. 174, 214–15.

54: *Rambles and Reveries* (N. Y., 1841), pp. 385–86, 399.

54–55: *The Italian Sketch Book* (Philadelphia, 1835), p. 193; (Boston, 1837), p. 219; (N. Y., 1848), pp. 420-23.

55: *The Optimist* (N. Y., 1850), p. 1.

57: *The Criterion* (N. Y., 1866), p. 46.

58–60: *Isabel* (Philadelphia, 1839), pp. 14–17, 87, 179.

60: *Leaves from the Diary of a Dreamer* (London, 1853), pp. 35, 64, 1, 51, 67, 66.

THEODORE S. FAY

61, 63: *The New-York Mirror*, XII (July 1834–June 1835), 4, 14, 282, 38, 52, 141, 293, 196, 390, 388, 61.

64–70: *Norman Leslie* (N. Y., 1835), II, 35, 145, 83–84, 83, 190; I, 14, 15; II, 37, 35, 36, 38; I, 15; II, 166, 46, 47, 96–97, 79, 84–85, 127, 68, 25–26, 57, 119.

71: *The New–York Mirror*, XIII (July 1835–June 1836), 149.

NATHANIEL PARKER WILLIS

73–74: *Pencillings by the Way* (N.Y., 1844), pp. 178, 173, 79.

75: *Melanie and Other Poems* (N. Y., 1837), p. 6.

76–77: *Dashes at Life with a Free Pencil* (N. Y., 1845), pp. 28, 95.

78: *Paul Fane* (N. Y., 1857), pp. 20, 182, 389.

HENRY GREENOUGH

81: *Ernest Carroll* (Boston, 1858), pp. 170, 101.

SARAH LORING GREENOUGH

84: *Lilian* (Boston, 1863), pp. 188–90.

HARRIET BEECHER STOWE

88: Charles Edward Stowe, *Life of Harriet Beecher Stowe* (Boston, 1890), pp. 300–301; *Life and Letters of Harriet Beecher Stowe*, ed. Annie Fields (Boston, 1897), p. 257; "Letters from Mrs. Stowe in Europe. No. III. The First Day in Rome," *The Independent*, IX (April 23, 1857), [1].

91: *Life and Letters of Harriet Beecher Stowe*, p. 285.

92–102: *The Writings of Harriet Beecher Stowe* (Boston, 1896), VII, ix, 257, 69, 167–68, 276, 137, 72, 83, 27, 118, 108, 71, 115, 275–78, 88, 142, 110, 97, 110, 51, 52; V, 353, 16, 69; X, 211; XII, 199.

HENRY P. LELAND

105–107: *Americans in Rome* (N. Y., 1863), pp. 4, [3], [9], 158, 124, 60, 123, 307, 308, 311. (Leland's passport, sketchbooks, and drawings are at The Historical Society of Pennsylvania, Philadelphia.)

ANNE HAMPTON BREWSTER

108: *Diary,* April 16, 26, 1858 (Library Company of Philadelphia).

110: *Diary,* May 10, 1858; *St. Martin's Summer* (N. Y., 1866), p. v; *Diary,* March 20, 1858.

112–114: *St. Martin's Summer,* pp. 224, 10, 43, 306, 101, 390, 154, 102.

CHAPTER III

JAMES FENIMORE COOPER

115: *Sketches of Switzerland* (Philadelphia, 1836), II, 217.

116: *The Letters and Journals of James Fenimore Cooper,* ed. James F. Beard (Cambridge, 1960), I, 361, 424, 425; II, 18; I, 425; *Gleanings from Europe: Italy* (Philadelphia, 1838), II, 211.

117: *The Letters and Journals of . . . Cooper,* II, 75, 80. *Gleanings . . . Italy,* II, 235, 234; *The Letters and Journals of . . . Cooper,* I, 418; II, 371; II, 335, 368; Cooper to Greenough, Aug. 9, 1836 (David Richardson, Washington, D.C.); R. E. Spiller, *Fenimore Cooper Critic of his Times* (N. Y., 1931), p. 148.

117–118: *Correspondence of James Fenimore–Cooper* (New Haven, 1922), I, 71.

118–121: *Gleanings . . . Italy,* I, 137, 215, 181, 182, 152, 54, 180, 203; II, 238, 20, 34–35, 38, 32, 156, 154, 8, 40–41.

126: *The Works of James Fenimore Cooper* (N. Y., 1895–1900), XXIII, 4.

128: *A Letter to his Countrymen* (N. Y., 1834), pp. 24, 15, 12, 15.

128–137: *The Works of . . . Cooper,* XXIII, 361, 313, iv, 16, 44, 53, 35, 245, 293, 301; XXX, 371; XIII, 286; XIV, 169; XIII, 290, 201; IX, 104; *Autobiography of a Pocket-Handkerchief,* ed. Walter

Lee Brown (Evanston, Ill., 1907), p. 208; *The Works of . . . Cooper,* XXV, 506; XII, 237; I, 224.

CHAPTER IV

NATHANIEL HAWTHORNE

139: "The French and Italian Notebooks by Nathaniel Hawthorne," ed. Norman H. Pearson (Yale Dissertation, 1941), II, 65; Hawthorne to Pierce, Oct. 27, 1858 (New Haven Historical Society); Hawthorne to Fields, Feb. 3, 1859 (Huntington Library, San Marino, Calif.)

139–140: "The French and Italian Notebooks . . . ," II, 277; III, 611; II, 339, 386, 346, 345.

140: Hawthorne to Fields, Sept. 3, 1858 (Huntington Library).

140–142: "The French and Italian Notebooks . . . ," III, 543, 551, 579; II, 418; III, 641–42, 657.

142: Hawthorne to Fields, Feb. 3, 1859.

142–143: *The Complete Works of Nathaniel Hawthorne* (Boston, 1883), VI, 16; VII, 256.

143–149: "The French and Italian Notebooks . . . ," III, 574; II, 229, 302, 606; II, 309, 393–94, 275; III, 503; II, 425, 58–60; III, 554–55; II, 376, 191, 388, 374, 388, 402, 404, 380, 191; III, 535; II, 191; III, 501; II, 140; III, 535, 501, 402, 653; II, 411, 159, 246; III, 537.

149: Hawthorne to Fields, Sept. 3, 1858.

152: *The Complete Works of . . . Hawthorne,* VI, 15.

154: "The French and Italian Notebooks . . . ," II, 201, 207.

155–157, 159–167: *The Complete Works of . . . Hawthorne,* VI, 90, 335, 374, 93, 478, 468, 347, 160, 515, 520, 521, 276, 249, 466, 477, 57, 15–16, [19], 445, 61, 378, 21, 185, 57, 19, 480.

CHAPTER V

WILLIAM DEAN HOWELLS

168: *Life in Letters of William Dean Howells* (N. Y., 1928), I, 41, 44.

169: *Venetian Life* (N. Y., 1866), pp. 20, 2; (Boston, 1907), p. 406; *Italian Journeys* (Boston, 1867), pp. 152, 151.

170: *Venetian Life* (N. Y., 1866), p. 30.

170–171: *Life in Letters of* . . *Howells,* I, 85, 44, 57, 178.

171–172: *Venetian Life,* pp. 25, 24, 27.

172: "Recent Italian Comedy," *The North American Review,* XCIX (1864), 391; "Italian Brigandage," *The North American Review,* CI (1865), 168; *Venetian Life,* p. 343.

172–173: *The Unity of Italy: the American Celebration of the Unity of Italy, at the Academy of Music, New York, Jan. 12, 1871* . . . (N. Y., 1871), p. 76.

173: *Life in Letters of* . . . *Howells,* I, 58; *Venetian Life,* pp. 343, 344; "Italian Brigandage," p. 165; *My Literary Passions* (N. Y., 1895), p. 162.

173–174: *Venetian Life,* pp. 207, 349, 149.

174–175: *My Literary Passions,* pp. 149, 155, 157.

175–176: W. D. to W. C. Howells, April 22, 1883 (Houghton Library, Harvard).

176: *Life in Letters of* . . . *Howells,* I, 338.

176–177: *Tuscan Cities* (Boston, 1886), pp. 132, 11, 107.

177: *Life in Letters of* . . . *Howells,* II, 245, 256.

177–178: *Roman Holidays and Others* (N. Y., 1908), pp. 79, 27, 25.

178: H. H. Boyesen, "Real Conversations. I. A Dialogue between William Dean Howells and Hjalmar Hjorth Boyesen," *McClure's Magazine,* I (1893), 6.

179: "The Turning Point in my Life," *Harper's Bazaar,* XLIV (1910), 165; Boyesen, p. 6.

179–180: *Venetian Life,* p. 3.

181: "Editor's Study," *Harper's Monthly,* LXXIII (1886), 641.

184: *Life in Letters of* . . . *Howells,* I, 370.

184–185: *No Love Lost* (N. Y., 1869), pp. 19, 34.

187: *A Fearful Responsibility* (Boston, 1881), pp. 162, 82; *A Foregone Conclusion* (Boston, 1875), p. 154.

188: *The Lady of the Aroostook* (Boston, 1879), pp. 207, 216, 319.

189: *A Fearful Responsibility,* pp. 156, 124.

190: *The Lady of the Aroostook,* p. 67; *A Fearful Responsibility,* pp. 108, 119.

191–192: *Indian Summer* (Boston, 1886), pp. 64, 120, 371, 116, 175, 89–90.

193: *The Landlord at Lion's Head* (N. Y., 1897), p. 437; *Ragged Lady* (N. Y., 1899), pp. 192, 299.

194: *Annie Kilburn* (N. Y., 1889), p. 15; *An Imperative Duty* (N. Y., 1892), p. 10.

195: *The Minister's Charge* (Boston, 1887), p. 108; *The Kentons* (N. Y., 1902), p. 115.

196: *Impressions and Experiences* (N. Y., 1896), p. 279.

196–197: *The Vacation of the Kelwyns* (N. Y., c1920), pp. 51, 151, 54.

CHAPTER VI

HENRY JAMES

[Since little attempt is made in this chapter to trace a development in James' handling of Italian material, the dates of individual works by him are not always given. Nor are quotations made consistently from one set of texts. All quotations from the travel sketches published during his lifetime are taken, for convenience of citation, from *Italian Hours,* which incorporates his last revisions. Most of the quotations from other works come from first editions of them. Occasionally both the first and the New York editions of a work are quoted, according to what seemed more appropriate to the point at hand. All manuscript letters quoted are in the Houghton Library at Harvard.]

198: *Notes of a Son and Brother* (N. Y., 1914), pp. 37, 39; *A Small Boy and Others* (N. Y., 1913), p. 269.

199: Review of Howells' *Italian Journeys, The North American Review,* CVI (1878), 337–38.

199–200: Henry to Mary Walsh James, Sept. 10, 1869.

200: Henry to William James, Sept. 25, 1869; to Henry James, Sr., Oct. 24, 1869, Jan. 14, 1870; *The Letters of Henry James* (N. Y., 1920), I, 24, 25; Henry to Mary Walsh James, Dec. 21, Nov. 21, 1869.

200–201: *The Letters of Henry James,* I, 23.

201: Henry to William James, Nov. 25, Nov. 21, Sept. 25 [1869]; to Mary Walsh James, Feb. 5, 1870; to William James, March 8, 1870; to Mary Walsh James, Feb. 5, 1870; *The Letters of Henry James,* I, 12.

202: *Selected Letters of Henry James* (N. Y., 1955), p. 40; Henry to William James, April 9 [1873], Jan. 8, 1873; to Mary Walsh

James, Jan. 26, 1873; to Elizabeth Boott, Dec. 10, 1873; *The Letters of Henry James,* I, 35; Henry to William James, May 31 [1873].

203: *The Art of the Novel* (N. Y., 1934), pp. 7, 135; *The Letters of Henry James,* I, 36–37; *William Wetmore Story and his Friends* (Boston, 1903), II, 206, 208.

205: *The Letters of Henry James,* 1, 417; II, 68; 1, 106, 345; James to Elizabeth Boott, Jan. 26, 1878.

205–206: *The Letters of Henry James,* II, 160, 77, 80; I, 194; 213.

206: Henry to William James, May 9, 1880; *The American Scene* (N. Y., 1907), p. 293; *The Letters of Henry James,* I, 74, 78; *Italian Hours* (N. Y., 1909), pp. 485–86.

207–208: Henry to William James, May 9, 1880; *The Art of the Novel,* pp. 6, 159–60; *Notes on Novelists* (N. Y., 1914), p. 47; *William Wetmore Story and His Friends,* II, 209.

208: *The Letters of Henry James,* II, 101; " 'Very Modern Rome'—an Unpublished Essay of Henry James," *Harvard Library Bulletin,* VIII (1954), 137, 124.

208–209: *Italian Hours,* p. 233.

209: *English Hours* (Boston, 1905), p. 12; *Italian Hours,* pp. 492, 347–48; *The Notebooks of Henry James* (N. Y., 1947), p. 363; *Italian Hours,* pp. 367, [427], 278, 312, 306–07.

210: *Notes on Novelists,* p. 281.

210–214: *Italian Hours,* pp. 502, 498, 426, 415, 207, 156, 157, 172, 291, 103, 211, 126, [85], 308, 369, 102, 285, 192, 176, 432, 184, 165, [161], 159, 78, 62, 310, 304.

214: *The Letters of Henry James,* I, 300–301.

220–221: *Travelling Companions* (N. Y., 1919), pp. 14, 15, 38, 51, 145.

222: *The Bostonians* (London, 1886), III, 70.

223: *The Portrait of a Lady* (N. Y., 1908), I, 370; *The Madonna of the Future* (London, 1879), I, 26; *The Notebooks of Henry James,* p. 57.

224: *The Spoils of Poynton* (Boston, 1897), p. 24.

226: *The Golden Bowl* (N.Y., 1904), I, 57, 56, 371.

228: *The Portrait of a Lady* (Boston, 1882), pp. 52, 226, 216, 195.

229: *Watch and Ward* (Boston, 1878), p. 123.

229–230: *The Portrait of a Lady* (Boston, 1882), pp. 215, 250, 257; (N. Y., 1908), I, 400; (Boston, 1882), pp. 308, 472; (N. Y., 1908), II, 7–8; (Boston, 1882), pp. 454, 455.

231–233: *The Wings of the Dove* (N. Y., 1902), I, 313, 228, 229; II, 158–59; I, 242; II, 167, 225, 167, 157, 162, 175, 190, 225, 202, 222, 225, 201, 233.

234–236: *The Golden Bowl,* II, 253, 368, 369; I, 13, 49, 43, 331.

236: *Roderick Hudson* (Boston, 1876), pp. 305–06.

237: *The Notebooks of Henry James,* p. 85; *The Awkward Age* (London, 1899), p. 76; *The Real Thing and Other Tales* (London, 1893), p. 27.

238: *The Art of the Novel,* p. 202.

239: *Roderick Hudson,* pp. 249, 84–85.

240: *The Princess Casamassima* (London, 1886), pp. 229, 379, 380.

241: *The Portrait of a Lady,* p. 506.

241–242: *The Golden Bowl,* I, 168, 201, 17, 341.

243–245: *William Wetmore Story and his Friends,* I, 6, 110, 229, 331, 329, 330; II, 226, 4, 224, 223, 227, 226, 227.

245: *The Art of the Novel,* pp. 40–41, 136.

245–246: *William Wetmore Story and His Friends,* I, 312.

246: "Hawthorne's French and Italian Journals," *The Nation,* XIV (March 14, 1872), 173; "Nathaniel Hawthorne," *Library of the World's Best Literature* (N.Y., 1896), XII, 22.

247: Review of Howells' *A Foregone Conclusion, The Nation,* XX (Jan. 7, 1875), 12; "William Dean Howells," *Harper's Weekly,* XXX (June 19, 1886), 394.

247–248: *William Wetmore Story and his Friends,* I, 296, 308, 309.

CHAPTER VII

262: *The Works of . . . Irving,* XIII, 17; *The Complete Works of . . . Hawthorne,* VI, 15.

263: James, *Hawthorne* (N. Y., 1879), p. 42.

264: Merton M. Sealts, *Melville as Lecturer* (Cambridge, 1957), pp. 130, 150–51, 153.

Index

Of historical persons, places, and works of art, architecture, and literature cited in the text (see also "List of Illustrations" and "Sources of Quotations"). References to fictitious characters are indexed under the name of the work in which they appear.